Exploding the Myth?

Studies in Defence Economics

Edited by Keith Hartley, Centre for Defence Economics, University of York, UK.

This series of monographs and edited collections adopts a wide definition of defence economics to cover all aspects of the political economy of defence, disarmament and peace.

Exploding
the Myth?

THE PEACE DIVIDEND, REGIONS AND
MARKET ADJUSTMENT

Derek Braddon
University of the West of England, Bristol, UK

Routledge
Taylor & Francis Group
New York   London

First published by Harwood Academic Publishers.

This edition published 2013 by Routledge

Routledge
Taylor & Francis Group
711 Third Avenue
New York, NY 10017

Routledge
Taylor & Francis Group
2 Park Square, Milton Park
Abingdon, Oxfordshire OX14 4RN

First issued in paperback 2014

Routledge is an imprint of the Taylor & Francis Group, an informa business

British Library Cataloguing in Publication Data

A catalogue record for this book is available from the British Library.

ISBN 13: 978-90-5823-071-3 (hbk)
ISBN 13: 978-1-138-00232-6 (pbk)

ISSN: 1062-046X

THIS BOOK IS DEDICATED TO MY MOTHER
AND TO THE MEMORY OF MY FATHER

Contents

Preface

For the last 15 years, economists at the Research Unit in Defence Economics at the University of the West of England, Bristol have been observing and analysing the evolution of the defence sector, regionally, nationally and globally as it adjusts to the dramatic changes in the world security and business environment.

This book draws upon much of that work and focuses principally upon the post-Cold War period. It includes analysis of both Western nations and those of the Former Soviet Union. The central theme of the book is an exploration of the interplay of market forces in the pursuit of a peace dividend, the long-awaited, substantial and enduring surge in prosperity and individual well-being that was expected to flow from the ending of the Cold War and its massive military commitments.

In the context of this theme, the precise purpose of the book is to examine the efficacy of market forces in responding effectively to the 'outbreak of peace' after 1989. It seeks to demonstrate that, while markets do respond to such severe exogenous shocks as the unexpected and sustained huge reductions in defence spending in the 1990s, they do so in a way that both creates a sub-optimal outcome for industry, government, economy and society and, thereby, calls into question the attainment of a significant and lasting peace dividend.

The book is aimed at a wide audience including academic economists, political scientists and teachers and students of business, but it is also intended to be readily accessible to defence industry practitioners and decision-makers as well as the general reader.

I am greatly indebted to my colleagues Paul Dowdall, Adrian Kendry, Jonathan Bradley, Dr Stella Maile and Professor Philip Lawrence for their support and inspiration during so many research projects over the last 15 years, and to Tanya Hill for her patient and authoritative guidance on Internet access. Without their dedication and enthusiasm, it would not have been possible to write this book. I am most grateful to Professor Keith Hartley for his invaluable advice and guidance as the work of the Research Unit in Defence Economics has developed; to Professor Garel Rhys for constant encouragement over the years; to Kathy Morris, Director of the government's new Centre of Expertise for Aerospace and Defence for her interest in the

Research Unit's work and for her unswerving support; and to the many hundreds of defence industry employees at all levels, members of the armed forces, Ministry of Defence personnel, academic colleagues and many others who have given so much of their time to make the Unit's research possible. I owe my wife, Fiona, an enormous debt of gratitude for accepting the additional burdens that accompany a project such as this and I am grateful to Gwyn Mostyn for the conceptual thinking and encouragement in 1983 that eventually led to the creation of the Research Unit in Defence Economics.

Any errors or omissions which remain in this work are entirely those of the author.

Chapter 1

AFTER THE COLD WAR: DEFENCE CUTS AND THE PEACE DIVIDEND

INTRODUCTION

The unexpected ending of the Cold War at the end of the 1980s, the collapse of Communism and the subsequent wave of economic and political liberalisation unleashed across the former Soviet Union, Eastern and Central Europe seemed to offer the world the opportunity to secure a genuine 'peace dividend' as a result of sharply declining defence budgets.

Such a 'dividend' was anticipated as, firstly, governments would be able to free resources previously committed to the defence sector in order to expand social programme provision, to reduce the burden of public debt or reduce tax burdens and to allow market forces to generate new demand patterns and consequently stimulate new economic activity. Secondly, with the elimination of the perceived Cold War threats, a cyclical resurgence of defence spending to Cold War levels was thought to be extremely unlikely. Those companies previously focused upon military production, in due course, with or without government support, would be expected to redirect resources into the production of civilian goods.

It was anticipated that such a desirable economic outcome would require both some time for the adjustment process to work and a high degree of flexibility in the main factors of production, so that the transition from dependence on military to civil production as a significant income and employment generator could take place smoothly and with minimal economic dislocation. From the start, however, it was clear that such crucial temporal and structural conditions for smooth adjustment were missing. The Cold War came to an end with an abruptness that could not have been predicted, leaving the mechanisms and procedures for the maintenance of global security and stability in some disarray. With one former super-power confronting unprecedented economic collapse and the other only able to maintain its global stance on the basis of enormous debt acquired principally from the creditor nations of Japan and Germany, severe economic dislocation and potentially serious political instability appeared inevitable. Clearly, a New World Order would ultimately emerge but, in the immediate aftermath of the Cold War, the mechanisms and processes by which it would appear were far from obvious. At the time, as Kuttner (1991, p. 112) put it:

> 'it is undeniable that the post-war era is at last over, and its governing assumptions, long since dead, can now be properly buried. And it is high time to think seriously about the design of a new post-hegemonic world system.'

Within months of the end of the Cold War, however, the issue of global security and the urgent need for a properly-structured New World Order were unexpectedly brought into sharp focus, first by the invasion of Kuwait by Iraq and the subsequent Gulf War; second, soon after, by the tragic events in Bosnia; and, most recently, by the Kosovo crisis. At enormous expense and with tremendous effort on the diplomatic and military fronts, the first post-Cold War crisis in Iraq was at least held in check. The ponderous nature and, at times, extraordinary ineptitude of the political manoeuvrings that preceded the humanitarian disaster in Bosnia, however, quickly revealed that a solution to the problem of maintaining global security and stability had barely been addressed and that the traditional security mechanisms were both out of date and ineffective. Despite the tragic experience of the Bosnia disaster, Europe and the United States seemed little better prepared to deal with the crisis in Kosovo that developed towards the end of the decade (see below). It was becoming clear that the nature of global conflict and its resolution had changed once and for all (see, for example, Connaughton, 1993). Vershbow (1999) noted that, in the late 1990s, NATO has to confront a completely different set of risks, including:

> 'regional conflict, weapons of mass destruction, terrorism, and the so-called "asymmetric" threats like cyber-warfare. These are the security challenges that NATO must now address.'

While many nations were left with no choice but to join forces in various global military 'fire-fighting' and humanitarian peace-keeping exercises in the early 1990s, and while the key players in global security provision continued to incorporate concepts such as 'rapid reaction force deployment' as part of their planned crisis response strategies, behind the scenes the governments of defence-dependent economies and defence supply companies were already beginning to react to the changing security and defence budget scenario (for an interesting overview of the budgetary implications of various defence scenarios in the early 1990s, see Franck and Hildebrandt, 1994).

In those nations with a high commitment to military expenditure, the welcome 'outbreak of peace' brought with it not only the prospect of a peace dividend but also significant economic and industrial problems, in particular for the defence industries and military infrastructures in the countries concerned (see, for example, Saunders (1990) for a discussion of the potential effects of deep defence cuts from an early 1990s perspective). While political attention focused principally upon these broader issues of re-assessing international security mechanisms and appropriate strategic response to global security 'hot spots', the potentially adverse economic consequences of the end of the Cold War were almost entirely ignored.

Politicians were only too pleased to welcome the end of the Cold War and the associated reduction in defence spending, highlighting the unprecedented opportunities it offered to enjoy an economic dividend from a more peaceful world. Not only did they largely ignore the scale and impact of the immediate economic dislocation from defence cutbacks and the considerable costs associated with genuine disarmament (for an interesting analysis of these costs, see Renner M., 1996) but, perhaps somewhat naively, they appeared to believe that the required redistribution of resources from the military sector into civil production and welfare provision would happen, quickly and easily, without significant government intervention and at minimal cost. The market, left to its own devices would, they argued, swiftly restore equilibrium and, at the same time, serve to generate new prosperity. A decade later, we can focus on precisely this market adjustment process and assess the degree to which it has responded effectively to the new pressures placed upon it. The role which government intervention can play in facilitating and enhancing the process of market adjustment following such a powerful exogenous shock as a massive and sustained reduction in global defence expenditure can also be explored.

Both of these issues are central to this book. After an introductory section which examines briefly the changes in the global geo-political environment, including arms control initiatives and their consequences, which have impacted upon both defence expenditure and the defence sector in Western nations, this initial chapter then identifies the scale of global defence expenditure cuts in recent years. The geographically-focused nature of these expenditure cuts are then examined to highlight both their regional distribution and likely economic impact. The chapter concludes with an overview of various dimensions of the peace dividend.

THE EVOLVING GLOBAL GEO-POLITICAL ENVIRONMENT OF THE DEFENCE SECTOR

While the search for successful alternative products and markets has long been a central strategic objective of many defence supply companies, the historic events of the late 1980s and early 1990s gave an added impetus to that quest. The end of the Cold War and the associated demise of Communism, the Soviet Union and the Warsaw Pact brought sharply into focus the issue of the appropriate level and content of defence provision among the major Western industrialised nations.

With the sudden 'outbreak of peace' in the 1990s, the international security environment has altered in a number of significant ways. From a situation where two super-powers, together with their allies, appeared locked in head-to-head conflict, with the doctrine of 'mutually assured destruction' central to their security thinking, that strategic view has now been transformed and is more concerned with managing global risks and establishing a high level of preparedness for dealing with isolated but strategically significant regional conflicts, rather than preparing to counter perceived super-power threats.

Until the late 1980s, the scenario upon which NATO based its military strategy (and for which member countries devised their defence budgets) was one described by Gansler (1998) as:

> 'a relatively predictable high attrition, extended duration, Central European [military engagement,] backed up with the threat of massive retaliation to deter nuclear-armed ballistic missile attack.'

Following the end of the Cold War, however, the most likely conflict scenario on the international stage is one involving, as Gansler suggests:

> 'more limited—but almost always, coalition—engagements. They will be fought with smaller, lighter, more mobile forces and equipment; with concentrated firepower precisely delivered from long range. Wars of attrition will be replaced by so-called "reconnaissance strike" engagements.'

The evolution of defence policy internationally for the immediate future, then, will be driven by a continual reassessment of the risk of regionally-focused conflict and will determine, within tight budget constraints, the shape, content and distribution of future defence provision and associated budgets. In terms of policy drivers relating to defence expenditure commitments in the advanced industrial nations, a number of key points are relevant. Following the end of the Cold War, the individual members of the United Nations (UN)—and in particular those of the Security Council—are no longer as sensitive to East/West alignments. Military strategy is now more concerned with the efficient provision of 'rapid response' units equipped to carry out swift and effective intervention to support peace keeping (James, 1995) and the provision of humanitarian aid rather than the maintenance of huge military capability, much of which will never be required.

Each major arms-producing nation, operating within a range of international treaties and other agreements (UN, NATO, EU, CSCE, G7, etc.) will be continually re-assessing its overall defence commitments within this evolving UN security structure, identifying the nature of the forces and weapons systems required to support the policy and the criteria required for deciding how, why and when to use them.

At the same time, Russia, which retained between 70% and 80% of the former Soviet defence industry following the dissolution of the USSR, continues to combine devastating military power with widespread economic and political instability. Significant, if localised, conflicts in highly politically sensitive areas of the world continue to break out, requiring the USA and her European allies in NATO to develop a flexible and appropriately equipped force structure which must have the capacity to be able to respond, rapidly and effectively, to each emerging threat to international peace and stability. While the Cold War 'threat perception' may have receded significantly since 1990, it is clear that the each NATO member nation will have to retain its military planning and force reconstruction capabilities, either singly or jointly. In doing so, defence policy and associated military expenditure allocations will have to take account of the long lead times involved in the production of defence equipment. As nations begin to work more closely together in the defence and security arenas, the potential for heightened efficiency and cost-saving in joint procurement and production will become increasingly obvious and will serve to further strengthen the drive towards industrial concentration and globalisation in the defence supply sector.

Accommodating the contraction in defence budgets at a time of considerable international political and economic instability is a substantial challenge. Exacerbating the situation further, however, is the fact that many of the arms producing nations will also confront serious funding constraints within each national public expenditure budget. Many governments, particularly those in the process of implementing the Maastricht criteria for European Monetary Union, have set explicit and stringent targets for the reduction of public debt over the next few years, implying that the resources available to fund defence commitments will become even more limited. The expenditure constraint problem is aggravated further by the fact that defence costs tend to rise persistently over time and between one generation of military equipment and the next (Kirkpatrick, 1995).

It is inevitable that future defence expenditure will have to be directly related to explicit military commitments and to be acceptably balanced against the other demands confronting governments, not least of which, ultimately, will be the delivery of some kind of perceived 'peace dividend'. Such may be the economic consequences of the cuts in military spending for defence-dependent regions, however, that this potential 'dividend' may have to be seen, finally, more in terms of the provision of regional support measures designed to help exposed localities overcome the adverse effects of the run-down in both the military base and/or defence industrial base of their local economies in terms of income, employment and environmental impact.

PEACE-KEEPING AND THE KOSOVO CRISIS

One of the most important developments in modern military strategy—and one which will have considerable longer term significance for global military requirements—has been the significant new roles which NATO and the United Nations have been called upon to play in the 1980s and 1990s (see, for example, Sandler and Hartley, 1999). In particular, these new roles have involved the widespread deployment of United Nations (and/or NATO) forces in a peace-keeping or humanitarian role. In 1998, the United Nations maintained some 16 major peace-keeping operations, deploying over 20,000 troops from 70 countries. The cost of maintaining such a peace-keeping role has varied over the decade from over $3 billion in 1993, 1994 and 1995 to over $1 billion in 1997 and in 1998. Included within this UN function are observer missions (such as those in Tajikistan, Liberia and Georgia); transition missions (such as that in Haiti); and stabilisation forces (such as that in Bosnia-Herzegovina).

Although it has centuries-old and highly complex roots, the current Kosovo crisis began in the early part of 1998 with widespread fighting leading to the displacement of over 300,000 refugees, principally Kosovan Albanians. In October 1998 a cease-fire was agreed which enabled these refugees to seek and find shelter and averted a major humanitarian disaster in the winter of 1998. Under the auspices of the OSCE (the Organisation for Security and Co-operation in Europe), a verification mission was despatched to the region but the hostilities resumed in January 1999. A peace conference was held in Paris in March 1999 to seek a peaceful resolution of the conflict but the terms were rejected by the Yugoslav delegation, despite clear NATO threats to adopt air-strikes if necessary against them, should hostilities continue.

On 24 March 1999 NATO began a series of air-strikes against Serbian military targets in the Federal Republic of Yugoslavia (FRY), designed to ensure full compliance with the UN Security Council Resolution 1199 of September 23 1998. These air-strikes were planned as the key component of the response by the international community to perceived Serbian aggression.

NATO forces were ordered to pursue a swift end to hostilities perpetrated by the FRY against Kosovan Albanians and were given the military objective of degrading the FRY military and security structure that had enabled President Milosevic to pursue the ethnic cleansing strategy within Kosovo. Over the following weeks, it became obvious that the air-strikes programme, hampered by poor weather conditions and natural concern to minimise civilian casualties, was taking much longer than anticipated to incapacitate President Milosevic's military machine. The number, frequency and intensity of air-strikes was stepped up and major efforts were made, sometimes with surprising success, at the political level within the Allied nations to preserve and, indeed, strengthen the unity and sense of purpose of those involved in Operation Allied Force.

After many weeks of intense bombing and with signs of growing discontent within his forces, President Milosevic finally accepted peace terms offered to him by EU envoy Ahtisaari and Russian envoy Chernomyrdin. With full United Nations authorisation, NATO troops were deployed with a peace-keeping remit to Kosovo on June 10 1999 when NATO airstrikes were finally suspended.

At this point, Operation Allied Force was replaced by Operation Joint Guardian which, under a United Nations Chapter VII resolution of June 10 1999, enables member states and international organisations to establish an international security presence in Kosovo and thereby facilitate the return home of up to one million displaced persons and refugees and the full withdrawal from Kosovo of FRY troops and militia. The force has a unified NATO chain of command (except for the Russian component) and is scheduled to eventually comprise 12,000 UK troops, 8,500 German troops, 7,000 French troops, 7,000 US troops, 2,000 Italian troops and 11,000 others from Canada, Finland, Greece, Lithuania, Norway, Poland, Portugal, Sweden and Turkey. Russia has committed some 10,000 troops to the multinational KFOR mission.

While the lessons of the Kosovo crisis have yet to be drawn and, indeed, the situation there (and in neighbouring regions and republics) is far from stable at present, the conduct of the allied campaign, the military strategy employed and the performance of very expensive and leading-edge high-technology equipment have all been called into question. It remains the case that the current conflict resolution policy of the United Nations or of NATO tends to be piecemeal, fragmented, cumbersome and often difficult to hold together for all allied participants. The world does not yet have the kind of modern security framework that could successfully underpin a genuine New World Order and experiences such as the Kosovan crisis point out only too starkly the present limitations on the capabilities of existing international organisations for swift and effective conflict resolution.

THE COSTS OF KOSOVO

The true cost of the Kosovo conflict, of course, has to be measured in the appalling suffering, loss of life and widespread damage associated with the humanitarian disaster that has unfolded in the region. However, after a decade of defence budget cuts, it is important to assess the financial cost of the allied campaign in Kosovo as well. A recent provisional estimate from the Centre for Strategic and Budgetary Assessments (CSBA) suggests that, by itself, the US share of the NATO air campaign during the Kosovo crisis amounted to between $1.8 billion to $3.0 billion; adding the costs attributable to the other allies increases the estimate to between $2.3 billion to $4 billion. Additionally, the share of peace-keeping costs to be borne by the US alone is estimated to amount to between $2 billion and $3.5 billion per year for the duration of the peace-keeping commitment. These are additional costs over and above the normal peacetime costs of the US military and exclude all of the costs incurred to date and those in prospect associated with the humanitarian assistance to Kosovo refugees and costs related to future rebuilding of homes, factories and other facilities.

ARMS CONTROL INITIATIVES

During the last decade, a number of important international arms control initiatives have been agreed and partially implemented which both helped to precipitate the end of the Cold War and intensified the pressures on the defence industry. Brief reference to three of these will be made here.

The INF Treaty, signed between the United States and the Soviet Union, and implemented from 1 June 1988 was designed to eliminate all short-range and intermediate range ground-launched ballistic and cruise missiles belonging to both superpowers. This implied that the Soviet Union would eliminate all of its SS-12, SS-23, SS-20, SS-4 and SS-5 missiles while the USA would eliminate all of its Pershing IA and II and the BGM-109G missiles (SIPRI Yearbook 1990). The treaty encompasses both nuclear and non-nuclear missiles (for further discussion of INF, see Bischak and Oden, 1991).

Secondly, the Treaty on Conventional Armed Forces in Europe was signed by 22 nations in November 1990 with the former Soviet Republics committing themselves to the Treaty in January 1992. Under this treaty, limits were placed on five categories of equipment deployed by both NATO and the then Warsaw Pact nations in an area of Europe reaching from the Atlantic to the Urals. As part of the limitation process, protocols were signed relating to data and information exchange, inspection schedules and Treaty interpretation and compliance.

Finally, under the Strategic Arms Reduction Talks Treaty signed in July, 1991, it was agreed that US and Soviet offensive strategic nuclear weapons would be reduced to equal aggregate levels over a seven-year period. Numerical limits were imposed on various kinds of strategic nuclear delivery vehicles and the nuclear warheads they carry. While progress with implementing START I continued, in March 1997, President Clinton and President Yeltsin clarified their understanding regarding the future implementation of START II and START III.

Despite the fact that one superpower involved in the agreements and treaties noted above has all but disintegrated since 1990, significant progress with such treaties serves to underline the degree to which the business environment surrounding defence supply companies has changed. Central to the new business environment for the defence industry has been the scale and pace of change in defence expenditure.

THE DECLINE IN DEFENCE EXPENDITURE

At the start of the 1990s, world military expenditure amounted to almost $1,000 billion per annum of which some 60% was attributable to military provision associated with the Cold War. (Hartley et al., 1993). Recent estimates suggest that global defence expenditure by 1996 amounted to some $796 billion, the lowest level since 1966 and about 40% below its 1987 peak (for an excellent discussion of world military expenditure, see Brzoska, 1995). In the US, defence expenditure has declined by about one-third since 1987 and US weapons procurement by about two-thirds. In addition, recent estimates for future US defence budgets suggest a further reduction in expenditure of 10% up to 2002.

While the downturn in US defence expenditure is clearly an important factor in hastening the restructuring and consolidation of the US defence industries, that expenditure still remains significant at around 80% of the Cold War 'average'. It has been estimated that world military expenditure declined by 1.3 percentage points of global Gross Domestic Product between 1985 and 1990 (Hewitt, 1991). Clements, Gupta and Schiff (1996) estimated that, during the period 1991 to 1995, the downward trend continued taking global military expenditure from 3.6% of world GDP in 1991 down to just 2.5% in 1995, with most of the military expenditure reductions occurring in the industrial and transition economies. Clements et al. found that, of 130 countries included in their study, 90 reduced military expenditure while 40 maintained or increased it over the period.

Where defence expenditure has declined, the sharpest reduction appears to have been in the former Warsaw Pact nations (with military spending falling by an estimated 5% of GDP) and Europe (falling by 1.7% of GDP). In the USA defence expenditure fell by an average annual rate of 4.4% over these years.

Using data from the International Monetary Fund World Economic Outlook database, Clements et al. estimate that for the decade 1985 to 1995, world military expenditure fell by almost 3 percentage points of global GDP, suggesting a total potential peace dividend of $345 billion, if actual military spending is compared to what it would have been using the 1990 ratio of military spending to GDP, or some $720 billion, using the 1985 ratio.

Clements et al. note that other military spending databases, while utilising somewhat different data due to the variation in definitions employed and the countries included, produce reasonably similar results, particularly those based upon data sets from the International

Institute of Strategic Studies (IISS); the Stockholm International Peace Research Institute (SIPRI) and the United States Arms Control and Disarmament Agency (ACDA).

Bischak (1997), taking a specifically US perspective on the defence cuts, notes that the crucial issue in measuring the 'savings' and, therefore, the potential for a peace dividend, is first deciding on a meaningful point of comparison. Set against the Cold War average for military expenditure in the US ($311 billion annually in 1996 dollars), the US only 'saved' some $24 billion overall for the period 1991 to 1995.

In the main, this is attributable to the fact that military spending in the US during the 1990s remained relatively close to this average, despite the cuts. Set against the comparatively high levels of military expenditure in 1989, when the first signs of the end of the Cold War were becoming apparent, however, yields a cumulative 'saving' from reduced military expenditure in the US of some $364 billion between 1990 and 1995. Alternatively, simply summing the annual military expenditure cuts since 1990 produces a total 'saving' of some $81 billion between 1991 and 1995.

Analysts at the Bonn International Conversion Centre (BICC, 1996) estimated that global military expenditure had declined from around 5.4% of global GNP in 1986 to some 3% in 1994. As a result, they argued that an additional 2.4% of the world's GNP had became available for non-military uses, representing the true peace dividend.

CHANGING DEFENCE BUDGETS

For ease of comparison, the data set out in the following tables draws upon the work of the International Institute for Strategic Studies and their annual estimates of national, regional and global defence expenditure. Tables 1, 2, 3 and 4 below indicate the degree to which defence cuts have been implemented in various countries and within NATO and NATO Europe and where defence expenditure has increased marginally or substantially over the period from 1985 to 1997, the latest currently available estimate. Defence expenditure estimates are shown at 1995 constant prices.

In Table 1, every country listed has experienced defence expenditure reduction during the 1990s to varying degrees. Hard choices over the distribution and scale of procurement expenditure have had to be confronted in each country. In the face of political uncertainty, perceived threat or other reason, some countries have made a strategic decision over this period to increase their defence expenditure (see Table 4).

TABLE 1: DEFENCE EXPENDITURE IN NATO COUNTRIES ($MN) AND SHARE OF GDP (%) TAKEN BY DEFENCE EXPENDITURE: 1985 AND 1997

COUNTRY/AREA:	DEFENCE BUDGET ($M):		SHARE OF GDP (%):	
	1985:	1997:	1985:	1997:
Total NATO	584,891	454,076	3.3	2.2
NATO Europe	206,033	173,363	3.1	2.2
United States	367,711	272,955	6.5	3.4
Canada	11,147	7,757	2.2	1.3
Belgium	5,863	3,769	3.0	1.6
Denmark	2,978	2,816	2.2	1.9
France	46,522	41,545	4.0	3.0
Germany	50,220	33,416	3.2	1.6
Italy	24,471	21,837	2.3	1.9
United Kingdom	45,408	35,736	5.2	2.8

Source: The Military Balance: 1998–1999; International Institute of Strategic Studies, London.

Although the data employed in Table 2 is perhaps not as reliable as in Table 1, given the problem of measuring military expenditure within the former Soviet bloc nations, the trend displayed here reinforces the judgement that it is in the former Warsaw Pact nations where defence cutbacks have been deepest. As made clear in Table 3, in the Middle East, an area where both the threat of conflict and the reality have been so prominent in recent years, extreme reductions in military spending have been observed for countries such as Iran, Iraq and Saudi Arabia while defence budgets have increased somewhat in Israel and Kuwait. As noted earlier, Table 4 indicates countries where defence spending has actually risen in the period 1985–1996 with significant increases in Japan, Taiwan and Brazil.

In the US, the Cold War build-up commenced in 1978 and reached a peak level of expenditure in 1987 due primarily to the vast expenditure associated with the Reagan 'Star Wars' initiative. After the 'outbreak of peace', following the 1993 Quadrennial Defence Review in the US (known as the Bottom Up Review), which made 'readiness' the

TABLE 2: DEFENCE EXPENDITURE ($M) AND % DEFENCE EXPENDITURE IN GDP IN SELECTED COUNTRIES WITHIN THE FORMER SOVIET UNION AND WARSAW PACT: 1985 AND 1997

	DEFENCE BUDGET ($MN):		SHARE OF GDP (%):	
	1985:	1997:	1985:	1997:
USSR	343,616	n.a.	16.1	n.a.
Russia	n.a.	64,000	n.a.	5.8
Ukraine	n.a.	1,324	n.a.	2.7
Bulgaria	2,331	339	14.0	3.4
Hungary	3,380	666	7.2	1.4
Poland	8,212	3,730	8.1	2.3

Source: The Military Balance: 1998–1999; International Institute of Strategic Studies, London.

TABLE 3: CHANGING DEFENCE EXPENDITURE ($M) AND % GDP TAKEN BY DEFENCE
EXPENDITURE IN SELECTED MIDDLE EAST COUNTRIES: 1985 AND 1997

	DEFENCE BUDGET ($M):		SHARE OF GDP (%):	
	1985:	1997:	1985:	1997:
Iran	20,258	4,695	36.0	6.6
Iraq	18,328	1,250	25.9	7.4
Israel	7,196	11,143	21.2	11.5
Kuwait	2,558	3,618	9.1	11.4
Saudi Arabia	25,585	18,151	19.6	12.4
Middle East/N. Africa	95,890	56,451	12.3	6.9

Source: The Military Balance 1998–1999; International Institute of Strategic Studies, London.

main target of US defence policy (with modernisation in second place) defence spending fell by a further 15% up to 1996.

At this time, after a decade in which the US has experienced both an absolute decline in military expenditure and a reduction in its share of the national economy, it is worth noting that the US military budget in 1996 was still only about one-tenth lower than average defence spending during the Cold War, a period which included the high-spending periods of the Vietnam and Korea conflicts.

Again, in the mid-1990s, the US defence budget, despite the cuts, still exceeded by a significant margin the combined defence budget of the next eight highest defence spending countries (Russia, Japan, France, UK, Germany, China, Italy and Saudi Arabia). The US also spent about 15 times as much on defence as five of the most potentially dangerous countries in the world, from which emanates much of the current and potential threat to world peace in the late 1990s: Iraq, Iran, North Korea, Syria and Libya.

TABLE 4: COUNTRIES OUTSIDE THE MIDDLE EAST WHERE DEFENCE EXPENDITURE HAS
INCREASED OVER THE PERIOD 1985–1997: ($M)

	1985:	1997:
Sweden	4,546	5,481
Switzerland	2,749	3,837
Australia	7,755	8,501
China	28,273	36,551
Japan	30,612	40,891
South Korea	8,962	14,732
Malaysia	2,513	3,377
Philippines	675	1,422
Singapore	1,692	4,122
Taiwan	9,171	13,657
Thailand	2,669	3,248
Brazil	3,347	13,944

Source: The Military Balance: 1998–1999, International Institute of Strategic Studies, London.

In February, 1997, the second Clinton administration submitted a defence budget request for some $265 billion for fiscal year, 1998. This defence budget request recognised that the US is the only country in the world with the military strength, mobility, logistical support and access to leading-edge communications and intelligence systems which allow it to undertake large-scale military operations with global reach. Consequently, the 1998 defence budget set out to maintain defence expenditure at a constant level, allowing for inflation, so that the US could expect to operate successfully in regional conflicts as and when they arose.

Taking into account the US Administration's defence spending plans up to the year 2002 and comparing them with the position in 1985, estimates suggest that there will have been a 33% reduction in spending on military personnel over the period, a 26% cut in defence operations and maintenance expenditures, a 54% reduction in procurement spend and a 30% fall in research, development, testing and evaluation budgets. For US defence manufacturers, the implications of this expenditure decline are serious and, in order to accommodate unforeseen contingencies, orders for existing major projects have been reduced. For example, Department of Defense procurement for the F-18 aircraft was cut from 1,000 to between 548 and 748 aircraft; that for the F-22 from 437 to 339; and for the V22 from 425 to 360.

From the mid-1980s onward, concern in the US about the scale of the domestic budget deficit created an anti-deficit coalition in Congress which, by amending Congressional budget procedures, limited discretionary expenditures, including defence. It is interesting to note that the US public deficit declined by an amount similar to the reduction in military budgets over the period. The association here appears to be more imaginary than real as much of the budget reduction can be attributed to recouping higher tax payments.

The 1997 Quadrennial Defence Review (QDR) set out clearly the future approach of the US to its military commitments. A new conceptual framework 'Vision 2010' has been adopted to ensure that the US secures and maintains 'full spectrum dominance', particularly in the collecting, processing and dissemination of critical information, essential to battlefield victory. The 1999 US defence budget continues support for this strategy with emphasis being given to financing the new technologies required to deliver 'full spectrum dominance' (for further discussion of this development, see IISS, 1998–99). This has important implications for industry, especially for those companies developing, manufacturing and servicing products relevant for the military's requirements for command, control, communication, computers, intelligence, surveillance and reconnaissance (C4ISR).

In general, among the European members of NATO, defence expenditure has also declined but less sharply. From an aggregate NATO Europe defence expenditure level of some $92.2 billion in 1985, peak expenditure was reached in 1991 at $95.1 billion, declining to $91.5 billion one year later (at 1985 prices and exchange rates).

This aggregate hides considerable variation. Defence expenditure in the United Kingdom fell sharply in the peak years between 1985 and 1992 (from $23.8 billion to $20.7 billion). Denmark, Greece, the Netherlands and Spain recorded only a modest decline in defence budgets. France increased defence expenditure to a peak of $22.2 billion in 1991 (from £20.8 billion in 1985) before declining to $21.9 billion in 1992. (UN World Economic and Social Survey, 1995).

The Bonn International Center for Conversion presents their military expenditure data somewhat differently. Table 5 below draws upon BICC datasets (BICC,1999) to highlight the extent to which military expenditure has changed over the decade from 1987 to 1997, the latest year for which estimates are currently available. The BICC data referred to here uses index numbers (with 1997 = 100) for selected years over the decade which are based on military expenditure data measured in millions of US dollars, using 1993 prices and exchange rates.

Again, the scale of the immense reduction in military expenditure in Russia, the FSU and Eastern Europe over the decade from 1987 can be seen in Table 5, together with the significant decline in the US, UK and Germany. The much less significant defence cutbacks in France and Italy over the same period are also quite striking. BICC data also reveals that, in 1997, the industrialised world contributed some 76% of total world military expenditure (estimated at $680.5 billion) and the developing nations the remaining 24%. BICC estimated that the US accounted for 42% of global military expenditure in 1997, Europe 30% and Asia 25%. Taking different geographic boundaries, it was estimated that the European Union contributed some 24%, the Organisation for Economic Co-operation and Development 75% and the Organisation for Security and Co-operation in Europe 68% of global military expenditure in 1997 (BICC, 1999).

Given national and institutional differences in the definition and calculation of defence expenditure, expert groups assessing and measur-

TABLE 5: MILITARY EXPENDITURES: 1987–1997

COUNTRY/AREA:	1987	1992	1997
U. S.	147	126	100
U. K.	146	122	100
France	109	107	100
Germany	170	125	100
Italy	103	105	100
Russia/FSU	778	168	100
East Europe	842	143	100
NATO	136	121	100
World	151	117	100

Source: BICC, 1999

ing military data tend to reach somewhat different estimates and readers may wish to compare and contrast further the estimates shown here with those emanating from analysts such as the Stockholm International Peace Research Institute (SIPRI) and the US Arms Control and Disarmament Agency (ACDA).

EUROPEAN POLITICAL DEVELOPMENTS

The trend within Europe, generally, towards what is perceived to be a permanent reduction in defence budgets and commitments reflects faith in a number of international security developments which, taken together, offer the prospect for enhanced global stability. Three developments in particular stand out as significant: the Partnership for Peace initiative signed in 1994 between NATO and its 'co-operation partners' from the former USSR and from Eastern Europe; the establishment of the Euro-Atlantic Council in May 1997 to expand the political aspects of the Partnership for Peace structure and increase the potential for practical military co-operation across Europe; and, again in May/June 1997, the agreements to sign the NATO-Russia Founding Act and the NATO-Ukraine Charter. Furthermore, at around the same time, the Czech Republic, Hungary and Poland were invited to begin the process of joining NATO, finally doing so in early 1999. While NATO Europe contributes about 40% of overall defence expenditure within the organisation, this expenditure declined by 9% in 1997.

Western Europe has, since 1992, been considering the possibility of broadening its arms procurement base to create a genuinely more open European market and a joint procurement agency for defence goods, a scheme championed by France with support from Germany. In 1996, France and Germany announced the formation of a joint procurement agency, expanded soon after to form the Joint Armaments Co-operation Organisation (JACO). To be included in this organisation, a country was required to have involvement in collaborative defence projects with at least one of the founding members. In November, 1996, 10 members of the Western European Union responded to the interest being shown in joint procurement strategies by creating the West European Armaments Organisation (WEAO) with a focus more upon research than upon development and production.

As part of the process of cost-saving, Western European governments have cut orders for existing products and have delayed production schedules. To date, no single major defence order or programme has been cancelled. Despite concern over project costs and design, the Eurofighter Typhoon project continues to be developed, involving the UK, Germany, Italy and Spain. Given the recent decision of Greece to purchase 80 Typhoons, the first confirmed export order for the aircraft, the decision to continue development and production seems to have been justified. Similarly, the collaborative European projects associated with the Anglo-Italian EH101 helicopter and the Franco-German Tiger attack helicopter continue to receive support. The UK's leading role in the development of a new frigate has been maintained, despite the uncertain commitment of France and Italy to the programme.

Similar or more extensive reductions in military activities and budgets have been experienced over the last 50 years, for example, after World War II, the Korean War and the Vietnam War (Grawe 1991). On those occasions, however, the arms race (underpinned by the perceived communist threat) made a cyclical resurgence of defence expenditure inevitable. Corporate response to the cyclical behaviour of defence expenditure in the past was aptly summed up by Smith and Smith (1992) as one where:

> 'The optimal response to transitory demand shocks ... is to maintain capacity to provide an option for the next upturn.'

Such a cyclical resurgence of defence expenditure is unlikely to recur in the foreseeable future however and, consequently, defence industries, the armed forces, the military infrastructure and the regional economies that depend for much of their prosperity upon these activities now have to adjust to fundamental and probably permanent changes in the level and direction of defence budgets.

For those observing closely the economic dimensions of the transition to the post-Cold War world, one of the main issues to address is the extent to which the economic well-being of specific defence-dependent regions within the major Western arms producing nations and their constituent defence companies and military infrastructures will be adversely affected by their exposure to defence cuts and the degree to which regional economic regeneration is possible without an extensive and targeted compensatory public expenditure programme (see Braddon, 1996a for a fuller discussion).

The principal economic problem and, inevitably, policy issue associated with the widespread contraction in defence expenditure is how best to counteract the consequent reduction in economic activity. In a situation where market forces are left to reallocate resources and restore equilibrium, as has been mainly the case in the Western nations since 1990, the adjustment process is likely to be long-term, slow and potentially damaging in economic terms. Historically, evidence suggests that the ability of defence-dependent companies and localities to diversify into alternative civil activities, generating equivalent income and employment, is extremely limited. Inevitably, unemployment in defence-dependent areas is likely to increase sharply without compensatory action by government, either directly or indirectly, to enhance the capacity for smooth and rapid regional market adjustment. From the start, therefore, it is important to be clear about precisely where the negative economic impacts of the decline in defence expenditure are likely to fall.

REGIONAL IMPACT

For defence-dependent economies, a significant reduction in defence expenditure will inevitably, at least in the medium-term, result in a sharp reduction in defence-related economic activity with labour-shedding, military base and industrial plant closure and, in some cases, considerable regional economic dislocation and decline. In most of the major arms-producing nations, defence production tends to be regionally focused (see Braddon, 1995, for further discussion). In the United States, for example, during the peak years of Cold War defence spending, more than half of all prime defence contracts were initially allocated to just six states. In the United Kingdom, almost two-thirds of direct employment in the defence industry was to be found in just three out of eleven regions. In Italy, five out of twenty regions received some 80% of all defence-related business. (Paukert and Richards, 1991; Short, 1981).

Many regions and sub-regions within the advanced industrial nations have, for decades, depended critically upon defence-related activities to support both employment and prosperity, particularly in periods when national and international economic recession would otherwise have seriously eroded their economic performance. The regional impacts of defence expenditure are considered further in Chapter 2. For most of this century—and especially during the Cold War—such reliance at the regional level on national defence expenditure appeared both eminently rational and economically beneficial. Although cyclical in nature, not only was such a significant level of military expenditure both predictable and likely to increase over time in real terms but its economic impact could be measured in terms of an associated 'permanent' level of regional employment together with higher-than-average incomes for many defence workers.

In the 1990s, however, the economic disadvantages of such defence-dependency have appeared only too rapidly and starkly. Deep cuts in defence expenditure during this decade, experienced by almost all of the world's most significant defence producers, have appeared to pose a serious threat to short-term national economic prosperity and, in some instances, even to long-term economic viability. Some analysts believe, however, that the longer-term negative implications of sustained defence cuts for the US national economy in particular might be over-stated. From this national economic perspective, even a twenty-five percent cut in defence spending (which amounts to only about 5.5 percent of the nation's annual gross product of goods and services) was not perceived to be sufficiently large to have a significant impact on the national growth rate, inflation rate or unemployment level.

From a regional or sub-regional perspective, however, the effects of reduced defence budgets on the defence industrial and technology base and on defence sector employees, companies and local communities could be much more significant. Massive and prolonged defence expenditure cuts will inevitably impact hard upon specific defence-dependent communities, entire regions and many skill-specific employee groups, especially where there is significant clustering of defence companies, military bases and other military-focused economic activity at the regional level.

As defence budgets continue to decline in most of the major arms producing nations, growing concern about the economic costs associated with defence-related economic adjustment is fuelling interest in the consequences of defence expenditure reduction on defence-dependent regions. In doing so, important questions are being raised about the level of sustainability of any ensuing peace dividend.

DEFENCE-DEPENDENT REGIONS

a) The United States

Of all the principal forms of public expenditure in the US, military spending is the most regionally unbalanced category and plays a particularly prominent role in what has been termed 'the warfare state' across the South and West United States. The defence industry in the US has tended to concentrate in the southern, western and north-eastern states and the high-technology emphasis of much defence production since the Second World War has brought to prominence new industrial regions such as Silicon Valley and Route 128.

One of the most important problems encountered by those researching defence expenditure and its economic impacts is the availability and veracity of defence sector data. Unlike most other major arms-producing nations, the United States makes available sufficient high-quality data on the regional distribution of defence expenditure to enable accurate state-by-state regional defence-dependency to be explored using a variety of measures. Using the share of total Department of Defense (DoD) purchases received by a state as a measure of its defence-dependency, California, Virginia and Texas emerge as the most dependent states. On the other hand, taking the share of total procurement in each state emanating from the defence sector, Alaska, Hawaii and Virginia head the list. The District of Columbia, Alaska and Hawaii appear most dependent if an employment share indicator is used, with California falling to 7th place in the rankings. Using instead the number of active duty military personnel located in a state as a measure of defence-dependency, California regains its predominant position in terms of defence-dependence (for a fuller discussion, see Kosiak and Bitzinger, 1994).

Clearly, the selection of an appropriate indicator to reflect the degree of defence-dependency (share of DoD purchases; number of defence employees etc.) will be extremely significant in determining which states appear in such ranking lists. To illustrate the point, it should be noted that while the state of Texas had the second largest number of people employed in the defence sector in the early 1990's, its ranking under the criterion of the Department of Defense share of total purchases, however, placed it as only the 23rd most defence dependent state in the USA.

At that time, it was anticipated that while US defence expenditure reductions would have a limited national impact on employment and business activity, the effects on specific regional communities would be much greater. Given an expected reduction in DoD defence-related purchases of goods and services between FY 1990 and FY 1996 of 26%—and a consequent anticipated private sector employment loss of some 814,228 jobs—it was anticipated that the impact would be distributed across the US depending upon the uneven distribution of defence-related economic activity and the wide variety of local and regional economies where defence bases and industrial plants were located.

Although much of the impact of defence contraction would inevitably be focused upon the states listed above (and on specific localities within them), even those states with a relatively low share of defence goods and services in total state-wide purchases such as Nevada, Illinois, Michigan, South Dakota, Montana, Wisconsin, Iowa, West Virginia, Idaho and Oregon will not ultimately be able to escape unscathed. Furthermore, while prime contractors and key first-tier suppliers may operate from relatively few principal locations across the country, they form the tip of a very large and wide-ranging industrial 'iceberg'—the apex of a defence industry supply chain or matrix (see Chapter 4) which will include a vast number of smaller suppliers operating from a multitude of different localities. The reduced income generation and employment loss associated with declining defence expenditure will, therefore, spread through the supply base of the defence industry, impacting upon economic activity and prosperity in locations that seem remote to the core areas of defence production.

In terms of income generation, some states are particularly defence-dependent. California, for example, received over $50 billion per annum from the Department of Defense at the start of this decade, $23 billion of which was attributable to aerospace contracts. This underlines the crucial role of military aerospace (and its symbiotic relationship with civil aerospace) within the overall defence sector, a point explored further elsewhere in this book. The Los Angeles region alone attracted one-tenth of the entire US Department of Defense aerospace contracts. In addition, California received one-third of the total US defence budget for research, development, testing and evaluation. Department of Defense expenditure at the end of the Cold War accounted for some 8% of the state's gross product, distributed between industries involved in aerospace, electronics, high technology/computing and manufacturing sub-contractors. Without question, targeted defence expenditure kept the Californian economy buoyant over the decades when other states and regions of the US have suffered economic recession. Such has been its defence-dependency, however, that the state's economy experienced a severe downturn in the mid-1990s due primarily to the defence cutbacks with unemployment one-third higher than the national average (Cohen and Garcia, 1994).

Markusen has made many important contributions to identifying the geographic incidence of defence expenditure in the United States (see, for example, Markusen, 1991 and Markusen, 1997a). She notes the striking difference in post-war urbanisation patterns and population movements between the US and Europe and the impact this had on fundamentally changing the relative importance of US cities and regions. Markusen observes that one of the important causes of the 'remarkable re-composition' of the US was the prominent economic role played by the military as a consumer of manufacturing output. As the nature of warfare has changed over time from primitive manual weaponry, through mechanical to electronic weapons, so too the industry itself has relocated to reflect these trends. In the main, since 1945, the trend has been for US defence production to move away from the traditional industrial heart-lands and instead develop in suburban sites in the 'defence perimeter' of the US, an area defined as an area stretching from the Boston area south through Connecticut, Long Island to Newport News, Huntsville, Alabama, and Melbourne, Florida, across the gulf states to Dallas and Houston, and encompassing much of the inter-Mountain west, as well as the Pacific coast.

Consequently, between 1950 and the 1980s, the New England and West North Central states first suffered relative regional decline, followed by the mid-Atlantic states and later the East North central states. Rapid regional job growth was experienced, however, in states southwest of Texas, Colorado and Washington with later expansion in the southern states.

Markusen points to strong political factors which have tended to accentuate the distribution of defence contracts towards the 'defence perimeter' in the post-war period and identified important economic consequences associated with the concentration of much defence activity in the 'perimeter' regions. In particular, she argued that the US population had become more spatially segregated than previously with particular regions becoming more defence-dependent, thereby increasing their vulnerability to potential defence budget contraction in the future.

Defence expenditure within regions is often very highly concentrated and the US is no exception. In Missouri, for example, defence spending is concentrated in the districts in and around St Louis (principally related to McDonnell Douglas operations) and in the district around Fort Leonard Wood. At the same time, taxes have to be paid to finance defence expenditure or raise revenue to cover associated government debt service requirements. An examination of the defence expenditure concentration issue and associated taxation impact two decades ago, focusing upon districts within US states which had received Pentagon contracts, identified 305 out of 435 districts as net losers. Only Maryland and Connecticut on the east coast possessed more gaining than losing districts. In the North East, there were 79 net loser districts out of 104; in the Upper Midwest, 95 losing districts out of 100. No states in the Midwest or the South had more gaining districts than those losing.

Specific military projects, too, can exert significant economic impact upon particular localities within states. Unlike the B1 bomber which had weapons systems that were built in every Congressional district bar two, most projects have a more focused economic impact. In the competition between the C-17 and C-5B aircraft for the military heavy airlift contract, the Government Audit Office (GAO) tracked geographic distribution of prime and first-tier contracts. GAO found that the C-17 impacted upon 14 states and 42 House districts, with 30% of programme spending in one Congressional district (the California 19th). For the C-5B, 29 states and 76 House districts were involved in the project with over 25% of programme spending flowing to California's 22nd district and over 22% to Ohio's 1st district.

As noted earlier, UK research (see Chapter 4) has identified some of the complexities in and the extraordinary inter-dependency of the supply network for defence contractors which will inevitably mean that even areas of the US which appear remote from the defence contraction scythe are unlikely to escape its damaging effects, exacerbated by the current practice of major defence prime contractors to revolutionise their supply base in order to enhance the competitive edge of defence sub-contracting and expand the geographic spread of this sector of the market. For many companies, particularly the smaller ones in the sub-contract defence sector, the only effective solution seems to be to sharpen local focus while maintaining global competitiveness, a difficult combination but one which can be realistically pursued with sufficient management training (see, for example, Kanter, 1995).

b) The European Union

The regional distribution of defence expenditure across the European Union (EU) was estimated in 1992, in the most comprehensive study of its kind, to assess the significance of military expenditure to the European economy. The study employed a 'threshold' indicator of twice the European average for the share of the regional labour force directly employed in defence (European Commission 1992) and applied this indicator to specific regions of the EU. Some 19 regions were found to be particularly dependent on defence industrial activity and a further 31 regions were identified as particularly dependent upon military base activity. The most defence-dependent regions of Western Europe based upon the location of defence industry were identified as Cumbria in the United Kingdom and Bretagne and Acquitaine in France. Regions which were identified as being heavily dependent upon the military base sector for employment included parts of Greece (Voreio Aigaio, Notio Aigaio, Kriti); Spain (Ceuta y Melilla); and Portugal (Acores). In a few critical cases, some regions such as Avon, Gloucestershire and Wiltshire in the United Kingdom and Friuli in Italy exhibited significant dependence for employment on both elements of defence sector activity, making them potentially very vulnerable to deep and sustained cuts in defence expenditure.

The regional distribution of defence industrial production within the EU depends partly on historical origins of the industry and on the nature and extent of the kinds of weaponry produced by indigenous arms industries across the Union. In the UK, for example, the emergence of a 'capitalist arms industry', together with the need to defend the British Empire, brought to prominence a significant range of new defence companies with specific locations including Vickers (Sheffield), Whitworth (Manchester), and small arms and ordnance works at Birmingham and Coventry. The Second World War saw the emergence of a military-industrial complex in Britain with key industries such as vehicles, aircraft and electronic engineering being transformed into major military industries with relocation for wartime protection to the North West and southwest regions. The southeast, however, remained the most significant centre of defence activity with a focus on metal fabrication and electrical engineering industries (see Lovering 1991).

The development of the new Cold War industries widened the regional scope of defence production activity through nuclear weapons (North West coast), aircraft (North and South London, rural southeast, Midlands, southwest, and parts of Lancashire. Defence electronics, in turn, expanded most in middle and southern England and East Anglia. Barrow became the centre of UK submarine production and Newcastle and Leeds specialised in tank production.

The last decade, however, has witnessed a major restructuring of the British defence industry which has yet to run its full course. Overall, the restructuring process has brought into prominence the high technology centres of southern England while reducing the significance of the more traditional industrial regions. At the same time, Lovering (1993) notes that:

> 'as production employment declined the remaining work has been relocated towards lower wage costs areas, notably away from the southeast, a process encouraged in the late 1980s by the boom in Southern land values'

In Germany, on the other hand, defence production associated with significant weapon projects (frigates, the Leopard tank and the MRCA fighter aircraft) has been relatively concentrated in Bavaria (principally, Munich), Hamburg and Bremen. However, industries in the regions of Friedrichshafen, Mannheim, Cologne/Dusseldorf, Frankfurt, and Kiel also benefit from these military projects. Considerable disparity in the distribution of contract awards from the Federal Office of Military Procurement strengthens the regional impact of defence procurement. In 1976, for example, in Bavaria, a region which attracts two-and-a-half times as much defence expenditure as Baden-Wurttemberg, the procurement payment per industrial employee was five times as high as that in North-Rhine Westphalia and nearly ten times as high as that in Lower Saxony.

Overall in 1991, 0.68m people (0.55% of the labour force) were employed in the defence industries of the European Union with a further 2.2m employed in the armed forces (1.7% of the labour force). Together with civilians employed by the military and dependants, aggregate defence-dependent employment across the EC totalled some

TABLE 6: EUROPEAN COMMUNITIES NUTS II REGIONS: INDUSTRIAL DEFENCE-DEPENDENCY 1991

UNITED KINGDOM:	Cumbria, Essex, Lancashire, Cornwall, Devon, Avon, Gloucestershire, Wiltshire, Hampshire/Isle of Wight
GERMANY:	Bremen, Oberbayern
FRANCE:	Bretagne, Aquitaine, Provence-Alpes, Cote d'Azur,, Centre, Limousin, Mid-Pyrenees, Ile de France, Basse-Normandie, Haute-Normandie.
ITALY:	Liguria, Friuli-Venezia Giulia.

Source: Commission of the European Communities, 1992.

3m people (2.4% of the labour force). As noted earlier, regional defence-dependence within the EC was calculated using a 'threshold' indicator of twice the European average for the share of the regional labour force directly employed in defence. Applying this indicator to NUTS II regions of the EC, 19 regions were found to be particularly dependent on defence industrial activity. (see Table 6 below).

A further 31 regions were identified as very dependent upon military base activity. (see Table 7 below).

c) Russia/Former Soviet Union

The paucity of information relating to the distribution of the defence industry within the former Soviet Union has, in the past, made measurement of its regional concentration difficult although the pioneering work of Cooper (1991) has greatly clarified the picture. Cooper has identified 760 significant defence facilities within the former USSR, including production enterprises, science-production associations, research institutes, design organisations and military-related 'closed' towns. Three-quarters of this total are located within Russian territory, a further 14.5% in the Ukraine, and the remainder distributed across the other republics. Newer 'electronics-related' production facilities tend to be less regionally concentrated that the more traditional defence industries.

Regions with very high levels of defence-related employment include the North-West, Urals, Volgo-Vyatka and Volga regions. Again, such distribution of defence facilities and production tends to be highly concentrated. At the 'oblast' level, Cooper identifies the most defence-dependent from the employment perspective as including: Sverdlovsk,

TABLE 7: EUROPEAN COMMUNITIES NUTS II REGIONS: MILITARY BASE
DEPENDENCY, 1991

UNITED KINGDOM:	Hampshire & Isle of Wight, North Yorkshire, Cornwall, Devon, East Anglia, Avon, Gloucestershire, Wiltshire, Lincolnshire, Berkshire, Buckinghamshire, Oxfordshire.
GERMANY:	Trier, Koblenz, Luneburg, Rheinhessen-Pfalz, Unterfranken, Schleswig-Holstein, Gieben
FRANCE:	Corse, Lorraine, Provence-Alpes, Cote d'Azur.
ITALY:	Friuli-Venezia Giulia, Valle d'Aosta
GREECE:	Voreio Aigaio, Notio Aigaio, Kriti, Dytiki, Makedonia, Anatoliki, Thraki, Ipeiros
SPAIN:	Ceuta y Melilla, Madrid, Murcia.
PORTUGAL:	Acores, Madeira
BELG/LUX:	Suxemburg

Source: Commission of the European Communities, 1992.

Leningrad (city), Moscow (city), Nizhnii-Novgorod (Gor'kii), Moscow (oblast'), Perm', Samara (Kuibyshev), Novosibirsk, Tatarstan (Tatar ASSR) and Udmurtiya. Cooper (1991) notes the great significance of defence production to some regions. In Udmurtiya, for example, a remarkable concentration of defence factories is located, involving all the important towns (Izhevsk, Votkinsk, Sarapul and Glazov) where defence industry facilities dominate the local economy. In this region, military production has been estimated to account for about 85% of total industrial output and some 60% of total employment.

Assessing regional defence-dependency instead by the share of defence industry employment in total industrial employment, the regions that appear most defence-dependent include: Udmurtiya, Nikolaev (southern Ukraine), Kaluga, Mariiel, Northern Kazakhstan, Omsk, Voronezh, Novgorod, Perm' and Vladimir. Turning our attention to the Ukraine, major weapon production is located in Kiev, Khar'kov, Dnepropetrovsk, Lugansk, L'vov, Nikolaev and the Crimea. Kazakhstan has important production facilites in its northern region and, in addition, some 7% of territory was used as weapons testing sites under the former USSR regime, including nuclear testing facilities at Semipalatinsk and space/missile test facilities at Baikonur. Overall, some 40% of the former USSR territory was occupied by the defence ministry for weapons testing purposes with considerable regional impact.

The scale of Russian defence cuts has been immense. Given the recognised problems of tracking and accurately measuring defence expenditure in the member states of the former USSR, military production estimates may provide a better guide to the severity of these cuts. Compared with 1990, by 1992 Russian tank production had almost halved (from 1,300 to 675); artillery production had fallen from 1,900 new weapons to around 450; military aircraft production had declined from over 600 aircraft to some 170; and submarine and surface ships output had decreased from 20 to 8 vessels. To underline the sheer scale of arms reduction in Russia during the 1990's, it has been noted that, according to Russian sources, arms production is being cut back on a huge scale—50–60 percent, and for particular weapon categories by even 90 per cent. Overall, the last decade has witnessed a major change in the fortunes of the Russian military-industrial complex and severely weakened its capacity to help rebuild economic prosperity. As Izyumov et al. (1995) commented:

'...probably no other part of the Russian economy and society has suffered more casualties than its former pride, the military-industrial complex

(MIC). Having entered Gorbachev's *perestroika* at the height of its might and privilege, the MIC now finds itself disgraced, isolated, underfinanced and shrinking beyond recognition.'

At first, in the wave of euphoria sweeping the Western world following the unexpected end of the Cold War, Western support for the newly-emerging quasi-market 'economies in transition' seemed politically strong and economically substantial, particularly for Russia, although some analysts questioned the appropriateness of the economic aid provided by the West (see, for example, Kennaway, 1995). With the near simultaneous collapse of the inefficient but reasonably stable structures of the command economy of the Former Soviet Union (FSU), the solid security framework of the Warsaw Pact and the established trading networks of the Council for Mutual Economic Assistance, most of the new nations of the Commonwealth of Independent States (CIS) found themselves immediately immersed in a market experiment of the most intense kind.

Initially, expectations were optimistic with expert western market analysts predicting that, with the appropriate policies firmly in place, the transition to a fully-functioning market economy, while difficult and potentially destabilising in the short-run, would eventually be successfully achieved. If ever the potential for a genuine and lasting peace dividend was possible, many Western observers believed that the CIS, and particularly Russia, offered the best opportunity.

Here was a military-dominated economy and society where, with much reduced need for military expenditure, a smooth transition to civil production to meet the needs of long constrained consumers should be possible. As the scale of the transition required became clear and some of the transition economies began to experience grave instability and near economic collapse, expectations became much more pessimistic and market outcomes became increasingly subject to highly destabilising speculative activity.

The Russian experience since the heady days of 1990, however, illustrates the degree to which that early optimism completely failed to recognise the cumulative and damaging impacts of the whole range of conflicting economic forces being unleashed (Braddon, 1996b; Klein, Gronicki, and Kosaka, 1992). With hindsight, it has become clear that to expect a military-based super-power command economy like that of Russia to adjust, rapidly and smoothly, to the changes required to transform that system into a world-class market economy with only minimal support from the West was undoubtedly over-optimistic. To believe that this could be achieved while simultaneously undergoing transformation to a post-Cold War economy, requiring the rapid reduction of its highly significant military-industrial complex, has proved to be completely unrealistic (see Braddon, 1997).

CONVERSION IN RUSSIA

In order to deal with both the deepening economic crisis and the changing requirements of the post-Cold War world, Russia had little choice but to attempt to secure a peace dividend through a rapid and radical down-sizing of the defence sector and a similarly rapid expansion of civil production. As a result, the conversion programme, unavoidably, lay at the heart of an effective economic recovery programme (see Bougrov (1994) for an excellent discussion of this issue). Conversion plans were aligned closely with strategies to enhance Russia's economic growth rate and specific targets were set for the elimination of shortages in supply of many consumer goods by the mid-1990s. For example, the output of refrigerators, freezers, televisions and radios were intended to increase by one-half, while that of vacuum cleaners was planned to double, together with a 33-fold increase in the output of video-recorders. The conversion plans envisaged television ownership within Russia increasing by 3 per cent per annum and refrigerators/freezers by 4 per cent per annum. Even then, it was expected that this would represent ownership levels within Russia three to five times lower than in the United States with additional concern about product quality.

The financial demands placed upon the Russian government to facilitate effective conversion were, however, immense, making the strategy impossible to deliver without substantial long-term external support. Ozhegov et al. (1991) noted that, between 1991 and 1995 alone, it would have taken more than R40 billion in capital investments to restructure existing production facilities, to create new productive capacity for the production of civilian goods and to moth-ball older specialised production facilities as required. Given the economic collapse in Russia during those years, investment resources were simply insufficient to make such funds available for effective reconstruction.

Despite the constant problems encountered by recent conversion strategies, it is important to note that the process of defence conversion has been actively pursued by the governments of both the FSU and, more recently, Russia, for several years. Indeed, the first real conversion programme was formally launched by President Gorbachev over a decade ago in December, 1988. Under President Yeltsin, the strategy continued with somewhat mixed results.

As Cooper (1993) notes, President Yeltsin's government inherited a Soviet defence conversion policy but without the financial means to implement it. As a result, to a considerable extent, most defence enterprises were left to their own devices in dealing with their difficult situation. In some cases, enterprises have shown considerable initiative in teaming with foreign partners and switching into civilian production. Unfortunately, other key enterprises have been unable or unwilling to make the transition and, consequently, have had to rely upon meagre state budget support or, where possible, limited credit on preferential terms.

The transformation of the most successful and politically powerful sector of the Russian economy was always going to be an essential but formidable challenge. While the defence sector has traditionally had a priority claim on managerial, labour and material resources, it also differed from other sectors of the economy in that it could offer employees strong incentives in terms of higher salaries, bonuses and fringe benefits and was the only part of the economy to encounter genuine international competition through the arms race.

While on the civil side of the economy there appears to have been a damaging gap between research, innovation and eventual production, there is no evidence that this has been a feature of the military sector. However, in common with defence industries in the West, these strengths have, in the past, been offset to some extent by the absence of incentives to economise on the use of capital, labour and material inputs in military production. Given its critical strategic role within the economy, now significantly reduced, and its unquestioned political influence, it seems certain that the military-industrial complex in Russia will remain a key player in facilitating or, perhaps, obstructing the process of overall economic transformation.

In general, analysts view the comparative failure of the conversion strategy in Russia during the 1990s as very discouraging (see, for example, Leitenberg, 1992). However, it is important to emphasise that the lack of real progress to date is attributable not to technical obstacles, but to political, bureaucratic and managerial barriers, as well as the more obvious financial constraints. Cooper (1993) makes the critical point that the defence sector itself remains a principal actor in the evolution of post-Communist Russia. Despite the experiences of the last decade, the Russian defence industrial complex still retains significant power and influence which it can utilise to undermine progress towards a market, mixed economy, if that does not appear to be in its best interests. Surprisingly (and perhaps somewhat perversely in the post-Cold War context), the defence sector remains in a position where it can have a major impact on the success or failure of the government's attempts to improve living standards. The degree to which Russia has been able to pursue the defence conversion option during the 1990s will be discussed further in Chapter 5.

THE PEACE DIVIDEND

Since 1945, total world military expenditure has been estimated at between $30 and $35 trillion (Felice, 1998, p. 36). Annual global military expenditure roughly equals the income of half of the world's population. Estimates suggest that just 12% of the military expenditure of the developing nations would be sufficient to provide primary health care for everyone; just 8% of the total would enable the provision of family planning to everyone and help to stabilise the world's exploding population by 2015. It would take only 4% of developing countries, annual military budgets to extend primary education on a universal basis and cut adult illiteracy by half. (Felice, 1998, p. 32).

With such vast global resources being dedicated to military activities over such a prolonged period of time—and with the opportunity cost dimension only too clear—it is scarcely surprising that analysts should anticipate that the so-called 'outbreak of peace' in the 1990s would be linked with the release of a significant proportion of military resources into alternative uses.

It appeared unquestionable at the time that the world was presented with an unparalleled opportunity to extract a large and lasting peace dividend from the diminution of the threat of ultimately self-destructive super-power conflict and the associated scope for massive cutbacks in armaments production and military infrastructure. To politicians and the public alike, the end of the Cold War appeared to offer a guarantee of significant economic rewards (for an early analysis of the post-Cold War peace dividend, see Dunne and Smith, 1990). The concern of some analysts with the significant costs associated with reduced military expenditure tended to be dismissed lightly and the peace dividend resulting from substantial disarmament was seen primarily in terms of enhanced consumption rather than as an investment process (see Hartley et al. (1993) for a fuller discussion of this point), although it was clear that the armed forces would themselves demand a significant share of the peace dividend in order to reconstruct their role, mission and responsibilities to meet new rapid reaction, peace-keeping and humanitarian requirements.

The economic analysis of the peace dividend process has tended to focus upon the opportunity cost dimension of military expenditure, often at the national level (see, for example, Dunne and Smith, 1984) and the literature has concentrated largely on two issues in particular: the impact of military spending on productivity (or the rate of growth of GDP over time); and the impact of military expenditure by government on the allocation of other varieties of public sector spending. In the literature, the predicted consequences of the peace dividend in terms of both faster economic growth and higher government expenditure on social provision are considered to be desirable goals, commensurate with improving national well-being. Yet, as Chan (1996) noted, there is considerable evidence to support the propositions that faster economic growth tends to exacerbate rather than resolve income inequity and also that high levels of government expenditure, through large public sector deficits and high inflation, can be detrimental to the poor, the intended beneficiaries of the government's welfare spending.

In the initial wave of optimism that followed the end of the Cold War at the beginning of the 1990s, there were heightened expectations of a peace dividend to be attained from the process of disarmament that would surely follow and attempts were made to estimate the scale and scope of the peace dividend for individual countries (see, for example, Smith, 1991). With a much-reduced demand for military output, a significant proportion of the vast expenditure which had, for so many decades, been absorbed by the resource-hungry military industrial complex could now be redirected to more socially-desirable purposes.

In particular, public and political expectations were high concerning the potential for improved public services (education, health, welfare) and rural amenities (see, for example, Dowdall and Braddon, 1995) and for enhanced private civil sector development, especially for civil research and development which, it was argued, had previously been 'crowded out' by high levels of defence expenditure. The scale of the task confronting such a dividend in alleviating human suffering and acting as a catalyst for social betterment was, of course, immense but significant improvements in the global human condition were thought to be possible even with a relatively modest peace dividend. Arias

(1997) noted that, for example, in the context of total global military expenditure of over $800 billion in 1995:

> 'If we redirected just $40 billion of those resources over the next 10 years to fighting poverty, all of the world's population would enjoy basic social services, such as education, health care and nutrition, reproductive health, clean water and sanitation. Another $40 billion would provide all people on the planet with an income above the poverty line for their country.'

Yet, it should not be overlooked that even in the poorest parts of the world, where the Cold War and its cessation had little real meaning or significance, military expenditure still remains high. Arias cites the case of sub-Saharan Africa, a region which has the highest proportion of people in poverty in the world and where, in 1995, military expenditure was approximately $8 billion (Arias, 1997).

Part of the problem of securing a genuine and lasting peace dividend is that the quest becomes entangled in the issue of how best the diverted military budget should be employed, who should receive it and for what purpose. As the United Nations emphasised in 1995, there is no unanimous agreement among analysts and political decision-makers on how best to reallocate the resources released by reduced military expenditures.

Another element of the peace dividend problem is that the process whereby such a dividend is acquired is quite complex and often difficult to fully understand. Brommelhorster and Dedek (1998) observe that some analysts see it as a process which starts with the release of financial resources and then, through a wide range of alternative uses, generates ultimately a series of 'positive' welfare results. They make the point that such a process, characterized as it will be by causes and effects, decisions and transmissions, is far more complex than commonly supposed by those who view the process simply in terms of reduced defence spending and the consequent reallocation of government spending in isolation.

Brommelhorster and Dedek propose a more appropriate methodology by which to explore the peace dividend process and suggest that the process should be considered in 3 stages, a resource dividend, a product dividend and a welfare dividend. The resource dividend from military cutbacks amount to the direct savings resulting from this strategy. However, it is very important to note that these direct savings are unlikely to amount to the actual reduction in military expenditure. Military build-up may be a costly business but disarmament is not necessarily low cost, a factor often neglected in simplistic estimates of potential real savings from military expenditure cuts. Eliminating weapon systems and military installations, particularly nuclear, is a high cost procedure and one likely to absorb a significant proportion of any ensuing peace dividend for many years. Similarly, if defence cuts mean substantial and prolonged unemployment, the cost of disarmament may again seriously erode a potential peace dividend.

The product dividend should occur as the resources freed from the military sector are redirected to the civil sector, in pursuit of greater production efficiency. The degree to which this process succeeds in generating a peace dividend will depend upon the relative efficiency of public and private, and military and non-military sectors of the economy. If a high level of defence expenditure does, in fact, contribute to impaired national economic performance, there may well be scope for enhancing national output and employment by a redistribution of defence budgets to civil activities. To achieve the dividend goal, at the micro level there would need to be evidence that the civil sector operates with higher productivity levels than the defence sector and, from a macroeconomic perspective, that private investment levels would increase as a result of reductions in public expenditure.

The welfare dividend would be captured by society as defence expenditure is redirected into social provision (health, education etc.) and, in turn over the longer period, such improvements in welfare provision translate into a healthier, better educated workforce.

The process whereby these theoretical stages of the peace dividend process occur is, in reality, either left to the market or, occasionally, becomes part of government strategy. In 1993, President Clinton committed the US to a plan of action designed to acquire precisely such a dividend and launched an ambitious plan, focused principally on economic conversion, as a means of securing significant civil sector enhancement in the transition to peace. Infrastructure improvements, employment training and the expansion of commercial sector research and development were all prime targets for the new strategy. Byler (1998) estimates that over the period 1993 to 1998, the peace dividend in the US may have amounted to as much as £81 billion. Of this sum, some $16.5 billion has been used to fund economic conversion projects with varying degrees of success, while about 80% has been redirected to reduce the federal deficit. To some economists, deficit reduction has a distinct economic impact which may, in turn, stimulate economic adjustment in a positive direction if interest rates decline in response to lower public sector debt.

The key ingredient in the Clinton strategy was the pursuit of dual-use technologies—a means by which both government and industrial research and development budgets could ultimately serve both military and civil objectives. The intention was to fund leading-edge technology developments in the civil sector and transfer them for military application wherever possible. The cost saving dimension of this strategy was, on paper, highly attractive to government and industry alike. By employing sub-systems and components designed for commercial use in military products, defence budgets could be significantly reduced or higher standard military products could be acquired for the same budget.

Furthermore, by harnessing technologies originally developed for military application to the production of both military and civil goods, economies of scope could be secured as output would be spread over a much larger customer base. In practice, however, the evidence of the 1990s suggests that the development of dual-use technologies and their application, while successful in some instances, confronts major problems in terms of corporate culture and the functioning of the defence market and that the current stated goal of US defence industrial policy for an integrated civil and military industrial and technological base—perhaps the most effective corporate route to a real and lasting peace dividend—remains largely inaccessible.

Klein (1997) makes the important point that, in attempting to understand the economic impacts associated with changes in military expenditure, it is essential to separate short and long term effects on goods, services and employment, emanating from budgetary adjustment. He also emphasises the need to treat with caution economic impact projections on both the demand and supply side. To understand the full impact on the supply side, a real analysis must also be combined with a monetary analysis, focusing upon the cost of capital and interest rates and incorporating the 'overall public budgetary position' (Klein, 1997) as well as impacts on international trade. Klein asserts that a peace dividend is already in existence and will become more significant over time. It is Klein's assertion that

> 'Adam Smith's invisible hand has guided "the market" in the allocation of the peace dividend. A dividend in the form of reduced global spending for military purposes has, in fact, been realized, but its distribution is not

visible to the naked eyes of the lay observer. But to the eye of the analytical economist, it can be seen.'

It is the view of this analytical economist, however, that while a peace dividend in the form of significant cost savings in global military expenditure may ultimately be realized, the transfer of these cost savings through market adjustment alone into a genuine, substantial, enduring and, in particular, visible peace dividend will be far more problematic.

BUDGET TRADE-OFFS AND THE PEACE DIVIDEND

In economic literature, it is frequently posited that defence expenditure exerts a negative influence upon national economic performance and some analysts report statistical results that appear to confirm this damaging relationship. In general, however, it has been extremely difficult to discover any convincing evidence that reductions in defence expenditure have a predictable and positive impact upon national economic performance. Superficially, one could argue that the improved economic performance of the US after 1990 is interestingly correlated with a period when defence expenditure was shrinking rapidly. A causal relationship, however, would be very difficult to prove.

Certainly, the reduction in defence expenditure represents a diminution of the role of the government in the economy and will undoubtedly exert some influence on economic performance through its effects on demand, deficit reduction or real interest rates. But the defence cutbacks will only be part of the fiscal story and the influence they exert may be positive or it may be negative as far as national economic performance is concerned. The empirical evidence distilled from the literature suggests that the defence expenditure/economic performance relationship tends to vary depending upon the country and time period under consideration with examples of both positive and negative relationship as well as, in some cases, no apparent relationship at all.

More directly, the peace dividend has at its heart the notion that expenditure on defence necessarily excludes—or 'crowds out'—that same level of expenditure on other forms of public spending outside defence. Governments are seen to have a direct choice between defence expenditure and that on, say, health, education or housing. Public spending devoted previously to the provision and maintenance of defence activities is often perceived to be easily transferable to other desirable public goods, thereby considerably improving living standards. This view is based on the supposition that all public goods necessarily compete with each other for a share of a limited public budget and, consequently, higher spending in one area will unavoidably reduce spending in another. Consequently, with this apparent negative correlation in mind, the end of the Cold War and declining military budgets raised public expectations for this kind of resource transfer.

Yet, in the literature, once again, it is difficult to find studies which offer incontrovertible evidence that such a direct and inevitable trade-off between defence and other public goods exists, and the concept of a zero-sum outcome in public expenditure budgets and their distribution is frequently challenged (see, for example, Russet, 1982 and Donke et al. 1983). Indeed, it may be that many of the relevant studies miss the point and, as a result, divert attention from what may become, ultimately, the source of the real peace dividend. In the US, for example, apart from the years when the Reagan administration implemented a massive build-up of armaments associated with the Star Wars programme, defence and public sector social spending have both increased simultaneously over time. The trade-off here, therefore, may be between public and private consumption or public and private investment, rather than the exclusion of public social spending in order to finance defence.

Furthermore, where consumption in both public and private sectors is paid for through borrowing, the trade-off is likely to be between current and future consumption, since additional consumption today will reduce the current capacity to invest and will impact adversely on future income and consumption levels as a result. Where public or private expenditure is financed by greater debt—and that debt, especially in terms of public sector debt servicing—becomes an economic problem in itself, it may well be that the peace dividend needs to be measured more in terms of debt reduction (with possible easing of interest rates as a result) than in terms of enhanced public sector social provision. Alternatively, where the burden of public sector expenditure is perceived to have driven up tax rates to a level at which serious disincentives to work effort, savings and investment come into effect, it may be that the peace dividend needs to be seen in terms of a supply-side stimulus to be derived from tax cuts, made possible as government expenditure declines due to defence cutbacks.

It is usually the case that governments plan their expenditure over relatively long periods of time and, when the economic situation allows, vary the aggregate level of spending to take account of desired goals and stated manifesto pledges. Despite the obsession with public expenditure constraint in the 1980s and 1990s in the major industrial nations, in line with the central tenets of monetarism and free-market economics, governments can and still do exercise the power to adjust the fiscal stance to accommodate the needs of the economy and their political objectives. The overall level of public expenditure, then, can be manipulated within reasonable limits, a possibility which effectively erodes the notion of any fixed-sum trade-off between defence spending and expenditure on other public services. Indeed, for much of the last half century in most of the major industrial nations, and at times in spite of the so-called monetarist counter-revolution with its emphasis on money supply control and public sector restraint, there has been a pronounced tendency for the public sector to expand and to absorb a greater proportion of national output over time.

Perhaps, though, the trade-off for the economy and society as a whole lies elsewhere. There is, for example, some evidence (see, for example, Eichenberg, 1984) that there may be a trade-off between defence (and other forms of public) spending and tax revenue. Eichenberg's results for the West German economy revealed no trade-off between defence expenditure and social spending but did identify the higher tax burden (especially social security payroll taxes) which seemed to accompany increases in the German defence budget.

In addition to the widely-perceived but, for the most part, apparently unfounded trade-offs that make the identification (and possibly the attainment) of a genuine peace dividend difficult, it is also a popular misconception to regard defence expenditure as necessarily socially disadvantageous when compared with the other forms of welfare expenditure implemented by government. Without concealing the precise purpose of defence expenditure, it is still necessary to remember that a significant proportion of the defence budget has a 'welfare' dimension, without which a large number of families would be worse off. Within the defence budget, large sums are dispensed in salary payments and additional services provided by the military include subsidies for health care, housing, education, transport and catering. Furthermore, as highlighted previously, defence expenditure can have a critically important role to play in the economic well-being of specific defence-dependent regions. In career terms, too, many generations of young people from less well-off backgrounds have found opportunity for personal advancement in the armed forces. Against the conventional wisdom, therefore, it may be that any socially beneficial effects emanating from a reduction in the resources going to the defence sector have to be adjusted to take account of the negative impact of defence budget cuts on these important 'welfare' aspects of the military infrastructure.

In discussions of the consequences of declining defence expenditure in the economics literature, the focus of attention, as we have seen, tends to be the fiscal stance of the national government and the degree to which a trade-off between defence and social expenditure exists. In many countries, local authorities and regional administrations play a significant part in funding public provision and studies tend to overlook this aspect of the fiscal stance, leading in turn to misleading results and policy implications. Assessing correlations and trade-offs between aggregate expenditure levels at the national level, then, may offer an incomplete picture of the real situation.

Recognising the complex nature and temporal dimensions of the policy-making process is also crucial to understanding how and when a peace dividend of any kind may appear. The choice to release expenditure 'saved' from the reduction of defence budgets in the form of additional social spending will have an immediate and mainly consumption-led impact on the economy. Even here, however, the timing will depend on the fiscal cycle, whereby various categories of government expenditure tend to change only gradually over time and sudden, large changes occur very infrequently. Government expenditure programmes tend to be incremental in nature and a social expenditure peace dividend would take some time to implement. Furthermore, governments need to address issues such as business cycles, political unpopularity at constituency level and associated lobbying, the imminence of election dates and so forth in deciding when and where to release new social expenditure.

Diverting, instead, such resources into public sector deficit reduction will tend to have a delayed impact and then will only show itself in a 'dividend' sense if interest rates fall and consumption and investment respond positively to the stimulus. Again, choosing to deliver a peace dividend in the form of lower taxation will change the nature and timing of the impact, since the eventual supply-side effects of this strategy will depend on which taxes are reduced, the income groups receiving the tax reduction and what they, in turn, choose to do with the windfall.

ALTERNATIVE DEFENCE SCENARIOS

Some studies in the United States have attempted to identify potential cost savings from specific changes that could be implemented in the US approach to security provision as part of the adjustment to a 'new world order'. At present, the US commits over $250 billion per year to its defence activities, domestically and globally, which represents expenditure of some $680 million per day to fulfil its world military role (Felice, 1998, p. 27). Estimates suggest that for each 1% of Gross National product committed to defence expenditure, the economic growth rate of the country concerned declines by 0.5% (Smith, 1980).

Kaufmann and Steinbruner (1991) have estimated the cost savings to the US from adopting a new security strategy whereby military provision, in partnership with other allied nations, is seen as entirely a defensive rather than an offensive activity with much smaller standing forces, nuclear arsenals and so forth as a result. With the emphasis on co-operation between nations on the security front and strict adherence to a defence-only code of practice, Kaufmann and Steinbruner suggest that the US could save over $420 billion in a decade.

O'Hanlon (1995) suggests that the US could easily and safely reduce defence expenditure by a further 10% per annum without reducing significantly its capacity to respond to global crises or to fulfil its global commitments. Such savings would add some $100 billion to the Clinton administration's projected cost savings from defence expenditure reduction over a seven year period.

At the more extreme end of the potential peace dividend scenario, Forsberg (1992) argues that the introduction of a genuine global 'co-operative security' strategy would release massive funds from the US military sector, potentially up to 80% of the budget, amounting to cost savings of some $180 billion per year.

Clements et al. (1996) found that those countries that implemented deep cuts in military expenditure during the 1990s typically (and, perhaps, surprisingly in the context of a peace dividend) also reduced non-military expenditure as well as their fiscal deficits. In this sense, then, the peace dividend could be measured in terms of any resulting stimulus to private investment, triggered by the deficit reduction and its impact on interest rates and market confidence. The authors also noted that there was some limited evidence to suggest that some countries have been able to support or increase their existing social spending, despite cuts in total public spending, due to military expenditure budgets shrinking.

Focusing specifically on the US, Bischak (1997) notes the conventional wisdom that, once again, the peace dividend emanating from defence expenditure cuts has been used to reduce the budget deficit, following the Budget Enforcement Act of 1990 which put in place barriers to attempt to move defence savings into other economic sectors. Bischak also notes, however, that an additional peace dividend has been generated by government through the financing of economic conversion and environmental programmes ($36.9 billion) via defence budgets. Between 1990 and 1995, Bischak suggests that modest increases in public spending of some $9.4 billion on areas such as infrastructure, construction, transportation, community, regional development, environment, community health and education and training were facilitated by military expenditure cuts.

ERODING THE PEACE DIVIDEND

All the analyses above assume that the decision to cut defence expenditure and divert the resources 'saved' into alternative forms of economic activity can be achieved in a relatively smooth, rapid and relatively cost-less manner. Such a desirable outcome, however, could only be attained if both market forces and government decision-making respond quickly to the changing environment surrounding the defence sector and ensure that resources do indeed move as they need to in order to minimise transition costs.

All the evidence suggests that, in reality, the process of transition from high to lower defence expenditure carries with it a whole range of additional costs which must be borne by the local, regional or national economy. These costs may include higher unemployment as defence industries and the armed forces shed personnel in response to the cuts; the consequent loss of income and expenditure and their multiplier impacts in regional economies, dependent on defence-related employment for their economic well-being; the very high financial costs of decommissioning nuclear, chemical, biological and other weapons and rendering them safe (see, for example, BICC, 1996); and a variety of other costs including personnel retraining, environmental restitution and so forth that will undoubtedly be required. Furthermore, in an unstable and turbulent world, the need for 'force regeneration' at short notice cannot be overlooked and there will be costs associated with the process of ensuring that, despite defence cuts, an adequate military response can be made in times of crisis.

Some analysts actually question whether there has been a genuine peace dividend at all and contend that, even if the potential for one has existed, that dividend has now been lost. In the US, Greider has concluded that the peace dividend that was anticipated following the end of the Cold War has not materialised. While US military expenditure has declined in recent years, it still remains very high compared with the average over time, yet the US military are now beset with problems relating to maintenance and the availability of spare parts as well as significant issues of low morale in the armed forces and an apparent shortage of 1,300 trained pilots in the Air Force. The US Joint Chiefs of Staff have warned Congress and President Clinton that the military sector is in danger of decline. It is becoming increasingly clear that reconstructing the armed forces to meet the defence and security requirements of the post-Cold War world will absorb a considerable proportion of any dividend that does eventually accrue.

Despite spending more than three times as much on defence as any other country, the US has reached a situation in which, according to Senator McCain of Arizona 'too much of our military is not ready to rapidly deploy into a conflict'. Greider lays the blame for this with the 'Iron Triangle' (see Adams, 1981), the so-called military-industrial complex uniting defence contractors, politicians in the Congress and the Pentagon and their tendency to fund leading-edge, high-technology and extremely expensive equipment, draining the defence budget and creating real problems in maintaining a modern and effective fighting force capable of rapid response to contain and defuse regional conflicts.

Similar vested interests are highlighted by Markusen (1997b) in reviewing recent literature on the dividend to explain why the US has demonstrably failed to demobilise after the Cold War ended and has all but reneged on its commitment to deliver a real and lasting peace dividend. Leaving post-Cold War adjustment primarily to the market to reallocate resources has failed to secure much in the way of peace dividend benefits for US citizens. Worse still, the initiatives undertaken by the US government to facilitate the transfer of resources from the military to the civil sector (discussed later in this book)—a crucial step in attaining a genuine peace dividend—have been undermined and ultimately reversed.

Finally, Allison et al. (1996) noted that the collapse of the Soviet empire left vast quantities of highly dangerous weapons-grade nuclear material in vulnerable stockpiles across the former Soviet Union (FSU), raising the alarming prospect of theft and eventual use by terrorists or rogue states. The authors note that on six occasions since 1991, unsuccessful attempts have been made to sell stolen Russian nuclear material. With sufficient nuclear material in Russian stockpiles to manufacture over 100,000 nuclear weapons (including an estimated

800 to 1,200 tons of highly enriched uranium and 200 tons of pluto-nium), held in security conditions which are described by the authors as: 'questionable at best, non-existent at worst', there is clearly great urgency attached to finding an appropriate solution. In 1991, the US enacted legislation introduced by Senators Nunn and Lugar which enabled the US to spend $300–$400 million per year to help dismantle nuclear weapons held in the FSU. The Nunn-Lugar Co-operative Threat Reduction Programme has a total budget committed by Congress of $1.5 billion and has four principal objectives: to destroy weapons of mass destruction; to transport, store, disable and safe-guard weapons of mass destruction before their elimination; to estab-lish verifiable controls on the proliferation of weapons of mass destruction, components and associated materials; and to prevent the global movement of scientific expertise associated with weapons of mass destruction that could otherwise encourage their proliferation (see IISS, The Military Balance, p. 15).

Allison et al. allege that this effort is minimal in the context of the scale of the problem and argue that the US needs to spend at least $30 billion (a sum roughly equivalent to the entire budget for the B2 bomber or the Trident nuclear submarine programme) to purchase, remove, secure and store Russian weapons-grade nuclear material.

CONCLUSION

In the initial wave of optimism that followed the end of the Cold War at the beginning of the decade of the 1990s, there were heightened expectations of a peace dividend to be attained from the process of disarmament that would surely follow. With a much-reduced demand for military output, a significant proportion of the vast expenditure which had, for so many decades, been absorbed by the resource-hungry military industrial complex could now be redirected to more socially-desirable purposes. In particular, public and political expecta-tions were high concerning the potential for improved public services (education, health, welfare) and for enhanced private civil sector development, especially for civil research and development which, it was argued, had previously been 'crowded out' by high levels of defence expenditure. The scale of the task confronting such a dividend in alleviating human suffering and acting as a catalyst for human bet-terment was, of course, immense but significant improvements in the global human condition were thought to be possible even with a rela-tively modest peace dividend.

In practice, we may observe that the market, in such a complex and difficult phase of economic history, has been found seriously wanting, leaving fundamental disequilibrium in its wake. While there are certainly a number of examples of military producers choosing to, and succeeding in, switching part of their operations into civil production during the 1990s, they have been the exception rather than the rule. By far the most notable corporate response to declining defence expenditure during the decade, which will be discussed further in Chapter 2, has been initial corporate contraction combined with rationalisation, generating a series of massive lay-offs of defence workers in the major prime contractors, adversely affected by defence cuts. This has been followed, in turn, by a similar adjustment process in the second and subsequent tiers of the defence industry supply chain as suppliers and subcontractors find their business also declining and respond with additional employee redundancies. In this sense, the market has certainly adjusted rapidly and smoothly to the reduction in demand for military products but not in such a way as to deliver a peace dividend or even a satisfactory equilibrium outcome. Instead, in many instances, the market has generated a sub-optimal outcome in the form of a peace 'tax' rather than 'dividend' for society in the form of higher unemployment, idle resources, and the failure to transfer these scarce resources into efficient alternative uses.

Furthermore, as will be argued later in the book, even the limited funding devoted to economic conversion in the US during the 1990s may be considered to be targeted in reality at meeting military rather than civil objectives, further diminishing the potential for a genuine peace dividend. The conclusion must be drawn at the end of the decade of the 1990s that, for the most part, the peace dividend has yet to be attained. Market forces have not, as yet, shown themselves capable of generating the kind of rapid and flexible adjustment processes that would transform the economic and social impacts of defence decline in a strongly positive direction. For economists and politicians persuaded of the supreme efficacy of the market in resolving the economic damage attributable to such exogenous shocks, the experience of the last decade (with respect to the peace dividend issue at least) must have been surprising. In this unique set of conditions, smooth and rapid market adjustment to a desired end has been exposed as a myth. Rather than economic adjustment to significant defence cutbacks leading to an easy and costless transition to securing a large and sustainable peace dividend, the process of market adjustment has in fact been characterised by a whole series of obstacles, delays and dis-equilibria. In turn, the adjustment process has been exacerbated by the need to bear significant direct and indirect costs necessary to ensure peace is maintained (for further discussion of these issues and reference to additional studies of the peace dividend, see Kirby, 1991, pp. 174–176; and Fontanel, 1995, pp. 563–590). These obstacles, delays and costs are to be found in the market responses of the defence industry prime contractors and their supply chains, the labour market, the conversion process and disarmament, technology transfer and dual-use technology development, among others. It is these key features of the process of economic adjustment in the defence sector which form the focus of the analysis in the following chapters and constitutes the main elements behind the myth of market solutions to major exogenous shocks in modern economies which is the central theme of this book.

REFERENCES

Adams G., (1981), *The Iron Triangle: The Politics of Defence Contracting*, Council on Economic Priorities.

Allison G., Cote O., Falkenrath R. and Miller S., (1996), *Avoiding Nuclear Anarchy: Containing the Threat of Loose Russian Nuclear Weapons and Fissile Material*, MIT Press.

Arias O., (1997) The Price of Peace, *BICC Bulletin*, No. 5, 1 October.

BICC, (1996), Global Disarmament, Demilitarization and Demobilization, *Conversion Survey 1996*, Bonn International Center for Conversion.

BICC, (1996), *Cost of Disarmament*, Bonn International Center for Conversion, Brief 6.

BICC, (1999), BICC Yearbook: *Conversion Survey 1999*, and at http://bicc.uni-bonn.de/milex/data-1997.html

Bischak G., (1997) *What happened to the Peace Dividend?* See http://www.webcom.com/ncecd/div.html

Bischak G. and Oden M., (1991) The INF Treaty and the United States experience: The industrial, economic and employment impact, in Paukert L. and Richards P., (eds) *Defence Expenditure, industrial conversion and local employment*, International Labour Office, Geneva, pp. 123–152.

Bougrov E., (1994) Conversion in Transitional Economies: The Case of the Former USSR and Russia, *Defence and Peace Economics*, Vol. 5, pp. 153–166.

Braddon D. L., (1995), Regional Impact of Defence Expenditure, in Hartley K. and Sandler T., (eds.) *Handbook of Defence Economics*, Elsevier Science B.V., North Holland, Ch. 17.'

Braddon D. L., (1996a), The Regional Dimension of Defence Economics: An Introduction, *Defence and Peace Economics*, Vol. 7.

Braddon D. L., (1996b), Economic Instability in Russia: The Price of Peace?, in Carlton D., Ingram P., and Tenaglia G., (eds) *Rising Tension in Eastern Europe and the Former Soviet Union*, Dartmouth, 1996.

Braddon D. L. (1997) Dancing on the Edge of the Chasm: The Struggle for Survival in the Former Soviet Union, in Carlton D. and Ingram P., (eds) *The Search for Stability in Russia and the Former Soviet Union*, Ashgate, 1997.

Brommelhorster and Dedek, (1998*), Changing Priorities of Military Expenditures and the Results of the Peace Dividend*, BICC Peace Dividend Project, September.

Brzoska M., (1995) World Military Expenditures, in Hartley K. and Sandler T., (eds.) *Handbook of Defence Economics*, Elsevier Science B.V., North Holland, Ch. 3, pp. 45–68.

Byler J D, (1998), *Washington Memo*, March-April, Volume XXX, No. 2.

Chan S., (1996), Romancing the Peace Dividend, BICC Conversion Survey, Bonn.

Clements B., Gupta S. and Schiff J., (1996), Worldwide Military Spending, 1990–95, *International Monetary Fund Working Paper*, No. 96/64, June, IMF Washington D.C.

Cohen S. S. and Garcia C. E., (1994), California's Missile Gap, *California Management Review*, Vol. 37, No. 1, Fall.

Commission of the European Communities, (1992), *The Economic and Social Impact of Reductions in Defence Spending and Military Forces on the Regions of the Community*, EC. Brussels.

Connaughton R. M. (1993), Swords and Ploughshares: Coalition Operations, the Nature of Future Conflict and the United Nations, *Strategic and Combat Studies Institute Occasional Paper No.7*.

Cooper J., (1991) The Soviet Defence Industry and Conversion: The Regional Dimension, in Paukert L. and Richards P., (eds) *Defence Expenditure, Industrial Conversion and Local Employment*, International Labour Office, Geneva.

Cooper J., (1993) Transforming Russia's Defence Industrial Base, *Survival*, Vol. 35, (4) pp. 147–162.

Dowdall P. and Braddon D. L., (1995) *The 'Peace Dividend' and Rural England*, Research Unit in Defence Economics, University of the West of England, Bristol, a report for the Rural Development Commission, February.

Dunne J. P. and Smith R., (1984), The Economic Consequences of Reduced UK Military Expenditure, *Cambridge Journal of Economics*, 8, pp. 297–310.

Dunne P. and Smith R., (1990), The Peace Dividend and the UK Economy, *Cambridge Econometrics*, Report No. 1, Spring, pp. 47–61.

Eichenberg B., (1993), A Payments Mechanism for the Former Soviet Union: Is the EPU a Relevant Precedent?, *Economic Policy*, 17 October

Felice W. F. (1998), Militarism and Human Rights, *International Affairs*, 74, 1, pp. 25–40.

Fontanel J., (1995) Economics of Disarmament, in Hartley K. and Sandler T., (eds.) *Handbook of Defence Economics*, Elsevier Science B.V., North Holland, Ch. 19.

Forsberg R., (1992) Defense Cuts and Co-operative Security in the post-Cold War World, *Boston Review*, 17, 3-4, May-July.

Franck Jr. R. E. and Hildebrandt G. G. (1994), Alternatives for Defense in the Post-Soviet World: A Guide for Economists to the US Debate, *Defence and Peace Economics*, Vol. 5, pp. 37–50.

Gansler J., Military and Industrial Cooperation in a Transformed, NATO-Wide Competitive Market, XVth International NATO Workshop on Political-Military Decision Making, Vienna, 22 June, 1998.

Grawe O. R., (1991) *Defence Rationalisation in the US*, mimeograph, Division of Economic Policy Analysis, Federal Trade Commission, Washington D.C..

Greider W., (1998), Fortress America, cited in *Peace Dividend: What happened to Savings?*, http://wvgazette.com/Editorial/PEAC1217.html

Hartley K., Bhaduri A., Bougrov E., Deger S., Dessouki A., Fontanel J., de Haan H., Intriligator M., and Egea A. (1993), *Economic Aspects of Disarmament: Disarmament as an Investment Process*, United Nations Institute for Disarmament Research (UNIDIR), New York.

Hewitt D., (1991) Military Expenditure: International Comparison of Trends, *International Monetary Fund Working Paper 91/54*, IMF Washington D.C.

International Institute for Strategic Studies (IISS), (1998), The Military Balance, 1998–99, Oxford University Press for IISS, October.

Izyumov A., Kosals L. and Ryvkin R., (1995), The Russian Military-Industrial Complex: The Shock of Independence, in Di Chiaro III J., (ed.) *Conversion of the Defence Industry in Russia and Eastern Europe*, Proceedings of the BICC/CISAC Workshop on Conversion, April.

James A., (1995), Peacekeeping in the post-Cold War Era, *International Journal*, 1, Spring.

Kanter R. M., (1995), *World Class: Thriving Locally in the Global Economy*, Simon and Schuster.

Kaufmann W. and Steinbruner J., (1991) *Decisions for Defence: Prospects for a New Order*, The Brookings Institution, Washington D.C., p. 70.

Kennaway A., (1995), *What is wrong with western aid to the FSU and Central and Eastern Europe and how to improve it*, Conflict Studies Research Centre, Paper M11, May.

Kirby S., (1991), Demilitarising Europe, in Kirby S. and Hooper N., (eds.) *The Cost of Peace: Assessing Europe's Security Options,* Harwood Academic Publishers.

Kirkpatrick D L. I.(1995) The Rising Unit Cost of Defence Equipment—The Reasons and the Results, *Defence and Peace Economics,* Vol. 6, pp. 263–288.

Klein L. R., (1997), *Economic Analysis of the Peace Dividend,* BICC Bulletin No. 3, Bonn International Center for Conversion, April.

Klein L. R., Gronicki M., and Kosaka H, (1992) Impact of Military Cuts on the Soviet and East European Economies: Models and Simulations, in Isard W. and Anderton C. H., *Economics of Arms Reduction and the Peace Process: Contributions from Peace Economics and Peace Science,* North-Holland, Elsevier Science Publishers B.V..

Knight, M., Loayza N., and Villaneuva D., (1995) *The Peace Dividend: Military Spending Cuts and Economic Growth,* International Monetary Fund Working Paper, Washington D.C.

Kosiak S. and Bitzinger R. A., (1994) *Potential Impact of Defence Spending Reductions on the Defence-Related Labour Force by State,* Defence Budget Project, Washington D.C., May.

Kuttner R., (1991), The End of Laissez-Faire: National Purpose and the Global Economy after the Cold War, University of Pennsylvania Press.

Leitenberg M., (1992), Non-Conversion in the Former Soviet Union, *The New Economy,* Vol. 3, (2), p. 11.

Lovering J., (1993), Restructuring the British Defence Industrial Base After the Cold War: Institutional and Geographical Perspectives, *Defence Economics,* Vol. 4., pp. 123–139.

Markusen A., (1991), The Military Industrial Divide: Cold War Transformation of the Economy and the Rise of New Industrial Complexes, *Environment and Planning, D, Society and Space,* Vol. 9, No. 4.

Markusen A., (1997a), The Post-Cold War American Defence Industry: Options, Policies and Probable Outcomes, in Inbar E. and Zilberfarb B-Z, (eds.), *Politics and Economics of Defence Industries in a Changing World,* forthcoming.

Markusen A., (1997b) How We Lost the Peace Dividend, *The American Prospect,* no. 33, July-August, pp. 86–95.

McCain J., (1998) cited in *Peace Dividend: What Happened to Savings?,* http://wvgazette.com/Editorial/PEAC1217.html

O'Hanlon M, (1995) *Defense Planning for the Lste 1990's: Beyond the Desert Storm Framework,* the Brookings Institution, Washington D.C.

Ozhegov A., Rogovskii E., and Iaremenko L., (1991), Conversion of the Defence Industry and Transformation of the Economy of the USSR, *Problems of Economics,* Vol. 34, pp. 79–94.

Paukert L., and Richards P., (1991) *Defence Expenditure, Industrial Conversion and Local Employment,* International Labour Office, Geneva.

Renner M., (1996), *Cost of Disarmament: An Overview of the Economic Costs of the Dismantlement of Weapons and the Disposal of Military Surplus,* Brief 6, Bonn International Centre for Conversion, March.

Sandler T. and Hartley K., (1999), *The Political Economy of NATO,* Cambridge University Press.

Saunders N. C., (1990), Defence Spending in the 1990s—The Effects of Deeper Cuts, *Monthly Labor Review,* October.

Short J., (1981), Defence Spending in the UK Regions, *Regional Studies,* Vol. 15, No. 2, pp. 101–110.

Smith R., (1980), Military Expenditure and Investment in OECD Countries: 1954–1973, *Journal of Comparative Economics,* 4, 1980, pp. 19–32.

Smith R., (1991) *Measuring the Peace Dividend in the UK,* Working Paper 9019, Department of Applied Economics, Cambridge.

Smith R. and Smith D., (1992) Corporate Strategy, Corporate Culture and Conversion: Adjustment in the Defence Industry, *Business Strategy Review,* Summer.

United Nations, (1995), *World Economic and Social Survey,* 1995, Current Trends and Policies in the World Economy, p. 198.

Vershbow A., (1999), from a speech by the US Permanent Representative on the North Atalantic Council, NATO, at the Crans-Montana Forum, Switzerland, 26 June.

Chapter 2

DEFENCE EXPENDITURE AND THE ECONOMY

INTRODUCTION

In order to understand the potential for a genuine and long-lasting peace dividend from the post-Cold War reductions in military spending, the inter-relationship between defence expenditure and the national and/or regional economy of a nation must first be explored. This will provide the context in which to identify and dissect the processes and transmission mechanisms through which a peace dividend may or may not be acquired. This chapter will offer an initial broad perspective of the economic linkages perceived to exist between defence expenditure and the economy relevant to the notion of a peace dividend and will, in turn, enable us to focus more precisely on specific critical areas of interest in the subsequent analysis. Since these linkages—and indeed the focus of this book—has much to do with the efficacy of market forces in facilitating economic adjustment to changes in defence spending, the chapter also offers an overview of the 'market forces versus government intervention' debate which has, for so long, pervaded economics, as such a contextual analysis is essential to understanding the remainder of the book. Finally, Chapter 2 takes the example of the labour market and examines employment transition in defence and similar industries, following severe exogenous shocks.

THE ECONOMIC CONSEQUENCES OF MILITARY EXPENDITURE

At the national and international level, the debate concerning the economic consequences of an increase or decrease in military expenditure has a long pedigree (see, for example, Udis, 1976; Brauer and Chatterji, 1993). Indeed, classical economists were well aware of the destabilising impact of both the outbreak of war and the eventual peace on the economy. Ricardo (1817, p. 265), commenting on the economic consequences of war and peace, noted that:

> 'The commencement of war after a long peace, or of peace after a long war, generally produces considerable distress in trade. It changes in a great degree the nature of the employments to which the respective capitals of countries were before devoted; and during the interval while they are settling in the situation which new circumstances have made the most

beneficial, much fixed capital is unemployed, perhaps wholly lost, and labourers are without full employment.'

Although some analysts (e.g. Kennedy, 1988) attribute American national decline to excessive levels of military expenditure, at the macroeconomic level they remain divided between perceptions of positive and negative economic benefits to be derived from sustained, high levels of defence spending. Positive effects are measured in terms of the contribution of defence expenditure to the maintenance of high and stable levels of employment, the stimulation and buoyancy of economic prosperity, the enhancement of export earnings which improve the balance of trade and the inherent stimulus to technological advance. The potential negative effects are usually measured in terms of inflationary pressure, reduced competitiveness and financial and physical 'crowding-out', where skilled labour and financial resources are drawn into the defence sector and away from the civil sector, damaging in consequence the nation's productive capacity in commercial markets (for a fuller discussion, see, for example, Sandler & Hartley, 1995, Chapter 8).

Conventionally, high levels of defence spending have been assumed (and sometimes empirically shown) to generate sub-optimal macroeconomic outcomes in terms of the opportunity cost of that expenditure. While defence expenditure can play an important role in reflating a demand-deficient economy, its economic legacy has frequently been viewed as being more inflationary and less employment-generating than alternative forms of public spending.

As Fontanel (1994) suggests:

'military expenditure does not lend itself readily to the traditional economic analysis of public expenditure. The optimum level of military expenditure is a concept that is prescriptive, political, strategic, psychological, economic and even moral, with the result that theoretical analysis of public property is relatively powerless when it comes to revealing the financial choices of defence. That is not to say that the economist can neglect the economic analysis of military expenditure, but there is the need to be aware that it has its limits and that it has a bearing on only one part of a multidisciplinary body of thought. Economists regard the level of defence as a monotonic function of military expenditure, whatever its form, the strategy and the arms that it procures, but only occasionally does economic rationality coincide with political and strategic rationality.'

Driven by political and strategic factors, one country's military expenditure can amount to a threat to others which, in turn, drives forward the arms race. Economists usually assume that such an arms race reduces world growth potential and hinders attempts to achieve economic development as it effectively wastes scarce resources. An alternative view, expounded by some analysts, suggests that there are circumstances in which military expansion could act as a stimulant to development as a result of the innovatory impetus of military research and development and, by their disciplined nature and need for high security, could prove valuable for the organisation of social labour. However, the majority of empirical studies suggest a sectoral substitution effect (reflected in the struggle to acquire resources between civil and military sectors of the economy); a temporal substitution effect (i.e. choosing between the present and the future) and a crowding-out effect (as a result of which investment is drawn into the military sector and away from the civil) attributable to military expenditure. In as far as these effects exist, military expenditure may be considered to have an adverse effect on economic development, even if, since it forms a key component of public spending, it may be responsible for increasing aggregate demand.

Over the last few years, however, a considerable amount of empirical evidence has appeared which questions the extent of this perceived difference in the macroeconomic impact between military expenditure and other forms of public spending. In general, although there is conflicting evidence on both sides of the debate, the emerging conventional wisdom seems to be that military spending has neither a positive nor negative effect on economic growth (Ram, 1995), is not uniquely inflationary, has an unclear relationship to productivity and technological development and, over time, does not create significantly different numbers of jobs. On the other hand, military spending does have a discernible and sometimes profound impact upon regions, sectors of industry and segments of the labour market in different ways from other federal spending (for an excellent review of the economics of disarmament, see Fontanel, 1994.)

As observed in Chapter 1, of all the principal forms of public spending in advanced industrial nations, the provision of defence services and associated production of defence goods exhibits a pronounced degree of regional concentration. While the end of the Cold War and the search for a New World Order and its associated 'security architecture' undoubtedly are acting as catalysts which will ultimately transform national economic systems, it will be at the microeconomic, regional and sectoral level within national economies that the most significant economic consequences are likely to be encountered.

THE ECONOMIC IMPACT OF DEFENCE EXPENDITURE

Early contributions to the literature on the economic impact of defence expenditure differed markedly in their conclusions with some studies identifying high-income US states and regions (New England, the Midwest, the Pacific coast) as benefiting significantly from US defence procurement in the period before the Vietnam war while others failed to identify any difference in the long run growth rates for states receiving high and low levels of defence spending. On the other hand, defence spending did have an impact on local economic growth at the sub-state level.

The precise economic impact of the Vietnam war also remained a matter for considerable conjecture. Evidence appeared to suggest that the war gave a stimulus to conventional armament production, thereby impacting most on the regional economies of the Midwest and Eastern seaboard of the USA. On the other hand, over the main period from 1964 to 1969, the defence procurement pattern in the US appeared to remain relatively stable with the major economic stimulus going to the West South Central states rather than the East and Midwest. There appeared to be no significant increase in the concentration of US Department of Defense procurement awards, almost half of which were taken by the states of California, New York, Texas, Connecticut and Massachusetts, representing approximately 28% of the US population. On the other hand, the share taken by Missouri, Pennsylvania, Ohio, New Jersey and Georgia did decline (with the first three suffering significant reduction in defence business in the post-Vietnam defence cutbacks) while that of Virginia increased sharply due to new shipbuilding contracts.

REGIONAL MULTIPLIERS

Economists have attempted to capture these national and regionally-focused economic effects related to varying levels of defence expenditure through various forms of impact analysis (see, for example, Saunders, 1990). Impact analysis seeks to estimate the consequences for regional income and employment of a given change in expenditure. The attempt to measure the economic impact of defence expenditure has conventionally been undertaken, usually at the regional level, through the estimation of regional multipliers. For a specific region which receives significant flows of defence expenditure from central government, this represents new income which will, in turn, stimulate consumption and other economic activities and generate additional income flows in the economy. The impact of defence expenditure within a region will differ depending on its scale and purpose and the nature of the recipient region itself.

These regional employment multipliers for the defence sector are simply logical extensions of the Kahn/Keynes employment/income multiplier process. As defence procurement budgets change, a series of economic chain reaction effects upon income and employment will be triggered as prime contractors in the defence industry adjust their business plans and corporate strategies to meet the new budgetary situation. As they react, purchasing requirements and associated orders of different magnitude pass along the supply linkages between companies within the defence industry and, eventually, reach companies in lower supply tiers that have no direct role in defence supply. Conventionally, this process is seen as a cumulative movement along established industrial supply chains with first round income effects being multiplied by second, third and other rounds as the process continues.

In addition to the direct and indirect income and employment effects generated along the supply chain following a change in defence expenditure, this new level of economic activity will have consequences for the spending power of those affected by the income or employment change. Consequently, it is necessary to include the additional consumer spending generated at each stage of the production process. These induced multiplier effects must also be incorporated in assessing the overall economic impact of a change in defence spending.

McDowall (see Hartley and Hooper, 1993, p. 58) estimated the induced multiplier effects of the Rosyth Naval Base in Scotland and found that due to expenditure by the 5,030 base employees (civilian and military) a further 1,628 jobs in the local Rosyth economy were generated through the induced effects of that spending. This implies that for every three direct jobs created by defence activity, approximately one additional job would be induced in the local economy (an outcome which is in line with the standard estimate for the UK economy of 1.2 to 1.3). Hartley and Hooper (1993) applied this result to the anticipated employment for the A400M (Future Large Aircraft) project and estimated that for the 5, 316 direct and indirect jobs that might be supported by the A400M project, a further 1,595 induced jobs could be generated through additional consumer spending.

Alternatively, where defence expenditure changes affect military bases and associated infrastructure, different but nonetheless significant income and employment effects will be experienced by local industry (through revision of construction or catering contracts, for example). In turn, these effects are likely to have a significant impact on prosperity. The economic impact of military base closures will be explored further in Chapter 5.

Studies of the economic impact of defence expenditure show a degree of variation in the local and regional multiplier estimates generated. In a study of the impact of defence spending on the economy of Portsmouth (USA), for example, Weiss and Gooding produced different multiplier estimates for different regional activities. Compared with a manufacturing sector multiplier of 1.78, Weiss and Gooding measured the multiplier associated with a naval shipyard at 1.55 and that for an air base at 1.35. The explanation for the lower multiplier estimates associated with, for example, the air base was that such defence establishments have a much higher propensity to import goods and services from other regions as government establishments tend to obtain their inputs through a central purchasing authority rather than simply purchasing inputs from local suppliers.

Depending on the precise locational constraints imposed on various multiplier studies, researchers have measured defence-related multipliers of 0.83 for defence industry in Lancashire (Demilitarized, 1991); 0.96 for a UK shipyard (ADCC, 1992); 1.27 for the UK electronics industry (ADCC, 1992); 1.33 for defence industry in Zaanstad (Demilitarized, 1991); between 1 and 2 for defence industry in Bremen (Demilitarized, 1991); 2.1 for German defence industry (IFO, 1991); and 1.5 for a UK aircraft factory (Aztec, 1992).

In general, however, recent estimates of regional multipliers in the defence industry suggest a range of estimates for employment, broadly between a value of one and two—i.e. for every direct job in defence production there are between one and two additional jobs indirectly supported through the supply chain (Braddon, 1995).

Variation in the multiplier-related economic impact of defence expenditure raises important questions when exploring the peace dividend potential of declining defence budgets. As noted earlier, it is often alleged by analysts that the multiplier effects associated with defence spending are significantly lower in comparison with multipliers emanating from other forms of government expenditure. As a result, defence spending is sometimes considered either to be wasteful of resources, inefficient, or less employment-creating than alternative forms of public expenditure.

Recent evidence, however, challenges this view. In a study of the economic consequences of the UK government's decision on a Chieftain tank replacement, Hartley and Hooper (1991) found that: 'there is little difference between the multiplier impact of defence and other types of government spending.' Comparing the gross output generated in the UK by £130m of final demand (the equivalent of purchasing 50–60 new Challenger tanks through the defence procurement budget), Hartley and Hooper estimated that defence expenditure matched the output-generating capacity of local government expenditure and exceeded that of the NHS, consumers expenditure and average central government spending, ignoring income multiplier effects.

Furthermore, while defence expenditure has historically been criticised for draining away much of a nation's science and engineering potential into an essentially non-commercial form of economic activity, a strong case could be made for its positive impact on high-technology development. Indeed, the strong association between leading edge technology industries and the defence sector can have important economic implications. In recent decades, defence procurement expenditure has undoubtedly played a very significant part in the development of much high technology industry with considerable economic impact. As Breheny noted almost a decade and a half ago in 1985 with respect to defence expenditure and regional development issues:

> 'a number of studies, particularly in the USA and the UK, have begun to address these issues ... . Most of these studies have arisen, in fact, as a by-product of investigations into the nature and location of "high technology" industries. Such studies have revealed the crucial role that defence procurement expenditure has played in the development of high technology, and particularly electronics, industries, both nationally and locally.'

The evidence seems to suggest that, where high-technology zones are concerned within local economies, significant spatial concentrations of key technology firms leads to strong agglomeration economies on the input side. As a result (and of crucial importance in analysing the real potential for a peace dividend) regional economies which attract defence, aerospace and other technology-dependent advanced manufacturing companies tend to generate, in turn specific locational advantages like more flexible and sophisticated labour markets, specialised input-output networks and high quality transportation networks.

In these regions, specialist supply companies have been developed to support the needs of high technology primes, technical knowledge and associated skills have been refined and the opportunity for inter-firm linkages has increased sharply. Together, these developments represent significant potential for agglomeration economies, attracting new industries to the region and acting as a strong stimulus to regional growth. To the extent that declining defence expenditure impacts adversely on the retention of regional high-technology centres and thereby threatens to erode their associated agglomeration economies, the scope for a significant and long-lasting peace dividend will be that much diminished.

Again, in a study of the Bristol sub-region of southwest England and the significance of the 'defence/aerospace nexus', Boddy and Lovering (1986) noted that:

> 'High technology industry in the region is found to be primarily identified with the aerospace industry, in terms of both products, process and occupational structure. Aerospace is central to high-technology industry as a whole in terms of subcontracting and purchasing, and through its domination of the labour market. The origins of the electronics-based aerospace sector are traced in the development of the aircraft and guided weapons industries as they related to the Bristol sub-region in the post-war period. This indicates the key role of defence-related production and Ministry of Defence procurement to the genesis and continuing importance of the advanced technology sector in the sub-region.'

Supplementing the significant magnet of defence and aerospace activity which attracts additional high technology industry into a region, Boddy and Lovering pointed to the additional stimulus of a clustering of several defence-related activities in a particular region, all of which draw upon (and ultimately will seek to enhance) a high-technology, communications and information gathering infrastructure, for example:

> 'There are a number of major users of information technology equipment in the southwest. These include GCHQ at Cheltenham, the MOD at Bath, Plymouth Dockyard, the Royal Signals and Radar Establishment at Malvern, the Navy at Yeovilton, and Westland Helicopters at Yeovil.'

The association between defence expenditure and economic performance is therefore both complex and difficult to quantify. Attempting to measure the relationship confronts a number of specific problems. Most national defence ministries present data relating to the distribution of military expenditure by recipient company headquarters, not by exact geographic incidence. Again, most attempts to trace the econ-omic impact of defence expenditure fail to capture precisely enough the multi-dimensional flow of inter-regional purchases relating to defence production by prime contractors and their sub-contracting partners. Furthermore, it is difficult to trace the implicit inter-regional tax burden shifts that occur due to the need to finance military pro-jects through fiscal means. Although this problem is a common one in analyses of the regional impacts of exogenous demands, there are some special aspects in the case of defence contracts. Finally, the rapidly changing technological nature of defence production and pro-curement over a relatively short time span implies that the impact of defence expenditure changes on output, employment and income in the 1990's will almost certainly be markedly different from that of, say, twenty years earlier, altering fundamentally, once again, the rel-ationship between defence spending and economic outcomes.

A number of important studies have been conducted to try to esti-mate the impact of defence on specific regional economies (see, for example, case studies in Paukert and Richards, 1991). Using input-output analysis, a 1971 study of the impact of defence expenditures on the St Louis Metropolitan economy found that defence spending of $2.3 billion in 1967 generated a volume of $3.1 billion in economic activity and $1.1 billion in personal income within the region. Employing an 89 sector input-output model (with technical coefficients derived from the Bureau of Economic Analysis Rims II input-output model) to examine the impact of prime defence contracts on the economy of the New York Metropolitan region, Warf and Cox (1989) found that in such a service-based economy:

> 'prime defence contracts and their associated taxes reallocate resources among industries, inducing a variety of positive and negative net effects on output, income and employment at the industry level.'

The majority of studies attempting to capture the economic impact of defence spending (as with other forms of public expenditure) have been demand-orientated. Supply-side aspects have tended to be either ignored or viewed as of secondary importance. Yet, recent research suggests that sudden and substantial variations in defence expenditure do impact directly and indirectly not only on prime defence contrac-tors but also on companies located in the supply chain of those major contractors, regionally, nationally and internationally. This creates an unstable and unpredictable business environment for these critical ele-ments of the defence equipment production process and will, in turn, trigger secondary market adjustments. As will be seen in Chapter 4, in many respects, it is the capacity of that supply chain to absorb the variations in defence-related demand, largely unaided by government, that will ultimately determine the capacity for regional and national economic regeneration and, in turn, help to restore regional and national prosperity in the form of a peace dividend.

In exploring the relationship between defence expenditure and economic performance above, the principal focus has been on how the regional or local economy adjusts over time to variations in the defence budget. In reality, of course, understanding the degree to which affected regions, sectors or industries can adjust, rapidly and smoothly, to such budgetary changes requires us to focus more precisely upon the market mechanism at work within these economies and to try to assess the degree to which that mechanism could (or perhaps should) facilitate transition. For non-economists, the debate about the efficacy of the market and the potential role of government within the economy must seem endlessly repetitive and immensely confusing. The next section of this chapter, therefore, seeks to provide a concise overview of these important issues.

MARKET ANALYSIS AND THE PEACE DIVIDEND

Central to discussions about the potential for realising a substantial and long-term economic dividend from the cessation of superpower hostilities in the 1990's lies the age-old debate about the efficacy of market forces and the merits or otherwise of government intervention. For the most part, market forces have been left to deal with the economic fall-out of the end of the Cold War although, as will be argued in the next chapter, in the US, governments have offered incentives to encourage market adjustment of a particular kind. Interestingly, of course, it has been a **reduction** in government intervention (i.e. through reductions in defence expenditure) that has initiated disequilibrium in the defence supply market; yet, in the main, governments have been slow to recognise a need for countervailing intervention to help restore market equilibrium and prosperity. As in many other areas of economic activity, the proponents and detractors of the role of the state in economic affairs continue to challenge one another vociferously. At the same time, the understanding of how both market forces and government intervention actually generate economic adjustment, together with their intended and unintended direct and indirect economic consequences, continues to be researched.

The economic analysis of markets in the late twentieth century amounts to a "competition of paradigms" (Lachmann, 1986) which forms the intellectual boundaries of much of the literature exploring market behaviour in recent years. The diversity of such models of market economics does not imply that some market models may be correct and others false. Historically, in economic analysis, intellectual reasoning produced theoretical constructs which have only been subject to serious empirical testing since the 1950s. In assessing possible economic outcomes from endogenous or exogenous change, therefore, much depends on the precise theory—or version of a particular theory—which is employed by the analyst. As Shackle (1972, p. 66) commented:

'in natural science, what is thought is built upon what is seen; but in economics, what is seen is built upon what is thought.'

Therefore, different models of the market process may be both relevant and valuable as frameworks to help us explore outcomes in markets for different kinds of goods and services, under a variety of economic conditions and at different times in economic history. As Lachmann (1986, p. 3) comments:

'To ignore such phenomena causing the diversity of market processes [would] blind us to the variety of circumstances that may shape market processes and prevent us from taking due account of the very forces that impel them and lend them shape.'

In examining a variety of approaches to market theory, Lachmann (1986, p. xii) makes the critically important point that:

'Economists must learn to surmount the artificial barriers which today separate them from historians as well as students of other social sciences. This is an urgent task made no easier by the circumstance that, since the darkness of the age of the reduced form fell upon us, several generations of economists have grown up who do not even know what they are separated from.'

THE ORTHODOX VIEW

For much of the last two centuries, the doctrine of free enterprise, supported by the twin pillars of free markets and free trade, has captured the minds of politicians and business decision-makers alike. From the initial seminal contributions of the 'classical' economists Adam Smith and David Ricardo to the more recent economic and political agenda set by influential 'monetarist' and 'new classical' economists such as

Milton Friedman, Robert Lucas and Patrick Minford, a free market analytical framework has been forged that has withstood not only the Marxist onslaught but also survived apparent emasculation by the 'state interventionism' of the Keynesian revolution.

Regardless of the challenge placed before them and despite their occasional flirtation with temporarily attractive alternative frameworks, economic decision-makers in government (particularly in the USA and Britain) sooner or later have returned to some variant of free-market economics, even if, in practice, these same governments still maintain a significant economic role as well. Like all ideologies, free market capitalism was founded on a set of central tenets, posited as essentially 'fundamental truths'. By ensuring the freedom of markets and permitting individual decisions to be motivated purely by well-informed self-interest, each individual, acting rationally, was perceived to actively pursue the maximisation of personal gain, subject however to competitive market pressures. It was concluded that the self-interested pursuit of maximum personal gain would, by means of the 'invisible hand' of the market, deliver an optimum economic outcome for society as long as competitive pressures were genuine and were fully reflected in the prices pertaining in each market.

Classical economists believed fervently in the power of market forces to attain natural equilibrium at full employment and so prevent the scourge of unemployment. To achieve this desirable goal, all markets in the economy had to be as free as possible. In practice, this meant that the labour market, the product market and the money market should all be allowed to operate freely so that equilibrium prices could be established by free market interaction in each case. At equilibrium, everything supplied would be consumed and there would be no resulting unemployment for any factor of production.

If unemployment did exist, it could only be attributed to market failure, due either to excessive power held by monopolists or trade unions or to excessive government economic activity which would inevitably, it was argued, distort the market. The government would have the obligation to eliminate excessive market power but would also be expected to keep its economic role to a minimum. To do so, the government would have to 'balance the books' and not allow a budget deficit to occur except in wartime, following which it would have to be immediately repaid.

The classical economists saw the producer as the key component in the economy, accepting the central tenet of Say's Law that 'supply creates its own demand'. If suppliers wished to produce, then people and other resources would be employed, generating in turn the income and expenditure required to consume what had been produced. Inflation would only occur where the government failed to control the supply of money, demonstrated uniquely in the so-called Fisher equation. Finally, to ensure that all idle money in the economy was put to work, it was necessary for savings and investment to be equal at all times. Classical economists believed that, through free market forces, this could be achieved. They believed that both savings and investment were determined by the interest rate which, if it was itself set by free market forces, would allow this critical part of the economy to reach equilibrium. Furthermore, both at the level of the company and the nation, it was essential that individuals should be free to make the most effective use of any comparative advantage they might possess, unconstrained by government intervention through excessive taxation, import restrictions or other forms of economic protection.

Pursuing the economic theory of markets a little further, what is often referred to as the orthodox Walrasian general equilibrium model of the market brings buyers and sellers together through the intermediary of a market auctioneer. The auctioneer conducts a process of 'tatonnement' or price bargaining and adjustment to achieve eventual equilibrium in a smooth, apparently co-ordinated way. Excess demand and excess supply will be gradually eliminated by this 'recontracting' process until genuine and stable market equilibrium in attained over time. It is not even necessary in this theoretical construct for an auctioneer to actually exist. All that is required is for economic actors to behave *as if* an auctioneer operates in their sector of the market.

Economic activity, then, is examined in terms of small adjustments made by individuals to the various economic stimuli to which they are exposed. Such a framework, often referred to in economics as neo-classical 'marginalism', postulates that, given the important assumptions outlined above, a genuine system of free markets and free trade will lead to an allocation of resources which will be optimal from the point of view of every individual and every company in an economy.

The neo-Austrian theory of markets differed somewhat from this neo-classical view. The neo-Austrian approach considers markets more in terms of a competitive process. Market behaviour is seen in terms of a selection process during which economic conditions continually change with the result that the market operates in a constant state of turmoil, encountering disequilibrium at times. This view of markets appears altogether more realistic in the context of the modern unstable global economy and is, in itself, a far more dynamic approach to explaining market behaviour. While different to neo-classical market theory, the neo-Austrian version of market behaviour nevertheless reaches the same fundamental conclusion—the market is the mechanism through which economic activity can best be co-ordinated (for an excellent discussion of the different theories of markets, see Thomson et al., 1991).

There is little doubt that in times of prosperity and economic expansion, where economies operate at or near to the full-employment level of national income, encountering only modest and occasional deviations, the equilibrating power of market forces can be extremely effective. In such conditions, the market mechanism appears able to correct, rapidly and smoothly, temporary movements away from full-employment. Market forces are at their most potent where the deviations to be absorbed and corrected are marginal in scale and originate in the context of a prosperous, expanding economy. In this instance, the market mechanism can be extremely efficient in its role as a powerful allocator of resources, if not always equitable in its redistributive function.

The situation is very different, however, where major systemic changes are concerned. Historical and current evidence suggests that market forces in the orthodox model can fail abysmally where the scale of change required and the associated expectations of consumers and producers extend beyond what would normally be experienced in the 'corridor' around full-employment. In such circumstances, the equilibrating mechanism of the market cannot deal adequately with major and sustained deviations from full-employment (or even from an equilibrium level of national income below full-employment).

Markets abhor conditions of extreme risk and prolonged uncertainty, particularly in an environment where the established 'modus operandi' of political and economic life has changed fundamentally. Deviations from equilibrium on a major scale tend not to be responsive to correction through minor price adjustments and, indeed, are more likely to be accompanied by significant adjustments in output and employment, long before the price mechanism can respond. In general, even in these difficult circumstances, the market mechanism will still attempt to secure equilibrium but, with prices no longer truly reflecting economic conditions or evolving social structures, its co-ordination role is constrained and false signals will be transmitted to the economy with sometimes devastating results. The breakdown of the market mechanism attributable to problems of information, co-ordination and time has been well-documented in the literature (see, for example, Leijonhufvud, 1981).

Equilibrium may be achieved in due course but at much lower levels of income and employment. More likely, a state of long-term dis-equilibrium will persist, generating economic instability and, poten-tially, weakening the economic base until it confronts the possibility of critical mass collapse. The model of general competitive equilibrium that evolved from these ideas—and the doctrine of laissez-faire that accompanied it—has played a critical role far beyond mainstream economic analysis and lies behind much of the political rhetoric of the last twenty years in the US and much of Western Europe. As Ormerod (1994) comments:

> 'The theoretical constructs introduced to economics over a century ago con-
> tinue to pervade discussions of policy. They provide both a strong bias
> towards—and an apparently strong rationale for—policies which move
> towards the creation of a free, competitive market. For example, the politi-
> cal and social agendas of Ronald Reagan and Margaret Thatcher were pow-
> erfully motivated by the logic of free market economics.'

The appeal of the competitive general equilibrium model in particular and market analysis in general to economists and political decision-makers ideologically committed to minimising the role of government in economic life was profound since it appeared to 'prove', with math-ematical precision, that business should be left as much as possible to its own devices, without help or hindrance from the state.

THE FAILURE OF ORTHODOXY AND THE KEYNESIAN INTERLUDE

Confronted with the economic cataclysm of the Great Depression in the 1930s, classical economic orthodoxy proved incapable of explain-ing either the origin or persistence of the disastrous economic condi-tions then prevailing. Keynes, the legendary British economist, identified natural processes within the business cycle as being respons-ible for the depression and revealed the inadequacy of market econom-ics in resolving the problem.

Keynesian economists explain natural business-cycle behaviour as being the result of shocks experienced by the economy due to sudden, unexpected changes in aggregate demand (i.e. anything which affects consumption, investment, exports etc.). So natural business cycles could be due to changes in desired investment resulting from changing expectations about potential return on that investment; or due to changes in consumers' patience or confidence in the future that will affect their desired level of saving (and therefore consumption). Keynesians would argue that most important shocks to the economy originate from these natural changes in behaviour that cannot be dealt with effectively by equilibrium adjustment in the market. Government intervention will be required to overcome them, so smoothing out the worst excesses of the business cycle.

The work of Keynes in explaining the origins and process of the Great Depression in the 1930s represented a complete break with the orthodox view. Keynes showed how markets have a tendency to self-destruct and indicated that a free market economy with no government intervention would inevitably lead to a situation in which prolonged and significant unemployment was the natural state. With dis-equilibrium being perceived now as the natural outcome of free market interaction following an exogenous shock, Keynesian logic propelled the government to the centre of the economic stage.

It would be the role of government to facilitate the recovery of prosperity by helping markets to re-establish equilibrium and begin again to generate employment and wealth. Through government expenditure and tax adjustments, essentially managing the level of aggregate demand, government could stimulate consumption and, through the multiplier-accelerator process, trigger off recurring rounds of new spending, driving the economy back towards a full-employment equilibrium state. To provide the financial injection, government would borrow idle capital from its own citizens and utilise that capital through a series of public works programmes to restore employment opportunities and increase private consumption. It is interesting and relevant to recall at this point that a significant amount of such intervention spending took the form of military contracts, providing both work and spending power in times of recession, thereby creating the concept of 'military Keynesianism'. The power of the multiplier was emphasised to over-turn the criticism of the orthodox economists that the doctrines of Keynesianism would generate highly inflationary outcomes.

Despite the potency of the Keynesian attack on orthodox market economics, a somewhat strange compromise was reached in the 1950s, a few years after Keynes' death. Belief in the power of market forces remained strong but—to avoid a repeat of the 1930s experience

of economic depression—governments began to use Keynesian intervention policies to secure and maintain full employment. The brief
Keynesian interlude, most prominently observed in Britain between
the mid-1950s and the mid-1970s, allowed governments a temporary
and ultimately ill-fated opportunity to influence economic outcomes
through the macroeconomic techniques of aggregate demand
management.

THE REVIVAL AND RENEWED FAILURE OF MARKET ORTHODOXY

At no point, however, did economists of a classical, market-based per-
suasion fully admit the defeat of their approach. To them, the
Keynesian revolution was viewed primarily as a necessary amendment
to orthodox theory which in no way called into question the fundamental soundness of their ideas. In essence, classical and Keynesian
economists struck a compromise, agreeing on an analytical framework
which became known as 'neo-classical' economics, reinforcing with its
name the supremacy of the classical mode of thinking about economic
issues in a market framework.

The compromise between the orthodox classical approach and its
Keynesian critics enabled the architects of the post-1945 global
economy to construct an international economic framework built
upon such key structures as the mixed economy and global integration
through a fixed exchange rate regime, while maintaining a formal
commitment to free markets, free trade and full-employment. The perceived failure of this unhappy marriage between marginal analysis and
macroeconomic intervention both called into question the Keynesian
approach during the 1970s and provided momentum for the rebirth of
orthodox free market and free trade ideology.

By the beginning of the 1970s, the apparently stable economic relationship that formed the cornerstone of Keynesian policy (the Phillips
Curve trade-off between inflation and unemployment) suddenly
became extremely unstable. Instead of a 'trade-off' between the two
variables, inflation and unemployment started to increase together.
The emergence of 'stagflation' as it became known meant not only the
collapse of the Phillips Curve relationship but—more important—
called into question the entire Keynesian policy framework and associated policy agenda for all political parties.

In the struggle to find a viable alternative economic framework and
a new policy, Keynesian economists were blamed for the emergence of
'stagflation'. Keynesians were credited with the creation of an

'inflation psychology' in the UK and USA, which suggested that inflationary Keynesian policies had gradually allowed the public to become used to inflation at successively higher levels, causing them to change their economic behaviour in such a way as to simply push inflation to even higher and more damaging levels.

Long-standing critics of Keynesian economics, led principally by Milton Friedman in the USA, constructed the Monetarist attack on the Keynesians and, in so doing, cleared a path for the return of free market ideology. The emphasis here was on restoring the economic power of the individual and minimising the intervention role of government. Quite apart from its powerful message concerning the limits to the economic role of government, monetarism sharpened the focus of the business community once again on the maximisation of shareholder value. As Wheeler et al. (1997, p. 34) comment:

> 'It has been the central belief of American academic Milton Friedman ... that increasing shareholder value is the over-riding moral obligation for the corporation. Indeed exercising any other act of social responsibility is in effect a tax on the wealth of the owners and is therefore akin to a socialist doctrine ... it is at least arguable that Adam Smith's iron rules lie at the heart of Friedman's argument and the so-called Chicago school of neoclassical economics.'

In essence, Friedman argued that the Keynesian policy of stimulating aggregate demand to attain full employment might work in the short-term but simply generated inflation in the longer-term. Keynesian intervention, therefore, amounted in Friedman's view to a recipe for inflation with, ultimately, not just the failure to derive real gains in terms of employment or output but also likely to culminate in the fundamental weakening of the economy.

During the late 1970s and 1980s, another group of economists offered an even more powerful critique of Keynesian economics and went on to fundamentally change economic thinking at the time. Their views were essentially founded in Classical economics (i.e. believing in the power of free markets and equilibrium) but added a completely new view of what determines the reaction of decision-makers to economic policy. This view—known as the 'rational expectations' approach—dominated economic thinking for most of the 1980s in the UK and USA and had a dramatic effect on political ideology and policy. By focusing upon the 'natural' rate of unemployment and stressing the **complete** inability of governments through demand management intervention policies to influence beneficially either the short or long term economic outcome new classical economics effectively returned the market to the centre of the economic stage.

Coincidentally, however, the attention of academics and policy-makers was captured by another school of thought which, while acknowledging the power of the market as the primary resource allo-cator, also proposed a role for government in helping strengthen the efficacy of market dynamics. The supply-side school, as its name implies, focused attention on the supply side of the economy and pro-posed mechanisms and policy measures designed to stimulate enhanced supply which, in turn, would generate higher levels of employment and income.

The supply-side school advocated government intervention designed to provide incentives to work, save, invest and take greater business risks, all of which were perceived to be crucial to the cause of econ-omic progress. Incentive mechanisms (for example, lower marginal taxes on high incomes) were recommended as vital stimulants to econ-omic growth. Weitzman (1984) suggested that economic growth could be better fostered by harnessing the sense of purpose and communal efforts of employees to the cause of corporate expansion and profit through widening share ownership.

This reborn market orthodoxy in the 1980s proved to be extremely powerful at the political level in the less consensual societies of the UK and the US. As Wheeler et al. (1997, p 34) note:

> 'In the 1980s, belief in the essential morality of Smith-Friedmanite econom-ics led first Margaret Thatcher, and then Ronald Reagan, to articulate extremely compelling, populist, political doctrines which virtually laid to rest the notion of interventionist economics as far as business and wealth creation in the English-speaking countries were concerned.'

In the case of the UK and several other countries in the 1980s, the policy of privatisation provided the first real opportunity for extending share-ownership more widely. By the late 1980s, such was the ideolo-gical grip of the market and supply-side economists on the political process, particularly in the UK, that leading government politicians were able to publicly herald the achievement of turning the UK not only into a home-owning but into a share-owning democracy.

MARKET DYNAMICS IN THE 1990s; THE METHODOLOGY OF IMPOTENCE

However, in recent years it has become increasingly apparent that the reformulated neo-classical economic framework—which in various guises has continued to dominate much of the mainstream economic literature in recent years by offering analysis of a neat, mathematically precise world—regrettably, bears little resemblance to the turbulent global trading arena that currently confronts business decision-makers in all industries and struggles to deal effectively with the economic fall-out of the historic changes taking place on all sides. As a result, there is strong evidence that the global economy—once again—confronts an economic malaise that conventional market-based economic theory cannot adequately resolve. Ormerod, for example, has noted that:

> 'The world economy is in crisis. Twenty million people are unemployed in Western Europe—America faces two severe deficits—and vast tracts of the former Soviet empire are on the brink of economic collapse. In this grim context, orthodox economics seems powerless to help. Teams of economists descend on the former Soviet Union proclaiming the virtues and necessity of moving to a free market system as rapidly as possible: systems of greater purity than those contemplated by Ronald Reagan and Margaret Thatcher. But despite governments in the former Soviet bloc doing everything they are told, their economic situation worsens.'

In an earlier analysis of the origins of recent economic problems, Lachmann focuses blame on the evolution of market economics.

> 'In looking at most of the models that have been devised by economic theorists in the last two decades we find little endeavour to depict traits of reality and less effort to accentuate them. Most of them are designed to reflect a network of relationships between variables, the parameters of which, one hopes, will find a counterpart in the regression coefficients of statistical time series. But the methodology of impotence ... which has come to dominate economics in the last few decades, has inspired its adherents with such a vivid fear of reality that they dare not touch it even at a few points of their own selection.'

What, then, is this 'reality' that conjures up such 'vivid fear'? It is not simply that the neo-classical framework cannot adequately encompass critical elements of time and uncertainty (see, for example, Shackle, 1972). It has more to do with the remarkable way in which the economic world has changed beyond recognition over recent decades and appears today, more often than not, to operate as if in a perpetual state of dis-equilibrium. The fault, according to Ormerod (1994, p. 208) lies in the fact that:

> 'For all its apparent mathematical sophistication, the core model of theoretical economics, that of competitive general equilibrium, is premised upon an entirely faulty view of the modern world.'

The heightened awareness of the deficiencies of equilibrium theory has, in recent years, served as a catalyst for the emergence and growth of what has been termed 'evolutionary economics' which replaces the formal mechanics of equilibrium adjustment with an approach more akin to a 'biological conceptions' approach to understanding economic change (see, for example, the excellent review paper by Nelson, 1995).

Taking this a stage further, as Wheeler et al. note, in a market economy economic actors play the game not by the rules of a competitive, open, fully informed, equilibrium-adjusting society but by implementing every possible device to protect market share, capture competitors' customers, secure market dominance and enhance profits. As a result, the 'invisible hand' of Adam Smith fails to deliver an optimum outcome, being replaced by 'the invisible elbow' (Jacobs, 1991), leading to the conclusion that: 'what the iron rules of free enterprise miss is the human element' (Wheeler et al. p. 15).

Furthermore, the age of relative stability and gradual change where marginal adjustment might have been thought of as representing real world adjustments has vanished. In its place is a turbulent, truly global and increasingly dynamic world system; a dynamic and ever-changing world to which the defence industries are increasingly being exposed. For this reason, a reworking of orthodox market economics to take account of major changes in the real economy has taken shape under the guise of what is termed the Rhenish model of capitalism which begins to offer a more coherent and realistic approach to understanding the requirements for economic advance in the late 20th century. The symbols of that economic advance are both numerous and, as Wheeler et al. indicate, striking. They include:

i)   a remarkable improvement in living standards in the rich industrial nations, coincident with a widening gap between them and the developing nations;

ii)   increasing emphasis upon the service sector of the economy in the industrial nations as mature economies increasingly switch resources from agriculture and industry to the tertiary sector;

iii) a change in social structure from class-based to hierarchical, with career ladders central to professional and bureaucratic organisations;

iv)   the development of a 'skewed meritocracy' in which recruitment is merit-based but where advantages of birth, school, and wealth still exert an influence on career opportunity and progress;

v)   the enhancement of women's role in the workforce and a significant change in gender relationships;

vi) a major expansion of the role of government since 1945, both in terms of employee numbers and expenditure, which has been only modestly restrained, if at all, by the post-1979 right wing attack on government activities;

vii) the associated expansion of the welfare state with huge public expenditure commitments to education, pensions and health, which, in some nations, appear to have reached unsustainable levels of public provision;

viii) the remarkable expansion of higher education, often seen as the major determinant of human capital, to include an unprecedented proportion of the relevant age-group;

ix) the dramatic increase in the role and power of giant private corporations which dominate so much of global business and argue for market freedom, while often adopting market behaviour that creates markets which are anything but free. For example, estimates suggest that the top 500 corporations in the world now control 70% of world trade and 30% of global gross domestic product (GDP);

x)   the rapid and apparently inexorable globalisation of business, creating as a direct result corporations which are 'wealthier' than many members of the United nations. In fact, of the largest 100 'economies' in the world, 51 are corporations. Mitsubishi's turnover exceeds the GDP of Indonesia; General Motors' that of Denmark; Toyota's that of Norway; Ford's that of Hong Kong and Turkey combined.

In addition to these critical changes in social structure and economic power over the last half century, by the 1990s, a new global economic system had evolved, built upon a very different set of values and structures to its predecessor. Economic integration across the world is now achieved through the interaction of global business, unfettered wherever possible by government intervention, with growth and prosperity often being pursued within self-protective trade blocs. Partly, this was because the attempts to construct a truly global macroeconomic co-ordination process to replace out-dated often national macroeconomic management programmes had proved singularly unsuccessful, especially in times of international economic recession. Hence, to survive and prosper in an unstable global economy, governments have had to both recognise and try to facilitate a revolution in global business organisation and management that is currently transforming the shape, content and modus operandi of the corporate sector and provide it with the kinds of support required to achieve desired ends, such as export market penetration.

In the turbulent international business environment of the 1990s, the simple notions of smooth and gradual market adjustment to economic change seem barely relevant. Individuals and corporations can no longer be seen as responding to the wishes of some unseen auctioneer to secure equilibrium outcomes. For example, most major companies now pursue their corporate goals by adopting business strategies which favour constant pro-active radical change—change which, in itself, sets the pace of market adjustment rather than responding to market conditions in a purely reactive way. To survive and prosper in the intensely competitive global marketplace of the late 20th century, such companies constantly redesign their business operations and corporate structure, defining and then accessing new markets.

For these companies, the essential means by which corporate redevelopment and market success are being pursued include 'boundary-lessness' (which refers to the ability to work effectively horizontally and vertically within the corporate hierarchy, incorporating a wide variety of different business functions and often in partnership with both customers and suppliers); speed in decision-making and implementation (which is achieved by eliminating superfluous layers of management, thereby creating a flexible and responsive business organisation which can readily seize market opportunities and adapt accordingly) and 'organisational stretch' (which identifies ambitious, long-term corporate goals, designed to push quality and efficiency standards to ever higher levels while encouraging employees to take acceptable risks in the interests of the business).

For leading global companies such as Shell, Boeing, General Motors, Toyota, Ford and Samsung, and increasingly for the major prime contractors in the defence industry, the time available for such strategic readjustment and corporate reconstruction tends to be very limited and the need for rapid and flexible response that much more urgent. That response now needs to encompass a much wider range of stimuli than ever before. It needs to address not only the requirements of enhanced market share, higher productivity and profitability but, more fundamentally, the demands of a wide array of economic, political and social agents with interests in securing broader environmental, ethical and other strictly non-economic objectives.

It is here that the Rhenish model comes into its own and forms part of the process of redefining the mechanism of the market which will both facilitate our understanding of economic events and outcomes and better enable decision-makers, both corporate and governmental, to respond effectively to dynamic global change. In particular, Smith Ring and Van de Ven (1994) make the important point that:

> 'As the uncertainty, complexity and duration of economic transactions within and between firms increase, it becomes increasingly important for scholars and managers to understand developmental processes of how equity, trust, conflict-resolution and procedures and internal governance structures emerge, evolve and dissolve over time.'

At the heart of the Rhenish model lies the notion of stakeholding which recognises the crucial inter-dependence and need for involvement of all relevant players in the market in the decision-making process. Consequently, the essence of the stakeholding approach is to challenge the age-old belief that the pursuit of enlightened self-interest in a competitive environment inevitably achieves an optimum outcome through the 'invisible hand' of the market. Indeed, as Hutton (1996 p. 251) notes:

> 'If information is held asymmetrically and your welfare depends in part on other people's strategies, the prosecution of undiluted competitive self-interest is often self-defeating.'

Recent economic experience in those countries which have most assiduously pursued the Rhenish approach to market activity suggests that this approach, too, may have its own problems to contend with. However, in the context of an economy confronting a sudden and massive exogenous shock such as the end of the Cold War, it does appear to offer an appropriate mechanism to facilitate change in the smoothest and most rapid way possible and as Ormerod (1994, p. 211)) suggests:

> 'by the rejection of the concepts of orthodox economics, of "rational" behaviour in a mechanical, linear world of equilibrium, progress can begin to be made to a more powerful understanding of how economies behave.'

DEFENCE CUTS AND THE LABOUR MARKET

The literature on the employment consequences of reductions in defence expenditure and disarmament is extensive (see, for example,

Richards, 1991, pp. 275–289). How, then, do markets adjust in response to sustained and substantial reductions in defence expenditure? In the next two chapters, the adjustment process in the product market and the implications for the defence industrial base will be explored in some detail. To conclude this chapter, however, the impact upon, and adjustment process within, the defence industry labour market will be considered (see Braddon et al. (1994) for a fuller discussion of these issues in the context of the UK).

Clearly, in most respects, the labour market response in the defence sector to a severe contraction in demand is similar to that experienced in any other major manufacturing industry. The literature on employment transition proposes two basic models of job search. Early contributions to the literature (see, for example, Stigler, 1962) proposed a marginal cost of job search model in which applicants seek a number of job offers and hold them until a decision point at which the marginal cost of further search is deemed to outweigh the benefit. Under this model, applicants will neither accept nor reject individual job offers, but will take batch decisions. This basic model has been extended to consider finite time horizons and the case where job offers are no longer available, as well as utility rather than income maximisation, and incomplete information (Gronau, 1971; Kohn and Shavell, 1974; Hey, 1979; McKenna, 1979; Wilde, 1979).

The alternative approach is reflected in the model proposed by McCall (1970). In McCall's model, individual offers are compared with a preferred option and a reservation wage level and offers are rejected until a preferred job is offered at or above the reservation wage level. The possibility that the search process may be influenced by the length of the job search must also be considered. After a period of unemployment the list of preferred jobs may be widened and the reservation wage reduced. This is particularly likely in a time of job shortage and unemployment (low demand), and when, for some reason, large numbers enter the labour market (high supply).

EMPLOYMENT TRANSITION IN NON-DEFENCE SECTORS

There are many examples of large-scale redundancies in other major industries over the last few decades from which we may glean some guidance as to the capacity of the labour market to handle sudden substantial surges in demand and supply. For example, in the contraction and closure of two large railway workshops in the UK following the Beeching plan for the future of railway services, estimates suggest that 37% of redundant employees went straight into new employment and a further 15% found employment within four weeks. However, 21% were still without work 10 months after the closure. Only 38% of the skilled and semi-skilled men found work in their previous trade and over a quarter took jobs as labourers, warehousemen and porters. The major employment problem was for older workers, with about 8% of the sample retiring up to a year early as a result of the closure (Wedderburn,1965). In the UK shipbuilding industry, evidence in the 1970s suggested that where redundant ship-workers found new jobs they tended to displace other workers (Mackay et al., 1980). In the steel industry, evidence from redundancies in Sheffield in the late 1970s suggested that even three years after redundancy, nearly sixty percent of redundant labour had not acquired new paid employment (Westergaard, Noble and Walker, 1989).

The coal industry, most notably, experienced a significant fall in employment in the UK during the 1980s and 1990s. When the government and British Coal announced the closure of 31 pits in October 1992, the industry had already lost some 150,000 mining jobs over a decade. Following the initial announcement, 34 pits were closed, including some operated by the private sector, leading to over 40,000 job losses. A number of studies have examined the experience of these redundant miners. The Coalfields' Communities Campaign conducted a series of surveys amongst redundant miners from 5 of the pits closed following the October 1992 announcement. At the time of the surveys, 44% of respondents were in employment, with 9% in training or education and 46% unemployed. Only 3% of the sample were self-employed. This relates closely to data from the Job Shops established by British Coal Enterprises at each pit, which show 37% of men who registered between October 1992 and November 1993 (covering most of those leaving the industry over the period) in employment and 42% out of work. The study found evidence of hidden unemployment in that 30% of respondents were claiming sickness benefit and hence were not on the register of unemployed.

Information on the nature of their new work was available for 294 respondents, 91% of whom were in manual employment. On average, respondents worked 41 hours a week for an average of £4.07 per hour, or almost £5 less than average pay rates for underground mineworkers and £3.50 less than the average for full-time male workers in Derbyshire. This implies that those miners who had found work had gone from above average pay to below average pay (Guy, 1994).

The unemployment experience of professional and executive workers tends to show a somewhat different pattern (Berthoud, 1979), which may be summarised as follows: professional and executives rarely become unemployed; once they do become unemployed, they take a long time to find new employment; unemployment is even rarer, and even more prolonged, for middle-aged professionals and executives; scientists tend to have greater difficulty in finding new jobs; and the speed of finding a new job depends on individual circumstances not personal behaviour. Clearly, there are lessons to be drawn from the experience of particular employee groups in non-defence sectors that are important for defence industry employees or Services personnel made redundant by the defence cuts of the last decade.

THE DEFENCE SECTOR

A study of defence conversion by the International Labour Office (ILO) summarised the results of the 1980s shake-out of the manufacturing labour force in industrialised market economies as a period when most governments aimed at increasing the flexibility of labour markets rather than seeking stability or security of employment. However, the study (see Richards 1992) found that:

> 'most displaced manufacturing workers have managed to find new jobs within a period of months, generally in a different occupation or industry. Better educated workers generally find jobs more quickly, less educated workers may take longer than average to find new jobs and are more likely to have to accept lower wages. Geographical mobility can help, but few workers are willing to move and many who do so will return. Older workers are least willing to move and likely to be re-employed. A sizeable proportion of displaced workers is likely to be unemployed for an extended period ... On average, displaced workers must expect an income loss, although a few may even gain.'

In a survey of studies of displaced workers in North America, the International Labour Office found that 67% of some 2.8 million US workers who lost their jobs between 1981 and 1986 were in employment in January 1986, and 18% were unemployed (see Richards, 1992). When expressed as a percentage of those displaced who remained in the labour force, the unemployment rate rises to 21%. The remainder had left the labour force.

The survey was conducted amongst workers employed for three years or more who had lost their jobs because of plant closure and relocation. Almost one-quarter of the women who lost their jobs had left the labour force compared with one in ten of the men. Older workers were also more likely to have left the labour force. Over a quarter (27%) of those made unemployed were without work for less than 5 weeks, while 19% were unemployed for more than one year. Higher levels of education reduced the duration of unemployment.

A comparison of earnings showed that 52% reported nominal weekly earnings the same or higher after finding new work. For 29%, the improvement in earnings was more than 20% above their previous jobs. At the same time, 30% were in jobs which cut their pay by 20% or more. This group included half the displaced steelworkers in the survey. Older workers, higher income earners, those with lower education levels and those in high unemployment areas were likely to suffer the greatest cuts in income. Each additional week without a job led to 0.3% to 0.4% lower earnings in a new job (Richards, 1992, pp. 303).

In Canada, nearly 400,000 workers lost their jobs through closure or relocation between 1981 and 1984. In January 1986, 25% of those displaced and still in the labour force were unemployed; this was more than double the unemployment rate for the labour force as a whole. Within this average, 34% of those aged 55 or over were unemployed. Those with higher education levels were less likely to be unemployed. Those in depressed regions and older workers took most time to find jobs, while more educated workers needed less time (Richards, 1992).

In Europe, Hesler and Osterland (1986) followed the 2,000 workers displaced following the closure of the A G Weser shipyard in Bremen in 1983. In early 1985 20% were unemployed and two-thirds were in employment. Between 22% and 35% had not experienced a period of unemployment. At the time, Bremen had an unemployment rate 4% above the national average, which rose over the year following the closure, suggesting that some of the displaced shipworkers took jobs which in turn displaced those in other industries. Over a quarter of those who found jobs were in less skilled work. Over half of the unemployed were over 50 years of age and two-thirds over 45 (see Richards, 1992).

Two studies were conducted of 800 people made redundant by Devonport Management Ltd in Plymouth, Southwest England, over the period from May 1989 to December 1991 (Gripaios and Gripaios, 1990 and 1992). At the time of the survey, 41.6% of respondents were employed by a firm and a further 9.8% were self-employed, with 33.7% remaining unemployed. The study found that workers over the age of 40 had a higher incidence of unemployment while more of those under 30 were in the other category, including students and training. The implications for the Plymouth region's economy was explored in Gripaios and Gripaios (1994).

Although Plymouth has a high unemployment rate relative to the southwest region, over 80% of those who had found a job and 75% of those self-employed had remained in the Plymouth area. Only 10% of the sample had left the two counties of Devon and Cornwall. For those gaining employment, however, their new occupational status revealed considerable de-skilling. This research confirmed the typical picture of redundant workers finding difficulty in obtaining new work, with those finding jobs often not using their skills and accepting lower pay. Many move from manufacturing industry to the service sector. The problems are more severe for older workers. Despite the difficulties, few move home to find new work.

In Lancashire, a survey of those leaving British Aerospace plants at Preston, Salmesbury and Warton found that only 8% had jobs in industry by the end of the study (Demilitarized, 1991). Again, a memorandum submitted by the Defence Industries Council to the House of Commons Defence Committee (the Sixth Report, written evidence, p. 37), refers to the experience of defence workers who lost their jobs in 1990 and commented that:

> 'Latest company studies of the effects of redundancy over three years on defence workers who lost their jobs in 1990, suggest that 33% were still unemployed, 34% had found only semi-skilled, or un-skilled work, only 29% had found employment in a manufacturing industry and 40% of those working were working at lower rates of pay in 1993 than they were earning 3 years earlier. The market's ability to generate new, quality industrial jobs has been demonstrably weak and shows few signs of improvement.'

The significance of large-scale redundancies during the 1980s is illustrated by the *Mass Lay-off Statistics Program,* initiated by the US Bureau of Labor Statistics in 1984 in response to the Job Training Partnership Act of 1982. This Act required the Secretary of Labor to develop and maintain statistical information on permanent large-scale redundancies and plant closings, and to report annually on the number of plant closures, the number of large-scale lay-offs, the numbers of workers affected and the geographical and industrial breakdown. Mass lay-offs were defined as those involving 50 or more personnel at one job site within a three-week period. Eight US States took part in the development of the Program in 1984. By 1992, California was the only state not participating. The Program ended in the winter of 1992. Over the course of the study, data were collected on some 533 defence-related layoffs covering some 110,950 workers.

The Mass Lay-off Program collected information on the jobs and industry from which workers were made redundant. In a separate survey of 19 of the largest US defence contractors, the CBO obtained data relating those workers laid off in 1991 by 13 large defence contractors. The job losses totalled 143,735 over the period 1988–1992, or some 21% of their 1987 employment. Most of the job losses took place in 1991 (8%) and the first half of 1992 (9%).

According to the Congressional Budget Office (CBO, 1993), the:

> 'available evidence indicates that displaced defence workers are undergoing about the same average duration of unemployment as other workers experiencing mass lay-offs. In the latter half of 1990, the exhaustion rate—defined as the ratio of those whose benefits have been exhausted to initial claimants two quarters earlier—was the same for displaced defence workers as for all displaced workers. Both groups experience exhaustion rates of about 17% to 18%. In 1991, as the recession took hold, the rate rose to about 22%, but the differences between the two groups remained too small to be significant.'

To summarise, then, there are a number of conclusions which appear consistently throughout the studies:

- many redundant workers cease to be unemployed (i.e. they accept a new job, enter training or education, retire or voluntarily leave the workforce) within a short period (typically within one year);
- those who remain unemployed are likely to do so for a long time (over one year, and often for many years);
- unskilled workers have more difficulty finding new work;
- older workers have more difficulty finding new work;
- most redundant workers do not move in search of work;
- the majority of workers accept lower skilled work and lower pay in their new job;
- the state of the local economy affects the outcome of redundancy;
- the way in which redundancy is handled by a company makes a significant difference to the well-being of those made redundant.

One of the few major studies of defence industry redundancies in the UK was carried out by combined research teams from the University of York's Centre for Defence Economics and from the Research Unit in Defence Economics at the University of the West of England, Bristol between February and July 1995.

The central element of the study was a large postal survey of those who had left employment in 16 defence companies located in the southwest of the UK during the years 1989 and 1994. Questionnaires were sent to some 10,347 ex-employees of these defence companies and 1,933 usable responses were received, a response rate of 18.3%. The data analysis from the study disclosed the following:

i)   most of the jobs lost were permanent and full-time.
ii)   some 25% remained unemployed at the time of the survey.
iii) most new jobs acquired were permanent and full-time.
iv)   some two-thirds of respondents earned less, and one-fifth more, in their new job than in their former employment in the defence industry.
v)   few defence jobs or skills were transferred to new employment.
vi)   there was evidence of job mobility but not geographic mobility.
vii) two-thirds of respondents found their new jobs satisfactory, although evidence suggested that respondents' expectations were not high and they no longer thought in terms of careers.
viii) qualified scientists and engineers tend to find employment more easily than others.
ix)   different industries in the defence sector shed different types of jobs.
x)   Ex-employees from the aerospace and electronics industries are more in demand than others.

Buck, Hartley and Hooper (1993, pp. 161–178), exploring the inter-relationships between the crowding-out dimension of military research and development expenditure and the issue of a peace dividend from reduced military expenditure, estimated potential employment impact for the UK. Their results suggested that a 10% reduction in UK defence expenditure would be associated with a 6% reduction in employment levels and commented that there may be a role for public policy in helping the economy absorb displaced defence industry scientists and engineers.

CONCLUSIONS

Without question, defence expenditure and associated employment and income-generating activity have a close and often symbiotic relationship with the national economy. While at the national aggregate level the impact may be modest over time, variations in national defence expenditure do impact significantly upon employment and income generation in local and regional economies. Furthermore, detrimental economic effects, attributable to defence cuts, may be transmitted less obviously but no less importantly to regions of an economy which have little direct defence dependence via the inter-dependencies of the supply chain or matrix which underpins defence production. Evidence suggests that the efficacy of the market mecha-nism in reallocating resources smoothly and efficiently, following a prolonged downturn in defence expenditure, may be called into ques-tion, offering scope for some form of government intervention in order to facilitate the process of generating a genuine and long-lasting peace dividend.

In this chapter, the labour market has been considered in order to illustrate the different ways in which the economic effects of sharply declining defence budgets, transmitted through the structure, opera-tion and inter-dependencies of the defence industry and its supply chain, may impact upon employment. These include:

a) job-shedding as part of the planned rationalisation of prime defence contractors. There is evidence from UK research in the 1990s that, critically, many prime contractors have initiated such rationalisation strategies in advance of an anticipated reduction in defence expenditure, utilising perhaps the end of the Cold War as a justification for corporate restructuring.

b) job-shedding as part of the planned rationalisation of small and medium sized enterprises in the defence sector, which recognise their strong business links with the defence prime contractors and, thereby, understand their exposure to defence cuts.

c) unplanned and sudden job-shedding by companies located in the lower tiers and levels of the defence industry supply chain, unaware of the degree to which their business is defence-dependent. Research outlined in Chapter 4 suggests that this lack of awareness of the eventual customer and their market situation has been a significant problem for many small and medium-sized enterprises, helping to explain why so many of these supply companies frequently find adjustment to the evolving market con-ditions so difficult.

d) additional and uncoordinated job-shedding as the defence indus-try's supply chain structure and interdependencies sets off a chain reaction of reduced demand throughout its component parts.

e) further job-shedding in the non-defence sectors of the economy as the regional multiplier consequences of reduced demand impact upon local business.

Similarly, this kind of employment impact can be expected from the closure or scaling-down of a military base, although the transmission mechanism may be different given the more insular nature of many military bases. Where defence industrial companies or military bases actually close, the labour market impact is unlikely to be contained within a neat set of geographical boundaries but will extend across local authority areas with variable severity, depending on the geographic distribution of defence suppliers, military bases and associated establishments and their suppliers. To the extent that reductions in spending on defence equipment will be accompanied by reductions in expenditure on military bases, establishments and their personnel, those regions of the UK which have concentrations of both defence supply companies and military manpower are likely to experience regional 'clustering' effects with considerable labour market impact. The economic impact and conversion potential of military bases are considered more fully in Chapter 5.

The degree to which regional economies with a significant defence sector can absorb the adverse impact upon employment and income of declining defence expenditure will depend largely upon the flexibility and responsiveness of the local and national labour markets and the potential for regional defence conversion. The capacity of the regional labour market to respond to significant adjustments in military spending will be affected by the mobility of displaced labour and the evolving skill profile required in any regeneration of the regional economy.

Defence-dependent companies in the industrialised nations tend to employ a larger number of professional, technical and skilled (craft) workers than the manufacturing sector generally. At the same time, however, they employ far fewer sales staff and semi-skilled workers. Furthermore, evidence suggests that the difficulty experienced by redundant defence workers in transferring to civilian employment differs markedly between occupational categories. Most redundant clerical and unskilled staff in the defence sector should be able to transfer relatively rapidly to the civil sector as long as the regional or national economy is in an expansionary phase. US research has shown, however, that the civil sector cannot offer comparable employment opportunities for some highly trained clerical staff, especially those working in unusual military support activities.

Again, there is evidence from diversification experience in Sweden, Germany and the USA to suggest that production workers, both skilled and unskilled, can be fairly easily transferred in certain circumstances from military to civil production. Sometimes, this is because of similarity in end-product (e.g. aerospace) or because of the similarity in the required employee task, even where the end-product is completely different. Some industrial sectors (such as the electronics industry) appear to be particularly well-suited to facilitating this transfer of personnel. Such production workers naturally would require an element of retraining. Experience suggests that this retraining period may be as short as three months and would be no more than that conventionally implemented by manufacturing companies wishing to redeploy their production personnel as part of a restructuring strategy.

Without doubt, the most difficult occupational groups to convert to civilian production will be the engineers, scientists and other technical personnel employed by defence companies and the managerial and administrative staff whose function is to support and direct specifically military business within the organisation. In the UK, estimates have suggested that about 60% of the design engineers and scientists are employed in the mechanical engineering industry although defence production accounts for only 7% of that industry's output. Furthermore, the French 'aero-naval' industrial sector (heavily reliant on defence contracts) employed in the 1970s five times more engineers, four times more technicians and nearly twice as many skilled workers as a whole. Research conducted in the USA and Europe suggests a number of reasons for this significant constraint on personnel transfer.

For engineers, scientists and other technical personnel, three barriers appear to exist:

i) the absence of sufficient 'cost consciousness' among defence engineers;
ii) the view of business managers that defence engineers are not well-suited to commercial work; and:
iii) the belief among engineers generally that the defence business requires more specialists and the commercial sector more generalists. If such highly trained personnel have a dominant influence

within the company, the standards applicable to military contracts are likely to be applied to civilian business with potentially disastrous consequences.

For managers and administrators, the problems of personnel transfer are different. Experience in the USA suggest two principal reasons. They are:

i)   the lack of experience in and familiarity with commercial marketing practices; and:
ii) the lower salary levels available in the civilian sector for such personnel. In some instances, there is evidence that middle-level managers may need considerable retraining because they have been accustomed to the practices and routines that are specific to dealing with a monopsonist customer such as a defence ministry.

Research which has focused on the problems encountered by displaced defence workers has confirmed a number of key explanatory characteristics. In common with displaced workers in other manufacturing industries, the greatest difficulty has been experienced by those aged over 50 years, female, members of a minority group, production workers with few skills, those geographically immobile, those unwilling or unable to move to a new industry, those unwilling to accept a pay cut, and those whose academic or technical qualifications were not acquired recently.

In almost every example of defence industry diversification into production for the civilian market, irrespective of the country concerned, the same barriers appear to recur. These include: slow product development; poorly estimated and uncompetitively higher costs; excessive quality characteristics; weak marketing and insufficient after-sales service, most of which are personnel/skill-related issues, at least in part.

For those members of the armed services becoming redundant as a result of defence cuts, there is a further problem as the employees released by the Services attempt to gain re-employment elsewhere at the same time as defence industries are releasing workers into the same labour market. This simultaneous increase in labour supply due to defence industry and armed forces contraction undoubtedly has presented a problem for those local and regional labour markets affected. It is likely that redundant labour in the armed services will initially seek employment in the area surrounding what has become their 'home base'.

Where such a region is dependent both on defence industry and on military base activities (such as the southwest of England), the absorptive capacity of the regional labour market must be questionable, even in times of relative prosperity. Where the national economy has recently experienced a recession—and defence-dependent regions have simultaneously lost their 'traditional' economic safety-net due to defence cuts—significant problems of excess labour supply at the regional level can be anticipated and may require local or national government policy response. More importantly, in a few highly defence-dependent geographic areas, intense clustering of defence industry facilities and military bases can be found. Simultaneous and significant redundancies in both of these sectors would, inevitably, threaten the prosperity—or possibly the economic viability—of such vulnerable localities.

The problems faced by particular occupational groups in the transfer process from military to civil work, then, may well be significant and, accentuated by problems in attracting sufficient inward investment to regenerate defence-dependent regional economies, may prove extremely difficult for the unaided labour market to resolve. In the major arms producing nations, the deep economic recession of the early 1990s, the slow and relatively weak recovery and the unprecedented reduction in manufacturing jobs and employment opportunities (over almost 3 decades) make the task of labour transfer from military to civilian production increasingly problematic and calls into question, once more, the attainability of a genuine and long-lasting peace dividend.

REFERENCES

ADCC., (1992), *The Impact of Reduced Military Spending on Local Economic Activity: A Case for European Community Assistance*, London.

Aztec., (1992), *Changing the Future*, Aztec Training and Enterprise Council, London.

Berthoud R., (1979), Unemployed Professionals and Executives, *Policy Studies Institute*, Vol. XLV, (582), May.

Boddy M., and Lovering J., (1986), High-Technology Industry in the Bristol Sub-Region: The Aerospace/Defence Nexus, *Regional Studies*, Vol. 20, Part 3, pp. 217–231.

Braddon D. L., (1995) Regional Impact of Defence Expenditure, in Hartley K. and Sandler T., (eds) *Handbook of Defence Economics*, Ch. 17. pp. 492–521.

Braddon D. L., Dowdall P. G., and Kendry A. P., (1994), Employment in the UK defence industry: Structural Change or Market Adjustment, in White M., (ed.), *Unemployment, Public Policy and the Labour Market*, Policy Studies Institute, London.

Brauer J., and Chatterji M., (eds), (1993), *Economic Issues of Disarmament: Contributions from Peace Economics and Peace Science*, New York, New York University Press.

Breheny M., (1988), *Defence Spending and Regional Development*, Mansell

CBO, (1993), *Re-employing Defence Workers: Current Experiences and Policy Alternatives*, Congressional Budget Office, Washington D.C., August.

Buck D., Hartley K. and Hooper N., (1993), Defence Research and Development, Crowding Out and the Peace Dividend, *Defence Economics*, Vol. 4.

Demilitarized., (1991), *Diversification of the European Military Industry*, Lancashire Enterprises, Preston.

Fontanel J., (1994), The Economics of Disarmament: A Survey, *Defence and Peace Economics*, Vol. 5, pp. 87–120.

Gripaios P. and Gripaios R., (1990), The Impact of Dockyard Redundancies at Plymouth, *Defence Analysis*, Vol. 6, (3), pp. 307–309.

Gripaios P. and Gripaios R., (1992), *An Analysis of Post-Redundancy Experience of ex-Devonport Workers*, southwest Economic Research Centre, Plymouth Business School, February.

Gripaios P. and Gripaios R., (1994), The Impact of Defence Cuts: The Case of Redundancy in Plymouth, *Geography*, No. 342, Vol. 79, (1), pp. 32–41.

Gronau R., (1971), Information and Frictional Unemployment, *American Economic Review*, Vol. 61, (2), May, pp. 290–301.

Guy N., (1994), see, for example, *Dole not Coal*, Coalfields Community Campaign, Barnsley.

Hartley K. and Hooper N., (1991), *The Economic Consequences of the UK Government's Decision on a Chieftain Replacement*, Research Monograph 1, Centre for Defence Economics, University of York.

Hartley K. and Hooper N., (1993), *The Economic Consequences of the UK Government's Decision on the Hercules Replacement*, Research Monograph Series 2, Centre for Defence Economics, University of York, February.

Hesler H. and Osterland M., (1986), *Bertriebsstillegung und lokaler arbeitsmarkt: das beispiel der AG Weser in Bremen*, Mitteilungen aus der arbeitmarkt und berufsforschung, Stuttgart.

Hey J. D., (1979), A Simple Generalised Stopping Rule, *Economics Letters*, Vol. 2, pp. 115–120.

Hooper N., Butler B., Hartley K., Braddon D., and Dowdall P., (1995), *Defence Industry Redundancies in the southwest Region*, Centre for Defence Economics, University of York, August.

Hutton W., (1996), *The State We're In*, Jonathan Cape, 1995.

ILO, see Richards (1992).

IFO., (1991), *Production of Defence Materials in GDR*, Institut fur Wirtsschaftsforschung, Munich.

Jacobs M., (1991), *The Green Economy*, Pluto.

Kennedy P., (1988), *The Rise and Fall of the Great Powers*, Random House, New York.

Kohn M. G. and Shavell S., (1974), The Theory of Search, *Journal of Economic Theory*, Vol. 9, (2), October, pp. 93–123.

Lachmann L. M., (1986), *The Market as an Economic Process*, Basil Blackwell.

Leijonhufvud A., *Information and Co-ordination: Essays in Macroeconomic Theory*, Oxford.

Mackay D. I., Mackay R., McVean P. and Edwards R., *Redundancy and Displacement*, Research Paper 16, Department of Employment, November.

McCall J. J., (1970), The Simple Economics of Incentive Contracting, *American Economic Review*, 60, December.

McKenna C. K., (1979), A Solution to a Class of Sequential Decision Problems, *Economics letters*, Vol. 48, (3), pp. 115–118.

Nelson R. R., (1995), Recent Evolutionary Theorizing About Economic Change, *Journal of Economic Literature*, Vol. XXXIII, March, pp. 49–90.

Ormerod P., (1994), *The Death of Economics*, Faber and Faber.

Ram R., (1995) Defence Expenditure and Economic Growth, in Hartley K. and Sandler T. (eds) *Handbook of Defence Economics*, Elsevier.

Ricardo D., (1817), *On the Principles of Political Economy, and Taxation*, 1951 edition: Cambridge, Cambridge University Press.

Richards P., (1991), 'Of Arms and the Man: Possible Employment Consequences of Disarmament', *International Labour Review*, Vol. 130, No. 3.

Richards P. J., (1992), Disarmament and Employment, *Defence Economics*, Vol. 2, (4).

Sandler T. and Hartley K., (1995), *The Economics of Defence*, Cambridge University Press, Ch. 8, pp. 200–220.

Saunders N. C., (1990), Defence Spending in the 1990s—The Effects of Deeper Cuts, *Monthly Labor Review*, October.

Shackle G. L. S., (1972), Marginalism: The Harvest, *History of Political Economy*, Fall.

Shackle G. L. S., (1972), *Epistemics and Economics*, Cambridge, Cambridge University Press.

Smith Ring P. and Van de Ven A. H., (1994) Developmental Processes of Cooperative Interorganizational

Relationships', *Academy of Management Review*; 19/1; pp. 90–118.

Stigler J., (1962), Information in the Labour Market, *Journal of Political Economy*, Vol. 70, supplement.

Thompson G., Frances J., Levacic R., and Mitchell J., (1991), *Markets, Hierarchies and Networks: The Coordination of Social Life*, Sage Publications and the Open University.

Warf B. and Cox J. C., (1989), Military Prime Contracts and Taxes in the New York Metropolitan Region—a Short Run Analysis, *Regional Studies*, 23, pp. 241–252.

Udis B. (ed), (1976), *The Economic Consequences of Reduced Military Spending*, Lexington Books.

Wedderburn D., (1965), *Redundancy and the Railwaymen*, Cambridge University Press, Cambridge

Weidenbaum M., Defence Spending and the American Economy: How Much Change is in the Offing?, *Defence Economics*, Vol. 1, No. 3, pp. 233–242.

Weiss S. and Gooding E., (1968), Estimation of Different Employment Multipliers in a Small Regional Economy, *Land Economics*, 44, pp. 235–244.

Weitzman M., (1984), *The Share Economy: Conquering Stagflation*, Harvard University Press, Cambridge.

Westergaard J., Noble I. And Alwker A., (1989), *After Redundancy: The Experience of Economic Insecurity*, Polity Press, Cambridge.

Wheeler D. and Sillanpaa M., (1997), *The Stakeholder Corporation: A Blueprint for Maximising Stakeholder Value*, Pitman Publishing, London.

Wilde L. L., (1979), An Information-Theoretic Approach to Job Quits, in (eds) Lippman S. A. and McCall J. J., *Studies in the Economics of Search*, North Holland, Amsterdam.

Chapter 3

___

DEFENCE INDUSTRY RESTRUCTURING AND THE MARKET

INTRODUCTION

Such was the scale and pace of political change sweeping through the former Soviet Union and Eastern Europe a decade ago that government and industry leaders worldwide, closely observing the evolving situation, were aware that the prevailing Cold War global security and business environment was about to change beyond recognition. Early in the 1990s, particularly in the US and Europe, governments began to signal significant reductions in current and future defence budgets, particularly in weapon procurement and military manpower requirements (for an interesting review of the impact of such reductions in a national context, see Lock and Vob, 1994). Initially, there was considerable uncertainty concerning the industrial implications of the scale, timing and consequences of major reductions in defence expenditure in the industrialised nations. Where possible, economists sought to improve the accuracy of economic modelling in order to help understand these implications (see, for example, Seiglie, 1992).

Over the last few years, the whole structure and modus operandi of the defence 'market' (if such it may be called given the important role played by government, often as a monopsonist) has changed fundamentally on both the demand side and the supply side. It is important to recognise that the significant defence expenditure reductions of the early 1990's followed a period in which, despite the massive commitment of public money to defence projects, governments had already begun to amend their defence procurement policies to secure significant cost savings and attain greater 'value for money'. Procurement reforms, such as the Levene reforms in the UK in the mid-1980's, had already fundamentally changed the nature of the business environment surrounding defence procurement and supply, placing greater pressure on defence companies to deliver enhanced efficiency and cost-effectiveness (Dunne, 1993, pp. 91–111).

The purpose of this chapter is to explore the supply side of the defence industry, focusing particularly upon the prime contractors. Initially, we will consider the important characteristics that differentiate a defence firm and its market from those firms which serve more commercial markets and note how these differences are changing over time. The initial corporate responses to declining defence expenditure levels during the 1990s and the variety of corporate strategic options employed as the decade progressed will then be examined. In particular, attention will focus on three options: market entry, market exit and corporate restructuring and rationalisation. Considerable attention will be given throughout the chapter to developments within the military aerospace industry, given the leading role this sector has played in the post-Cold War industrial restructuring process. The remarkable merger trend in the US aerospace industry will be considered in some detail and the consequent attempts by European nations to respond effectively to this new and immensely powerful competitive challenge will be explored. Case studies at the regional and programme level are incorporated in the chapter, where appropriate.

THE DEFENCE FIRM

At the outset, it is important to emphasise the key historic differences between a company that serves primarily the military sector and one which focuses on a normal commercial market. DiFiilipo (1991) provides a valuable taxonomy for comparing military-focused companies with commercial-focused companies. Commercial-focused companies sell their products domestically to many customers and, usually, no single customer can exert undue influence on their corporate strategy or production process. Such firms operate in markets which are usually competitive in nature but, even where oligopolistic situations prevail, companies still have to scrutinise costs carefully to prevent loss of competitive advantage. Most of these firms have the potential through long and sizeable production runs to pursue economies of scale and, in recent years with the advent of flexible manufacturing, economies of scope. Such companies enter into contracts in commercial markets which are binding, especially with regard to cost. Typically, cost over-runs do not occur and these companies are expected to generate profit from careful investment and self-financed research and development programmes. A commercial-focused company, operating in a competitive environment, will normally seek to minimise waste, inefficiency and costs to retain and expand its share of commercial markets.

On the other hand, a military-focused company usually sells its products to a single purchaser (the government defence procurement agency) and, occasionally, to similar defence agencies or procurement departments from other nations. This results in such government agencies having a considerable degree of influence over the company and its production. Although nominally there is a competitive environment for some defence equipment (e.g. combat aircraft), governments still in general tend to support their own 'national champion' where appropriate and genuine market competition is often non-existent. With the advent of procurement reforms over the last two decades, however, the competitive element of global defence markets is becoming more pronounced. Historically, until the defence procurement reforms, cost was not a major concern for military-focused companies; rather the pursuit of leading edge technology and, consequently, the attainment and preservation of military competitive advantage was paramount. As a result, military-focused companies had little real cost-consciousness and with governments keen to change military specifications frequently to ensure technological edge, there was a strong tendency towards cost over-runs and programme delays. DiFillipo contends that profits as a percentage of investment in such companies tended to be significantly higher than in commercial-focused companies since governments provide significant financial support for research and development investment. Such was the significance of government decision-making for military-focused companies for much of the Cold War period that the term 'Military Keynesianism' was coined to describe the symbiotic nature of the government-defence industry relationship, especially in the United States (see Cypher, 1982, for further discussion).

Increasingly, however, the combination of defence procurement reforms, competitive tendering, and the changing nature of both defence supply companies and the industry itself has begun to reduce and remove the differences between these two kinds of companies. Many companies now operate in both military and commercial sectors of the market and the drive towards dual-use technology is likely to further eliminate these differences. Nevertheless, many military-focused companies still do not operate under normal market conditions; an important point to remember in exploring the variety of corporate responses to defence cuts outlined below.

INITIAL CORPORATE RESPONSE

Strategic corporate response to the changing business environment facing the defence industry in the early 1990's comprised both reaction to the forecasts of significant and sustained defence expenditure reduction over the years ahead and, in some cases, what may be seen as delayed response to the more competitive, cost-conscious approach of the procurement reforms. The initial response among prime contractors in the defence supply industry was to begin to shed labour and to adopt other strategies designed to secure rapid cost reduction, including exit from the industry (Taylor, 1993, pp. 115–117). As the UK National Economic Development Council reported in 1991:

> 'in general, companies have responded to the situation by a drastic reduction in workforce and a streamlining of their operations. Some companies have sold all their defence interests and... others are in the process of seeking new avenues within defence since there are some new opportunities as the MoD moves towards contractorisation.'

As a second distinct element of the evolving business strategies pursued by defence supply companies in the post-Cold War world, the search for conversion and diversification opportunities became— perhaps for the first time with any serious intent—a major priority in new business development, despite the recognised difficulties inherent in such a process and the complex and uncertain business conditions prevailing at the time. Research focusing on southwest England in the early 1990s (CBI, 1993) explored this dimension of the emerging corporate rationalisation in the UK defence industrial base. In line with the analysis above, the research found that most defence supply companies located in the highly defence-dependent southwest region of the UK responded to defence cuts in the 1990's by seeking to maintain their competitive position in the market through the introduction of internal restructuring strategies (usually incorporating considerable redundancy programmes) and external strategies aimed at securing cost saving, enhanced efficiency, flexibility and, critically, new market penetration. To target new markets, the majority of defence supply companies affected have pursued a combination of new product design and development while refocusing their activities to access new geographic markets; adopting a joint venture/strategic alliance path to effective diversification; setting up distinctive new business ventures and attempting to change their market profile through acquisitions and mergers.

As part of the restructuring process, therefore, many prime defence contractors in the Western nations initially had little choice but to adopt new corporate strategies, ranging from market consolidation through diversification and conversion to, ultimately, complete divestment of defence divisions (see Dowdy, 1997). Table 8 below provides examples of the variety of such corporate responses in the immediate aftermath of the end of the Cold War in the years between 1990 and 1994.

It is argued that the industry has now entered the 'fourth and final phase' (a phrase coined by Norman Augustine, former Chief Executive Officer of Martin Marietta) in which large defence companies with different, or sometimes similar, attributes then merge in an attempt to reduce costs even further. Recent examples of this phenomenon include mergers in 1994 between Northrop and Grumman and between Lockheed and Martin Marietta. The strategy here is to reduce central organisation and research and development costs while enabling the new organisation to spread the risk of potential project cancellation or cutback over a greater range of weapons systems.

The formation of strategic alliances, technology partnerships and, within the supply and sub-contract network of the defence industry, the pursuit of partnership sourcing, has accentuated the industrial revolution taking place in this sector. The essence of market survival in the turbulent business world of the 1990s appears to lie in the pursuit of strategic flexibility, targeting the building of critical capabilities to secure competitive advantage (Hayes and Pisano, 1994), no less for the defence industrial base than for any other critical sector of the economy. For defence contractors, these organisational, managerial and production-related changes have accelerated their evolution into what is known as M-form, multi-divisional organisations. As a result, sharper market focus and enhanced production flexibility have enabled such companies, especially the large prime contractors in the defence sector, to implement wide-ranging corporate rationalisation decisions.

In general, then, confronted with the prospect of a prolonged and substantial reduction in defence expenditure, these companies have:

a) attempted to increase their share of a declining defence market through enhanced efficiency and cost reduction;

b) concentrated more on core business activities, pursuing long-range market positioning strategies, while targeting realistic short-term opportunities;

c) pursued collaborative policies to share costs and risks, both horizontally and vertically, with the aim of benefiting from new defence procurement decisions; and tried to enhance their civil business, harnessing and transferring technology and other operational aspects from their defence business.

TABLE 8: INITIAL CORPORATE RESPONSES TO THE REQUIREMENT TO RESTRUCTURE: 1990–1994

Ford (USA) IBM (USA) General Electric (USA)	Divestment of defence divisions to companies such as Loral and Martin Marietta.
Ferranti (UK)	Pursued consolidation but, after financial problems, was forced to divest.
Racal (UK) Thorn-EMI (UK)	Attempted to divest defence business but, ultimately, forced to consolidate. Racal gained civil market knowledge from space sector; moved into civil aircraft and satellite communications. Joint venture with Honeywell to supply civil airliner market.
General Dynamics (USA)	Refocused on core defence business—tactical aircraft, tanks, nuclear submarines and space projects. Divested peripheral business such as small civil aircraft and missiles.
Loral (USA)	Expanded core defence business by acquiring defence activities of US blue chip companies which had entered and then exited defence market.
GEC (UK)	Consolidated position by acquisition (with Siemens) of Plessey, divisions of Ferranti and the Yarrow shipyard.
Vickers (UK)	Consolidated position in UK tank production by acquiring Royal Ordnance tank factory.
British Aerospace (UK)	Consolidation through acquisition of Royal Ordnance factories in 1987 and diversification through acquisition into the construction (Ballast Nedam), car (Rover) and property (Arlington) markets.
The Dowty Group	Identified product/sector/or technology offering opportunity for growth; separated activity within the Group and used 'product champion' to foster growth; continual monitoring of need for investment, organic growth or acquisitions.
Easams Limited (UK)	Largest single diversification of the company out of defence market was software division. developed fourth generation computer software and moved into civil markets: stock control; leisure information; transportation, flight monitoring and sales processing.
Integrated Networks (Northern Telecom Ltd) (UK)	Moved into new product area (military integrated networks) and then diversified into civil markets, initially police, utilities, and shipping. Moved up the 'value chain' from manufacturing to service provision.
Logica (UK)	Exploited their capacity to build and manage large software systems projects under conditions of high security. transferred products and skills mainly successfully to intelligence operations; satellite observation; telephony; telegraphy; data communications; and business services.
Redifon (UK)	Identified new markets for existing products; redefined market from defence to 'radio communications market' and developed new products to target market; extended technology base to seek new opportunities.
Bofors (Sweden)	Merged with Kema Nobel in 1984 to reduce defence-dependency. Found that conversion was difficult at the time due to the fact that some 80–90% of Bofors employees lacked direct civil counterparts and there was little civil marketing experience within the company upon which to build a conversion strategy.

INITIAL MARKET RESPONSE IN A REGIONAL SETTING: THE CASE OF SOUTH-
WEST ENGLAND

To capture these industrial responses more accurately, a research
project was undertaken in 1993 which focused on defence companies
and their response to the changed environment of the 1990s in the
southwest region of England. At the start of the 1990's, the southwest
region of England (with a population of 4.7 million and a GDP of
some £40 billion, similar to that of Norway and greater than Greece,
Portugal and the Republic of Ireland, was one of the most defence-
dependent regions of the country. The region received some £3.38
billion of defence expenditure per annum, approximately 19% of total
UK defence expenditure, compared with the southeast's share of £7.1
billion or over 37% of the total. In terms of per capita defence expenditure, the southwest region attracted about £720 per capita in 1990,
considerably more than twice the national average and substantially
greater than the southeast region (£407). Within the region were
located divisions of most of the important UK defence companies
including British Aerospace, Rolls-Royce, Fairey Hydraulics, TI
Dowty, Smiths Industries, Thorn EMI, FR Group, Siemens Plessey,
Westland and DML and many of their principal suppliers.

Detailed analysis of the corporate responses of the thirty most
defence-dependent companies in the southwest region provided recent
evidence of how such companies initially reacted to the dramatic
changes of the 1990's. These responses, and the success with which
they are pursued, will have a profound impact on the economic well-
being of the southwest region. Since there is no reason to suppose that
these corporate responses are particularly unique to this region,
important trends can be observed that will have significance for most
other regions where defence industry forms a core element of the local
economy.

Research findings suggested that about three-quarters of the 30
most defence-dependent companies in the southwest region had experienced significantly reduced orders in the first three years of this
decade with more than half expecting that this trend would continue
over the medium term. One fifth of these major defence companies
had experienced actual order cancellations between 1990 and 1993
with the same number expecting the trend to continue. Almost two-
thirds of these highly defence-dependent companies had experienced
significantly reduced business enquiries since 1990 with almost as
many expecting this to continue in the future.

Following announcement and implementation of defence expenditure cuts by government after 1990, some 37% of highly defence-dependent companies in the region had already implemented significant redundancies up to 1993 with 43% expecting to do so in the next few years. Between one fifth and one quarter of highly defence-dependent companies in the region had experienced serious skill loss with half of the companies expecting this to be a problem in the future. A similar proportion had taken strategic decisions to reduce price and extend credit arrangements between 1990 and 1993.

Parallel with this survey of highly defence-dependent companies in the region, a similar investigation of the 'broader population' of companies was undertaken within the study for comparative purposes and to attempt to identify how much of the adjustment taking place could be attributed to general economic factors associated with the deep recession of the early 1990's as opposed to contraction in the defence market. In virtually every case, the data indicated that the problems experienced by the defence sector and the degree to which it was responding were dramatically higher than for southwest industry in general. The evidence makes clear the degree to which the defence-dependent sector of the southwest economy has been adversely affected by the defence cutbacks in a very short space of time. There is no reason to suppose that the impact in other similarly defence-dependent regions would be significantly different.

Furthermore, the research project produced some interesting findings concerning the manner in which vulnerable highly defence - dependent companies were responding in terms of both evolving market consolidation and new market strategies. To pursue market consolidation, 70% of defence-dependent companies in the region were planning in 1993 to implement major cost reduction programmes (with inevitable labour market and supply chain implications). Again, 60% were redeveloping and refining existing products for the changing defence market. Some 57% of defence-dependent companies were pursuing new customers for existing products while almost half of the companies were engaged in significant programmes of corporate restructuring, most through new joint ventures and strategic alliances.

To target new markets, over three-quarters of companies were pursuing new product design and development; 69% were seeking new geographic markets; 50% intended to take the joint venture/strategic alliance path to effective diversification; 23% were setting up a distinctive new business venture and 20% were changing market direction through acquisitions and mergers.

The findings of this survey tend to confirm at the regional level the conclusions of the Dussauge 'strategic management matrix' in exploring the possible corporate responses to be expected of a defence firm, perceiving a declining market for its output. The 'real-world' mixed strategies outlined above indicate that the response of firms operating in the defence sector to declining demand will depend on how significant that business is within their overall sales portfolio and their perceptions of viable market opportunities and threats.

To deal with the difficult business environment of the 1990's, the majority of defence supply companies have pursued a strategy involving a retreat to core business with peripheral activities spun off to sub-contract and/or a combination of new product design and development while refocusing their existing activities to access new geographic markets; adopting a joint venture/strategic alliance path to effective diversification; setting up distinctive new business ventures and attempting to change their market profile through acquisitions and mergers. Companies have had to choose between four options: market entry (perhaps surprising in the context of the 1990's defence business environment); market exit; corporate restructuring through acquisition/merger and/or pursuing diversification and conversion opportunities. In the remainder of this chapter, the first three of these options will be explored. In Chapter 5, the conversion and diversification option will be examined further with, in Chapter 6, due reference to the technological dimensions of this post-Cold War adjustment process.

MARKET ENTRY: COMPETITION AND CONTRACTING-OUT IN THE DEFENCE SECTOR

One of the interesting corporate responses to the post-Cold War contraction in defence budgets and the drive for greater value for money in defence spending has been for some companies to enter the defence business from outside at what may seem the worse possible time. The reason for this new interest in market entry has much to do with the introduction of competitive tendering and contracting-out by defence ministries in the UK and US, enabling interested companies to access for the first time the potentially lucrative business of servicing the MoD or DoD. One market, therefore, appeared to offer companies significant new business opportunities—the market created by opening up specific parts of MoD operations to outside contractors as part of the government's drive for enhanced value for money in public expenditure (see Braddon et al., (1996) for a fuller discussion of these issues).

For many years, defence ministries world-wide had been criticised for the application of insufficiently tight financial control mechanisms in both the defence procurement process and in the provision of 'in-house' defence services. At times such criticisms have been sharp indeed, highlighting what was seen as 'inadequate stewardship of public money' (see, for example, the 8th Report of the UK Public Accounts Committee, 1994). Persuaded by the logic of the market economists in the 1980s, governments began to press for enhanced 'value for money' in defence provision, pursuing this goal initially through an intensification of competition in defence supply together with the replacement of potentially lucrative cost-plus contracts for industrial suppliers to more limiting fixed-price contracts.

As the objective of liberating market forces became more widely accepted in political agendas around the world, even traditional and almost sacrosanct areas of public goods provision were gradually exposed to market pressures in the guise of privatisation, deregulation, contracting-out, competitive tendering and market testing. The arguments for such market-liberating devices focused upon the need to reduce large and unsustainable public sector deficits; to avoid or at least limit welfare losses believed to be associated with public ownership; to prevent the potential abuse of monopoly power; to overcome perceived x-inefficiency; and to restore incentives that would encourage innovation in product and process design. It was argued that such devices would act as catalysts for change in the public sector and serve to sharpen and enhance their economic performance.

The defence sector was no exception, although its modus operandi has crucial dimensions—such as national security issues and life-critical quality requirements in defence equipment—which do distinguish it from many other areas of economic activity and could limit the applicability of the market-liberating approach. Clearly, the private sector already plays a highly significant role within defence provision, principally on the equipment manufacturing side, although some countries prefer to retain at least part of that manufacturing process under government control. With a genuinely competitive framework in place, however, it was anticipated that further market exposure would be possible within the defence sector, especially in the provision of support services.

The application of the market-liberating approach to defence has stimulated considerable debate (see, for example, Sandler and Cauley, 1975; Sandler and Murdoch, 1990) given differing views on the extent to which defence is a pure public good, with the attendant characteristics of non-excludability and non-rivalry. Furthermore, unlike most other industries, the defence supply industry faces an unusual pattern of demand and, at the present time at least, is undergoing rapid and fundamental structural change. At the same time, while the dramatic changes that have dominated the geo-political landscape since 1989 appear, on the one hand, to signify a significant reduction in perceived threat, on the other, the uncertain and unpredictable global environment that has emerged could be seen as widening the threat and fundamentally changing its nature.

In general, contracting-out in the defence sector is most appropriate for functions that can be clearly defined and operated under franchise arrangements, such as waste removal, catering, cleaning services, accounting, transport and similar activities. In addition, the need for a wide range of maintenance services offers potential opportunities for private contractors. In the United States, for example, the Department of Defense has been particularly innovative in offering new market opportunities to private contractors during the last decade. This strategy was reinforced in November 1997 when Secretary of State for Defence Cohen introduced the defence reform initiative, a sweeping reform of the way the DoD conducts its business. This initiative radically restructured the DoD to reduce costs and enhance efficiency, retaining only those functions that were perceived to be 'governmental' in nature with all other functions intended to be competitively sourced to gain 'the performance and costs of market forces'. Key defence activities such as aircraft maintenance, early-warning provision, supply depot management and many other highly sensitive DoD functions have been offered for private sector provision. However, some of these DoD initiatives raised concerns at the political level about security and other considerations relating to private sector provision of key military services and these concerns led, in turn, to demands for much tighter limits on the extent to which the DoD could pursue the contracting-out process.

Similarly, in the UK the contracting-out or competitive tendering approach was introduced to inject market forces more directly into

the heart of defence procurement, reducing costs and sharpening competition. In the UK, by 1993, over 100 Ministry of Defence functions
had been contracted-out. These included such diverse activities as air
traffic control, dockyard operation, gardening, lecturing, operational
analysis, radar maintenance and waste disposal. In certain cases, for
example the contracting-out of military hospital cleaning, it has been
estimated that significant cost savings of some 40% were attained
(Uttley, 1993). While many MoD support services have been subjected
to 'market-testing' in the drive for enhanced efficiency, actual contractorisation has remained somewhat limited in practice. Uttley cites
ancillary support services within the MoD (such as cleaning, laundry
services and specialist management activities) as examples of successful
contractorisation with associated cost savings. To broaden the scope
of contracting-out to encompass the more complex core areas of MoD
operation, however, is likely to be more difficult for all parties
involved.

At the political level within the UK, increased private sector involvement in MoD activities has been accepted as economically desirable,
subject to the constraints of security, sound management and value for
money. For many private sector organisations, whether or not already
active in the defence sector, the process of contracting-out offers a
significant range of new market opportunities to explore. In terms of
market entry, what motives underpin their interest in entering potentially problematic and previously inaccessible markets?

Clearly, for the private sector organisation, the principal motive for
market entry into the provision of MoD core activities or support services will be the possibility of capturing economic rent and the associated acquisition of new profit opportunities. In line with the standard
literature on property rights and public choice, such private sector
organisations are viewed as groups of individuals, operating as a team,
bound together by contractual arrangements. If such organisations can
be managed in such a way as to minimise waste and inefficiency, compared with their public sector counterparts, enhanced performance
and reduced costs will result. To deliver this outcome, it is argued that
the management process requires effective incentive mechanisms, with
the profit motive best fulfilling this role.

Further sustaining the theoretical competitive advantage enjoyed by
the private sector, public choice theory (Tullock, 1976; Buchanan,
1978) has long asserted the proposition that politicians and state-
employed managers tend to focus more on their own self-interest,

rather than the public interest which they are supposed to protect. Without the constraint of the profit motive, organisations within government will tend to pursue a range of strategies such as 'budget maximisation, risk aversion, over-manning and non-optimal pricing, employment and investment.' (Ott and Hartley, 1991).

The crucial point in theory, then, is that private sector organisations, where property rights underpin the profit motive, have a clear incentive to out-perform public sector organisations in terms of allocative and productive efficiency. Allocative inefficiency can occur where public sector organisations lack a competitive environment which ensures efficient resource use. Productive inefficiency can occur where an organisation fails to minimise costs, often because incorrect internal organisational signals generate non-maximising behaviour. The organisation's performance is therefore adversely affected because its internal incentive and accountability structure is not designed to ensure an optimal outcome.

The international evidence comparing the relative efficiency attributes of public and private sector organisations is not conclusive. Borcherding et al. (1982); utilising the results of more than 50 studies from 5 countries, argues that public sector organisations tend to display higher unit cost structures. Yet Millward (1982) was unable to find support for the superiority of the private organisation on efficiency grounds from North American studies.

Despite the determined attempt by government to reduce the share of GDP taken by public expenditure, state bureaucracies tend to retain extremely large budgets. As such bureaucracies are compelled to shrink and become "consumers" of goods and services provided by external private operators, a significant part of the budget will be diverted to this activity, offering entrants to the newly-contractorised market potentially lucrative rewards.

For a profit-focused private sector organisation, the untapped potential profits to be derived from implementing market-based efficiency measures in the former public sector will attract those companies already performing a similar role in the private sector or those wishing to diversify into new areas of business activity. As well as the profit motive, additional stimulants to market entry may include the potential for valuable synergies between a company's existing business activities and its intended role in the newly contractorised market. Such synergies can include opportunities to generate economies of scale, scope and experience which can yield lower production costs;

the rationalisation of market supply to secure a quasi-monopoly position for the most efficient firm in that new market in the longer term; and the opportunity to develop more focused and effective financial management.

The scope that the contractorisation process offers for the eventual attainment of higher market prices for the provision of specific services than those considered currently acceptable under state provision is likely to be a further powerful motive for entry. Overall, within the market-testing and contracting-out approach, the private sector has to be able to demonstrate the capacity to offer defence support services more cheaply and more efficiently than 'in–house' providers. By offering flexible staff provision, efficiency gains from market-driven capital investment, and an improved factor-mix to achieve greater technical efficiency, private sector companies can, arguably, pursue cost-minimisation strategies beyond the scope of their public sector counterparts.

Two kinds of private sector organisations are likely to be interested in competing in the defence supply contractorisation process with the objective of attaining a quasi-monopolistic supplier role for specific services following the competition phase. First, some of those companies currently supplying defence ministries with defence equipment and other services may have both the managerial expertise and capacity to be able to switch their business activities away from traditional areas and into those currently being sought from the market. Research in the UK in the early 1990's confirmed that the major defence contractors and many of their first tier suppliers were indeed seeking precisely these kinds of new business opportunities in order to address the threat confronting them as military expenditure declines. In general, the emerging strategy from companies seeking to gain military contracts seems to be one of long-range market positioning, while also targeting realistic short-term opportunities. Both elements of the emerging strategy, particularly for the largest defence contractors, are appropriate in switching the business focus from military production to the provision of military support services, while helping to meet the immediate diversification requirements of defence supply companies in the evolving post-Cold War commercial environment.

Secondly, private sector organisations that currently operate only in non-defence markets may be attracted into the defence contractorisation process if they perceive potential cost advantages as well as clear opportunities for the extension or transfer of existing managerial functions and capacity into new business activities. While a large private organisation may have a business focus in pharmaceuticals, engine manufacture, power generation, food retailing or a range of such activities, it may be that their true business strength lies in the 'managerial' skills and capacity that they can bring to bear upon an organisational problem. For such companies, this is likely to be their most marketable asset in gaining access to the emerging military business opportunities.

For both types of private sector organisation, however, considerable barriers to entry exist which may deter or delay entry into the market for defence support services. For the military-serving company which, traditionally, has tended to operate in a monopsonistic market producing sophisticated technical goods for the military, the principal barrier to market entry in a competitive contracting-out process could be cultural in nature. Although the reforms of the last decade have undoubtedly eliminated much of the historic tendency towards cost-overrun, excessive profit-making, waste, inefficiency, and in some well-documented cases, fraud and corruption in many military-serving companies, limited experience of genuine open tendering in a new market with many active competitors may prove a significant barrier.

Companies which are primarily non-military in their business focus may be better positioned to take immediate advantage of new market opportunities in the defence sector. Managerial expertise is dedicated to ensuring a competitive edge in their principal markets on price, expected profit margins, quality, delivery time, after-sales service and other key respects and it may be possible to transfer these managerial capabilities into these new market opportunities. Costs are continually scrutinised to ensure that the competitive edge is maintained. Furthermore, the attainment of economies of scale and scope will be a principal objective in such organisations. The competitive environment is their natural home and entry into the new areas of the defence sector being contracted-out would seem an appropriate strategy to employ. For such companies, the new market opportunities appearing in the defence sector are certainly contestable.

Nevertheless, several significant barriers to entry also exist to confront these companies. First, the transactions costs associated with gaining access through competition to a market where conditions are set and monitored by a public sector monopsonist could be considerable and may not be recouped, should the competitive bid fail. Secondly, having gained access to the new market, such firms may have to confront (perhaps for the first time) the critical requirements of the 'public interest'. This may include the need to operate within the constraints set by government-established regulatory bodies limiting price and/or profit levels or, particularly in the defence sector, the need to meet stringent security requirements or life-critical quality and safety standards, both of which have significant cost implications. For example, in pursuing the contractor operation of the Atomic Weapons Establishment during the 1990's, the most stringent safety and security monitoring system was imposed on the successful contractor. A new Ministry of Defence Compliance Office was established to ensure contractor compliance with safety requirements with the authority to terminate immediately any activity deemed unsafe. At the same time, the MoD retained the power to set and monitor security standards to be maintained by private contractors.

While the emerging markets in defence sector support services are clearly open to access by new entrants, the initial entry costs may be prohibitive to private sector organisations when set against the longer-term potential for profits. While such new markets may be opened up to competition, there is little chance that, in practice, the operation of these markets will remain genuinely open. In exchange for a quasi-monopoly position in the new defence market after the tendering process has ended and the winning contractor has been selected, the government is certain to set tight safety, security and public interest constraints on the company's activities which, inevitably, will limit its decision-making freedom in this most sensitive of operational areas.

In the UK, the drive towards more market-driven defence procurement has been intensified recently with the SMART procurement initiative and the developments associated with the UK Strategic Defence Review (SDR). Viewed as yet another attempt to reduce costs and enhance efficiency in the procurement and defence production process, SMART procurement will attempt to eliminate some of the more glaring deficiencies in the previous approach. A National Audit Office report on major defence projects in 1998 noted that 25 major defence projects experienced cost over-runs of the order of £3 billion in addition to delays of more than 3 years with, to say the least, uncertain equipment performance at the end. Considerable cost savings are anticipated from the SMART procurement initiative, perhaps of the order of 30% (Hartley, 1998), with government estimates amounting to savings of £2 billion over 10 years (SDR, 1998).

MARKET EXIT

Among the range of options open to prime defence contractors, leaving the industry altogether is a significant step, particularly where the defence sector has been the main focus of their corporate activities. A great deal of investment will have been tied up in plant and equipment, little of which is likely to be transferable to civil production. The costs of exit will be significant unless a successful diversification strategy has been in place for some time.

Among US companies choosing to leave the defence business in the 1990's were Westinghouse, a major defence supplier for over a quarter of a century which sold its defence business to Northrup Grumman; Tenneco, which divested itself of Newport News, the largest naval shipbuilder in the US; Loral, which sold its defence division to Lockheed Martin, in order to focus on the civil space market; and the Hughes Corporation, part of General Motors, which pursued a highly successful diversification strategy into telecommunications, satellites and automotive products, allowing it to move rapidly out of the defence market yet maintain its earnings potential, while shedding over 14,000 jobs in the process.

DEFENCE INDUSTRY RESTRUCTURING

For many decades, particularly in countries such as the US, the UK and France, the business of defence procurement and supply was conducted through a process of interaction between national defence procurement agencies and their nationally-based prime defence contractors with very occasional forays into the external market. Unlike almost any other major industry, defence production remained remote from the global market (except in the marketing of that production as exports) and consequently, until recently, was spared the structural and behavioural changes necessary to survive and prosper in that dynamic global marketplace. A somewhat cosy relationship between government and these large corporations inevitably developed which eroded further competition in the market and was criticised for encouraging inefficiency, cost over-run and occasional corruption.

With the advent of procurement reforms, fixed price contracting and a more competitive market for defence goods, the seeds of a major restructuring of the defence supply industry were sown. The deep and prolonged defence budget cuts in the 1990's made such restructuring both more urgent and more dramatic in scale. The exogenous shock

which the defence cuts represented at the time was of such consequence that the scope for marginal adjustment in the market to restore
some kind of acceptable equilibrium simply was not possible.
Fundamental and far-reaching change was required that could only be
achieved through a series of economic seismic shocks during which
giant corporations shed a great deal of labour, downsized and rationalised their organisations and operations, returned to core business
and shed peripheral activities and, ultimately, joined forces to form
powerful and potentially more resilient defence companies. The pace-
setter in this revolution in defence supply was the United States.

By any measure, corporate response in the US defence industry to
the evolving post-Cold War business environment has been remarkable. Prior to 1993, significant transformation of US defence companies was already under way (Mandel, 1994, pp. 175–197). During the
period from 1993 to 1998, however, the structure, capabilities and
market power of the US defence industrial base has been fundamentally altered. What appears on the surface to be a natural free market
restructuring process, initiated and carried through entirely by the
industry as it adjusts to the changed business environment of the
1990s, in fact can be seen as the result of imperfect market behaviour,
fuelled by speculative action by investment bankers and subsidised
heavily by government.

At the same time, US defence mergers appear to have triggered off a
desire to achieve a similar wave of consolidation in the European
defence industrial base. Furthermore, in the European context, in the
absence of a meaningful and operational joint European defence and
procurement strategy within the Western European Union, large
European defence firms are, like their American counterparts, setting
the pace, significantly ahead of most governments. As a result, mergers
in Europe are also being pursued without the essential preliminary
step of a deep-rooted and far-reaching review by European govern
ments (except in the case of the UK's Strategic Defence Review) of
their precise future defence requirements and, consequently, without a
proper evaluation of the kind of defence industrial base that will be
required to meet these objectives. It is at the European level that such
a review is now urgent.

SETTING THE PACE: RESTRUCTURING AEROSPACE

On both sides of the Atlantic, by far the most significant steps towards
defence industry restructuring have taken place in the aerospace indus-

try. This sector, far in advance of any other part of the defence business, is engaged in a truly remarkable phase of consolidation and rationalisation which will create over the next few years a market for aerospace products which will be dominated by a few giant corporations and strategic partnerships, locked in a head-to-head battle for supremacy in the global marketplace. Indeed, the experience of the 1990's makes it only too clear that, in terms of US and European aerospace market share and competitive advantage, that battle has already been joined.

Given that the aerospace sector has clearly taken the lead in defence industry restructuring during the 1990's, much of the rest of Chapter 3 will focus primarily on this sector to identify and explain the ways in which the market has—or has not—operated effectively in response to the defence spending downturn.

Half a century ago, excluding helicopter and general aviation manufacturers, the UK possessed eighteen aircraft manufacturers, France nine, post-war Germany none and the US eleven. Thirty years ago, the number of aircraft manufacturers in the UK had fallen to two with four in France, three in Germany and seven in the US Currently, the UK and Germany possess one major aircraft manufacturing company each with two in France and three in the US. This extraordinary degree of industrial concentration has been matched by huge growth in the civil and military sides of the business with aerospace turnover in 1996 amounting to some \$53.6 billion in Europe and \$96.4 billion in the US. Table 9 below shows the ten largest aerospace companies in the world in 1998 by sales.

Compared with the largest of the US aerospace giants, the problem confronted by European aerospace companies becomes clear and helps to explain the planned merger between British Aerospace and GEC

TABLE 9: THE WORLD'S LARGEST AEROSPACE COMPANIES BY SALES (\$ BILLION): 1998

1	Boeing/McDonnell Douglas	45.1
2	Lockheed Martin	27.9
3	BAe/Marconi	21.3
4	Raytheon	10.6
5	United Technologies	10.3
6	Aerospatiale	9.6
7	Northrop Grumman	9.2
8	Dasa	8.8
9	General Electric	7.8
10	Allied Signal	6.4
11	Thomson-CSF	6.0

Source: Flight International, various, 1998.

Marconi's defence division, discussed later in this chapter. Furthermore, beyond Europe, a similar picture emerges with several relatively small aerospace companies trying to compete against giant US corporations. This includes companies such as Bombardier of Canada ($3,303m); Mitsubishi Heavy Industries of Japan ($3,166m); Kawasaki Heavy Industries of Japan ($1,732m); Israel Aircraft Industries ($1,691m); Ishikawajima-Harima of Japan ($1,135m) and Embraer of Brazil ($794m).

DEFENCE INDUSTRY RESTRUCTURING IN THE UNITED STATES

Following the end of the Cold War, the initial strategic adjustment of US defence supply companies was quite varied. General Dynamics chose to sell off some of its defence units and reduce the scale of its operations; Lockheed, Northrop, and Martin Marietta decided to commit themselves even more deeply to the defence supply market and, therefore, pursued appropriate mergers within the industry; TRW, Hughes and Rockwell adopted a pro-active stance to achieve internal diversification. Such strategic diversity was only to be expected at a time of such fundamental change in the industry and great uncertainty about the future business environment in the defence sector. However, fairly rapidly this diversity was replaced by a kind of 'conventional wisdom' evolving as a strategy focused upon mergers and divestments creating a small group of immensely powerful defence supply companies. Markusen (1997) makes the point that:

> 'the fashioning of America's new military industrial conglomerates is a joint project of three groups: Wall Street investment bankers, contractor CEOs and CFOs, and running as a poor third partner, the Pentagon. The role of the first, financial partner has been far more important in the phenomenon than is reflected in press accounts. In fact, Wall Street has performed a near miracle, engineering a strategy which has kept military contractors profitable despite post Cold War demobilization.'

Markusen argues that the crucial influence of investment bankers in the defence industrial restructuring process has produced a generation of senior corporate managers who will tend to favour shorter term stock appreciation and dividends over longer term investment. Following a financially successful decade in the 1980's, when the Reagan arms build-up was its height, large US defence manufacturers, endowed with substantial cash reserves and prime property locations, became an attractive prospect for restructuring and rationalisation by investment bankers as the post-Cold War business environment changed.

Some large US defence contractors were resistant to the merger trend, most notably Hughes, TRW and Rockwell. These companies were significantly less defence-dependent than many other larger contractors and were able to reduce their dependency still further (see, for example, Oden et al., 1996). Nevertheless, the relentless pressure for restructuring in the US defence industry ultimately also enveloped Hughes and Rockwell in the merger process.

The clear signal from the US government to US defence companies in 1992 that corporate restructuring through mergers was inevitable, and indeed required, precipitated a wave of industrial consolidation which has effectively reduced the US defence sector to very few key players (Dowdy, 1997, pp. 88–101). To encourage this process, the government provides corporate tax breaks under the Morris Trust tax scheme, through which it is possible for US companies to negotiate and conclude a merger and generate considerable tax savings in the process. It has been estimated that Lockheed Martin, for example, stand to save some $6 billion through 1999 and about $2.6 billions each year thereafter. It can be argued that this kind of merger subsidy effectively constitutes an indirect grant from the US government, enabling the company concerned to divert such funds into alternative areas such as R&D, marketing or cost reduction strategies.

In the US, unlike Europe, the unification of civil and military aerospace interests, under-pinned by extensive and deep-rooted government research and development programmes, has taken place with remarkable speed in the last 5 years. Between 1992 and 1997, 32 defence companies were concentrated into just 9 with the loss of 1 million jobs.

CORPORATE RESTRUCTURING

Lockheed Martin was formed from the merger of Lockheed with Martin Marietta and divisions of Loral, General Electric and General Dynamics. At one level, the merger represented a strategy of vertical integration and, in common with some other recent mergers within the US defence industrial base, brought together defence-electronics business and information systems to target one of the few parts of the *defence* market that is currently expanding. As a result of the merger, Lockheed Martin became one of the biggest defence companies worldwide with global sales of over $14 billion and attracted about 9% of all DoD prime defence contracts in the mid-1990's. The new corporate entity has a leading role in military aircraft, space launch, space systems, military and commercial satellites, electronics, information and systems integration. Although defence remains clearly the core business of the company, Lockheed Martin also operates commercially in markets as diverse as energy and environmental markets, civil aerospace, information technology and related services and electronics. New business opportunities have arisen in air-traffic management control systems, electronic toll systems, industrial and defence waste management, and electronic information transfer systems. Since 1990, corporate rationalisation has reduced employment by over 47,000. (For a fuller discussion of Lockheed Martin's evolving post-Cold War corporate strategy, see Augustine, 1997, pp. 83–94).

The decline in US defence spending in the 1990's and the consequent tightening of the defence supply market drove two vulnerable companies together, Northrop and Grumman. Again, rationalisation of these two businesses cost over 36,000 jobs in the 1990's. The acquisition of Westinghouse's defence electronics business increased their dependence on defence contracts and, as a result, Northrop Grumman has shown less interest in the conversion and diversification routes to corporate survival and expansion.

In the case of Raytheon, the capture of E-Systems and the defence divisions of Hughes and Texas Instruments created the leading player in the US defence electronics industry and the third largest US defence contractor in terms of sales. Over the years, Raytheon had been following a policy of business diversification with acquisition and technology transfer strategies taking it into civil and commercial areas such as air traffic management and communication satellite chips.

In 1996, the announcement of the impending merger of Boeing, an aerospace giant with a strong commercial sector pedigree, and McDonnell Douglas sharply raised the profile of defence activities within the Boeing organisation, and with it the prospect of greatly enhanced opportunities for military/civil synergies and technology transfers. Having already acquired the defence and space business of Rockwell International for $3.2 billion, the merger with McDonnell Douglas should increase defence share to about 40% of Boeing's projected $48 billion revenue for 1997. The merger is an example of horizontal integration within the industry. McDonnell Douglas, for example, manufactured the F 15 and F/A18 fighter aircraft, the C17 transporter, the Apache gunship, and (with British Aerospace), the Harrier jump-jet and Goshawk trainer. Boeing, on the other hand, contributes parts to the advanced F 22 fighter aircraft and, with

Lockheed Martin, won the contract to build the prototype Joint Strike Fighter, the AWACS early-warning aircraft, the Chinook and Comanche helicopters and the Osprey helicopter/aircraft.

The far-reaching restructuring of the US defence/aerospace sector is still not complete. The ill-fated Lockheed Martin-Northrop Grumman merger was perhaps 'a merger too far' but further potential consolidation between key players in the US aerospace and defence industry should not be ruled out nor, indeed, future corporate liaison between US giant corporations in the industry and some of their European counterparts.

PURPOSE OF THE MERGERS

The economic analysis of mergers suggests that they may take one of three forms; horizontal integration, under which competitors in the market would pool their resources and facilities, which is usually undertaken to eliminate excess capacity in the industry; vertical integration, under which a company acquires its suppliers or customers and which is usually undertaken to reduce a company's external transactions costs or protect supply or market access in competitive oligopolistic situations; or, thirdly, market extension mergers, enhancing and expanding a company's product range, generating the potential for beneficial economies of scope.

In the 1990s, while some of the larger defence industry mergers appear to offer the potential for horizontal integration, analysts argue that defence companies in the US have pursued mergers designed to extend their market. Oden (1997) shows that, in the US, the aim (and certainly the effect) of defence industry mergers in the 1990's has been to expand the range of defence equipment and services that a company can offer to the Pentagon. In doing so, the merged organisation can effectively trade-off gains and losses of different weapon programmes and help to protect itself against adverse procurement decisions.

As a result, we observe an interesting situation in the US at the moment. The interplay of oligopolistic market behaviour and reactive government intervention has generated an apparently sub-optimal outcome (see Kovacic and Smallwood, 1994). Significant amounts of public money have been deployed to encourage mergers in the defence industry in order to secure cost savings from rationalisation; yet it is now clear that such rationalisation has not, as yet, taken place. The broad range of weapons systems remains relatively untouched, giving the veneer of competition in the marketplace, and enabling the

Pentagon to claim that the (apparently) 'competitive' outcome is sufficient to justify merger reimbursement expenditure. Sapolsky and Gholz (1997) suggest that the absence of production line and plant closures in the US during a period of procurement cuts of around 70% since 1986, together with a remarkable phase of corporate restructuring, is evidence that the US defence industry mergers are not designed primarily to reduce production capacity. Indeed, a large number of defence supply companies are currently operating at far below capacity and large numbers of defence industry workers have been made redundant.

Markusen (1997) supports this view, although she does identify some exceptions, noting that:

> 'Hughes' purchase of General Dynamics missile division did result in the consolidation of the two lines in a single locale. But in weapons system after weapons system, duplicative shipyards, aircraft plants and other production facilities are kept going in a variant of the famous Kurth (1992) "follow-on" imperative. Indeed, the case of General Dynamics' Seawolf submarine demonstrates that having a single producer of a particular weapons system is no assurance that it will be easy to eliminate capacity which is no longer needed.'

There is also little evidence of vertical integration in the defence industry explaining much of the merger phenomenon. Vertical integration would draw together prime defence companies and their supply/sub-contract requirements within a single corporate structure. Evidence suggests that subcontracting and outsourcing have both increased with many smaller companies in the defence industry supply chain benefiting from higher levels of merged firms outsourcing (Oden, Markusen et al. 1996). Earlier we noted that the Lockheed Martin merger could be seen as an example of vertical integration in the industry. However, at another level, Markusen (1997) cites Lockheed Martin as a good example of a large company leading this out-sourcing phenomenon where she states that the company is:

> 'on record as boasting of its new vision of itself as a virtual corporation; maintaining a shell of management, design and systems integration capabilities while buying components and expertise when needed over the bumpy defense procurement cycle'.

As the next chapter will illustrate, however, other forms of vertical integration in the defence supply industry are rapidly taking shape with potentially profound business implications. Prime defence contractors are restructuring their supply chains and, in some cases, attempting to establish very strong business links with high quality key suppliers on a partnership basis. These issues will be discussed in detail in the next chapter.

THE ROLE OF THE PENTAGON

Under the first Clinton administration, the then Secretary of State for Defence, Les Aspin. initiated a major review of precisely what the US defence industrial base should comprise. This review was swiftly abandoned in order to free up private sector initiatives to reconstruct the defence industrial base. The export of some high technology weapon systems was permitted by the Pentagon as a means of protecting the business prospects of US defence manufacturers during the period of severe defence cuts in the domestic economy. More importantly, under Secretary of State for Defence, William Perry, a scheme was agreed to reimburse companies for the cost associated with the merger process. As a result of the implementation of this scheme, large US defence contractors remained generally profitable during the defence cuts of the 1990's, an unprecedented development given the damaging profit consequences for contractors of earlier defence expenditure contractions such as those after World War I and II. Korea and Vietnam.

While the rapid and massive restructuring of the US defence industrial base can be seen as partly market-driven, it is clear that government (in the form of the Pentagon) have also played a significant part. The role of government in this process has been to provide the financial stimulus to encourage and facilitate the merger and acquisition process. While having little influence on the practical outcome of the consolidation process, the US government still intervened, after a great deal of lobbying, to provide the crucial financial compensation magnet that attracted key industrial players to pursue expensive mergers. The justification given for the deployment of public funds to support the merger process was that such mergers would, in return, generate substantial future savings. This merger subsidy amounts to billions of dollars with, for example, Lockheed/Martin applying for over $1 billion in merger cost reimbursement (Korb, 1996) and indeed, has helped to preserve the profitability of US defence companies as Pentagon procurement cuts bit deep into their traditional markets.

Markusen (1997) notes that reimbursement is possible for the following range of costs:

> 'court costs for opposing worker severance suits or for attempting to lower local property tax assessments, costs involved in destroying productive capacity that might otherwise have been sold to competitors, and costs incurred in moving people and equipment to lower cost and union-free regions, any of which would spark social protest if widely understood. Socially benign purposes, such as severance pay and worker adjustment assistance (but not conversion or civilian job creation) can also be covered.'

The critical role of reimbursement in the context of US defence industry mergers is highlighted by the sheer scale of payments: over $1 billion was claimed from the government by Lockheed Martin over the four year merger process to date and a similar amount is expected to be claimed by Boeing as its new relationship with McDonnell-Douglas develops over time. Also, in the absence of reimbursement payments, some analysts believe that the merger process might not have taken place at all.

Markusen (1997) makes the important point that merger cost reimbursements:

> 'act as powerful incentives favouring the creation of 'pure play' defence conglomerates and have distorted contractor strategy-making. They have rewarded contractors for divorcing military from civilian operations and staking their fortunes on building market share in a stagnant if not shrinking domestic and world market rather than pursuing defence conversion and diversification strategies'.

The argument used to support merger cost reimbursement is that the Pentagon would enjoy future savings in the form of lower prices of weapons from the scale and scope economies acquired in the process of defence industry consolidation. Where a company, following a merger, finds it necessary to close a plant and make employees redundant, it can request that the costs associated with these actions can be added to existing cost-plus contracts, thereby ensuring that companies make a profit on these consolidation activities as well as on their more normal operations.

While potential cost savings may attract merger reimbursement support, the fact that such potential is rarely ever realised seems to be ignored. Studies of early subsidised mergers revealed that only 15% to 25% of the anticipated cost savings have actually been achieved (GAO, 1995).

ECONOMIC AND POLITICAL CONCERNS

The consolidation process in US industry has undoubtedly created enhanced market power for the key industrial players in their dealings with the Pentagon. Not only is efficient pricing under threat from the emergence of this relatively non-competitive market but, particularly in the case of a high technology industry such as defence production, market failure is exacerbated by information asymmetry problems. In such a market situation, consumers are at a continual disadvantage as only the supplier really possesses full knowledge about product cost and performance, even after detailed product review by the defence ministry procurement team. In such circumstances, real costs will always be difficult to gauge and where, despite the introduction of cost-focused 'value for money' initiatives, quasi-cost-plus pricing still exists in practice, industrial restructuring leading to greater consolidation in an industry will allow private contractors to acquire a greater proportion of consumer surplus by restricting output and driving up prices.

In May, 1997, Paul Kaminski, the Director of Acquisitions for the Department of Defense, suggested that a mechanism was now required to identify possible imminent defence industry mergers which might adversely affect Pentagon procurement. Some analysts, most notably Ann Markusen, have suggested that the Kaminski 'early warning system' has arrived too late to prevent disadvantageous aspects of market power arising from the consolidation process. As Markusen (1997) puts it:

> 'The move comes more than three years too late, after the mammoth mergers imploding huge companies like McDonnell Douglas, Lockheed, Martin Marietta, Boeing, Hughes, Loral, Northrop, Grumman, Rockwell, Raytheon and scores of smaller firms into a few gargantuan defense-dedicated contractors'.

Markusen also makes the interesting point that, outside America, the US defence industry consolidation through mergers is attributed to a Pentagon—led initiative to secure massive economies of scale—and perhaps scope—in defence production and further strengthen pereived US dominance in the global arms market. As a result, she argues that such mergers have intensified pressures for consolidation among European defence contractors and could ultimately serve to undermine the prospects for transatlantic cooperation. Since most European consolidation has so far taken the form of mergers and rationalisation within individual countries, Markusen believes that US defence industry mergers have increased the likelihood of the emergence of an essentially 'national champion' European outcome rather than the evolution of one or more genuine pan-European partnerships.

Fundamentally challenging this external view of US defence industry mergers, Markusen contends that the Pentagon has not designed and implemented a pro-active industrial base policy and, furthermore, implies that it lacks even the data and analysis on which to construct such a strategy. This is not an example of government-led industrial restructuring but derives its momentum and rationale from the interaction of two sets of markets, the defence supply market and the financial market. Markusen (1997) alleges that, in practice, the Pentagon has simply

> 'acquiesced in a strategy initiated by Wall Street investment bankers and a select group of corporate CEOs. Although the mergers have been rationalized as cost-saving moves, driven by budgetary imperatives, they have been chiefly motivated by expectations of short term financial gain and long term enhanced market power and political clout'.

Politically, too, it can be argued that the merger process gives the defence prime contractors enhanced geographic reach and, as a result, is likely to increase their capacity to lobby effectively for a greater commitment of public funds to support the defence industry, especially support for the promotion of existing weapons system production. For example, Markusen points out that, in 1996, powerful lobbying in Congress added $11 billion to the Clinton defence budget, mainly for additional orders of existing weapons and for larger R&D contracts for ballistic missile defence.

While the US government appears to be genuinely committed to the attempt to encourage corporate strategies of dual use, conversion and weapon system cooperation, in practice its other strategies of allowing high technology military export and subsidising mergers have given large defence supply companies confusing signals

In the defence industry supply chain, the picture is somewhat different. Markusen (1997) notes that there are many examples of successful diversification that have taken place among the ranks of small and medium-sized defence companies in the US. She argues that this success is due to a combination of factors including the expansion of large firm outsourcing, cash reserves and local economic development and conversion assistance, often federally funded, which have all enabled smaller firms switch key technology and skilled personnel into new civilian product lines. In terms of the transmission mechanism by which military-to-civil resource switching can be achieved, successfully generating a peace dividend, it appears to be this sector which offers the greatest potential. However, as Chapter 4 will indicate, it is also the sector most at risk from the unprecedented changes currently sweeping through the industry.

The principal rationale proposed to explain the merger movement among large US defence companies in the 1990's is that the process has been a necessary market-led response to enable industry to adjust, smoothly, rapidly and efficiently, to defence procurement budget reductions amounting, in some cases, to some 70% in real terms, with the implication that plant and production line closures would result from the consolidation process. The evidence suggests that, in reality, the remarkable transformation of US defence industry in the 1990s has come about through a mixture of pragmatic corporate and reactive governmental strategies from which the corporate sector in particular has extracted benefit; the investment bankers in terms of stockholder returns and the merged defence supply companies in terms of enhanced market power, nationally and globally.

DEFENCE INDUSTRY RESTRUCTURING IN EUROPE

The problem for Europe in terms of its competitiveness in the global defence market is stark indeed and reflects a similar position in many other more commercial markets. Put simply, there are too many manufacturers of almost all products in Europe and rapid consolidation and rationalisation appear to offer the only real solution.

For example, in the US, there are 3 manufacturers of missiles compared with 10 in Europe; 2 manufacturers of military aircraft in the US compared with 6 in Europe; 5 major defence electronics companies in the US compared with 8 in Europe; 2 manufacturers of tanks in the US compared with 10 in Europe; and 4 major shipyards in the US compared with 14 in Europe. Making things more difficult for European players is the additional fact that the US defence budget (at around $270 billion annually) is more than twice that of Europe (around $120 billion annually). In the defence business generally, then, intense competition from the much more highly concentrated US industry requires rapid and wide-ranging European restructuring in order to be able to offer effective market response.

With the end of the Cold War, most West European defence budgets began to decline sharply in real terms, falling by one-third on average across Europe in the period 1987–1997. Within this, while Italy and the UK reduced their procurement budgets by about the European average, in Germany the procurement budget was more than halved in the decade. In France, the procurement budget continued to increase until 1990 and has since fallen by over one quarter. Interestingly, the defence industry employment consequences of such budget cuts have varied widely across Europe, raising important questions about the freedom and efficacy of market forces to respond to such a recessionary shock. In France and Italy, while military output reductions have been very significant, the implications for employment loss have been much less serious. By comparison, in the UK the reduction in defence industry employment greatly exceeded the cut in military output.

While, as we have seen above, the pace of change in the US defence industrial base has been remarkable during the 1990's, the response across Europe has been both limited and much delayed. Indeed, Steinberg (1992) considered that the opportunities for trans-European consolidation were always somewhat limited. Nevertheless, changing market conditions in the defence industry m the early 1990's made some real response inevitable (Walker and Willett, 1993, pp. 141–160). At the same time, however, political considerations at the national level, encompassing the need to protect the perceived economic interests of individual countries within Europe and their industries; the differing views of European governments about the need for defence industries to be privately owned; and the complex and time-consuming discussions on the restructuring of European security and defence procurement architecture, have all served to delay rapid adjustment within Europe to the requirements of the post-Cold War age. In essence, defence production within Europe was seen as one of the few areas of business where national interest, especially measured in terms of guaranteed security, was at risk.

Nevertheless, the dynamic adjustment process observed in the US in recent years has, however, had a catalytic effect upon the restructuring debate within Europe and, consequently, in the late 1990's, attention is focused currently on the potential reshaping of European defence contractors as they attempt to respond to the emergence through mergers and acquisitions of powerful US competitors.

In a limited way, however, European defence industry restructuring is nothing new (Brown, Brown and Campbell, 1990), although previous examples mainly took the form of joint ventures and strategic alliances. Early examples include the formation of Sepecat by the UK and France to build Jaguar; the formation of Panavia and Turbo-Union by West Germany, the UK and Italy to build Tornado; and France and West Germany joining forces to build Alphajet. With growing aerospace and defence capabilities in Europe, demand grew in the late 1960's for European co-production of US systems. Direct US sales to Europe of key defence systems began to be replaced with co-production deals for the F104 Starfighter, the Hawk and eventually, to the so-called 'deal of the century', co-production of the F-16 in the 1970's.

Through the establishment of bilateral Memoranda of Understanding between Western European governments and the US DoD to pursue reciprocal defence procurement and remove trade barriers and 'buy national' laws, technology transfer became possible instead of simple work-sharing arrangements. By the mid-1980's, European defence producers had effectively regained the required level of maturity to be able to offer advanced technologies and highly sophisticated defence systems to the global market in direct competition with the US.

In the late 1980's, well before the end of the Cold War and despite the Reagan-Thatcher arms build-up and associated high defence budgets, the environment of military business was already beginning to change fundamentally. It was becoming increasingly obvious that there was an urgent need to seek enhanced integration of military and civil technologies and, possibly, of defence industry suppliers in order to compete effectively in the global market. Elsewhere in industry, such changes were commonplace as the potential impact of the Single European Act was already serving to sharpen competitive conditions.

At the European level, a number of mergers and joint ventures in defence research, design and production have been established on a national and, occasionally, on a cross-border basis (see, for example, Gummett, 1996). Examples include GEC's acquisition of VSEL in the UK and Finmeccanica's link-up with Agusta and Alenia in Italy at the national level, and trans-nationally, the formation of joint venture companies such as Eurocopter (from the merging of the helicopter business of Aerospatiale and Deutsche, more recently Daimler, Aerospace) and joint venture programmes, such as Eurofighter; the purchase of Plessey by Siemens of Germany and the UK's GEC.; and the merging of the space business of GEC Marconi and Matra. The Airbus partnership, a highly successful trans-European joint venture (soon to restructure into a single corporate entity) was, until recently, focused primarily on the civil aerospace sector. The company has now established the Airbus Military Company to consolidate and expand its defence market interests and seek dual-use and other technological synergies and scale and scope economies in design, development and production for both the civil and military markets.

Joint ventures have not been exclusively European, of course, and there are many instances of European/American collaboration. One current example is the Boeing team for the Joint Strike Fighter aircraft which includes British companies such as Rolls-Royce, GEC-Marconi, Flight Refuelling and Messier-Dowty as well as Fokker and Phillips from the Netherlands (Sears, 1998).

In general, however, while trans-national European defence industry ventures and programmes have been successful (Hartley and Martin, 1993), they have suffered from inefficiencies and inflexibility due to the constraints imposed on them at times by conflicts of interest at both the national political and individual corporate level. Consequently, the difficulty in securing the real cost savings, enhanced efficiency and asset-sharing synergies that would be likely to flow from the establishment of a genuinely 'European ' defence industrial base has continued to weaken the European response to the emergence of the US giants in the industry.

By the late 1990's, as a result of these and other defence/aerospace mergers and acquisitions, the West European defence industry now consists of a few large companies displaying a kind of 'national champion' dimension, operating at varying stages of consolidation, surrounded by a number of inter-connected networks of large first-tier suppliers and subcontractors.

In the UK, for example, in the aerospace sector, design, development and production at the platform level is mainly focused upon British Aerospace; that for the naval sector is centred principally upon GEC; and the land sector remains more fragmented. In Germany, the aerospace and space sectors are dominated by a vertically integrated national champion, Daimler-Benz, (now Daimler Chrysler Aerospace) with naval and land sectors more fragmented. The situation differs markedly in France where most of the defence industry, until recently, remained in public ownership with several companies operating in the three principal defence sectors, although the gradual move towards privatisation of the French defence industry will undoubtedly create a strong drive towards consolidation in the future.

The limited restructuring of Europe's defence industrial base over the last few years has created a kind of alliance structure (see Dussauge and Garrette, 1993) in which companies appear to work in partnership where such a strategy suits individual corporate interests and where doing so serves to protect and maintain an acceptable power balance within a strongly oligopolistic market. (For a fuller discussion of these issues, see Anthony, 1995; Hartley, 1996; Skons, 1997). This tendency has predicated against the formation of large, stable corporate entities to date and has tended to favour project-based collaboration, reflecting both the diversity of goods produced in the defence market (and, consequently, the fragmentation of that market) and the varying technological attributes of industry players within Europe.

RESTRUCTURING THE EUROPEAN AEROSPACE/DEFENCE NEXUS: THE CASE OF A400M—THE FUTURE LARGE AIRCRAFT

To replace its existing and ageing tactical military transport aircraft, Europe needs a new aircraft which can carry a large payload in a flexible manner rapidly over long distances. To deliver the required degree of cost-effectiveness in the new 'value-for-money' environment of modem military procurement, such an aircraft must have a multi-role operational capability and be considerably more economical under operational conditions than existing military transport aircraft. In addition it must utilise the best elements of modem aerospace technology; those proven in existing civil and military programmes and those being developed for future generations of aircraft.

The Future Large Aircraft (FLA), recently re-named the A400M, has been designed to meet the agreed airlift requirements of eight European nations: Belgium, France, Germany, Italy, Portugal, Spain, Turkey and the United Kingdom, as formally specified in the European Staff Requirement (see Lawrence and Braddon 1998 for a fuller discussion of the issues raised in the following section). To meet this requirement, a military transport aircraft would have to possess several key characteristics in order to be able to carry out effectively its future role in military missions, such as rapid reaction force deployment and humanitarian operations, where intervention is needed to deal with natural disasters or regional conflicts. Such essential characteristics include:

- long range capability to allow flexible deployment;
- the ability to land on short, soft runways so that cargo can be supplied direct to deployed forces in theatre;

- a cargo hold capacity that can enable large payloads to be carried containing the whole spectrum of modem military vehicles and helicopters engineering and relief equipment;
- a high cruising speed to facilitate rapid deployment of troops and equipment;
- the capacity to operate effectively at low speed so that airdrops can be carried out direct to target zones;
- the ability to operate autonomously on the ground in order to enter and leave target areas as rapidly as possible under difficult operational conditions.

In line with this European Staff Requirement remit, A400M has been designed to carry out both logistic as well as tactical missions and can operate effectively on both hard and soft airfields. It can carry military forces, vehicles, helicopters and equipment of most kinds and, since it can be refuelled in flight, has an extensive radius of action. The aircraft will be built to high civil design standards, incorporating the advanced technology which has become the Airbus hallmark. The aircraft's capabilities include: a cruise speed of M 0.68 at altitudes up to 37,000 feet; a top horizontal speed of M 0.72; performance of low level tactical missions at 300 KCAS fully loaded; the capacity to reverse and turn in confined spaces; soft field landing ability and an autonomous loading/unloading cargo system, freeing it from the constraints of dependence upon ground facilities at large, vulnerable airfields.

Two other military transport aircraft pose a serious challenge to A400M in the market, the Lockheed C130J and the Boeing C17. The C130J is essentially a remodelling of an extremely old design and in speed, range and payload is considered by many analysts to not even approximate the performance of A400M. US military transport aircraft undoubtedly have a deserved solid reputation based upon their deployment with European air forces over many years. However, recent widely reported difficulties at Lockheed with the C130J, regarding unanticipated stall characteristics associated with the airflow from the blades of the new engine, have clearly shown that US manufacturers are not infallible. Indeed, what analysts find remarkable is that this problem was not detected through routine flight testing designed to evaluate the effective integration of airframe and power units.

Significantly, whereas A400M is expected to meet all of the European Staff Requirements, the Cl3OJ meets less than half. A400M also has a much larger cross section size than the Cl30J, designed to accommodate all the various kinds of loads required for conflict intervention or humanitarian operations that might be required by a European rapid reaction force. The aircraft cargo compartment has been specifically structured so as to ensure the best balance between space availability and payload. Furthermore, A400M can carry twice the payload significantly further than the C130J for a projected initial price which is only roughly 50% greater, but, taking cost of ownership into account, for a price which, over the lifetime of the aircraft, is likely to be approximately the same as the C130J.

Another competitor, the C17, does meet all of the specifications set out in the European Staff Requirement, but apparently not on all missions. A400M and the C17 can both carry over 95% of British Army vehicles and, although A400M cannot carry the main battle tank, there is no need for it to do so under Joint Rapid Reaction Force requirements. The Cl7 does have a significant advantage in terms of payload, being able to carry about twice the capacity of the A400M over roughly the same distance. However, analysts have observed some operational limitations imposed on the C17, caused by its volume, weight and the wake vortex, where turbulence from the aircraft imposes a high value for horizontal separation.. This problem necessitates a significant separation distance between C17s on operations involving the deployment of airborne forces with consequent logistical problems. The operational case for A400M is further strengthened by the fact that, powered by four turboprop engines, the aircraft has a strategically valuable rapid descent capability which cannot be matched by either C17 or C-130J. A final point of relevance here is the A400M's soft field capability. Quite simply A400M can operate in environments denied to C17 and offers far superior tactical flexibility.

The proposed A400M is also attractive regarding value for money. Compared with a potential price for A400M of $75m, the C 17 (including power units) costs approximately $200m. In simplistic terms, then, it would be possible to purchase 2–3 A400Ms for every single C 17. The A400M is therefore a cost-effective aircraft which both meets fully the requirements of the European air forces and provides enhanced fleet flexibility, permitting a fleet 2–3 times larger for the same expenditure as the C 17. Furthermore, the C 17 is such an expensive aircraft that fleet size would be very small, implying a huge loss of capacity each time one aircraft was damaged on mission or undergoing major maintenance.

A400M also offers the strong possibility of significant supply chain benefits for European industry with BMW/Rolls-Royce and/or Snecma/MTU providing the engines and Messier-Dowty and/or Ratier involved in the propeller manufacture. The advanced composites industry will also benefit from A400M purchase through the carbon fibre structure which utilises new technology and will enable Europe to retain leading edge technology in wing design and production.

Of critical importance, however, is the fact that A400M will be manufactured by the Airbus Industrie partnership, emanating from a new military division of the emerging Airbus single corporate entity. The economic and technical arguments for A400M are underlined by the clear commercial and technical success of Airbus Industrie. In 1997 Airbus delivered over 200 large commercial aircraft to customers and secured an order backlog of 450 aircraft. These sales to a customer base of more than 130 airlines have resulted from a solid commitment to technical innovation and lower operating costs. Airbus's success has clearly impressed the US. In 1993 Presidential economic adviser Laura d'Andrea Tyson remarked that "Airbus had achieved technical parity with Boeing", (Tyson, 1993, p. 155).

The success of Airbus civil aerospace market penetration has been vital to European exports and the health of the whole European aerospace industry and wider economy. In 1996, the pick-up in the European aerospace industry's turnover of 12% was almost entirely due to civil sales. This excellent performance in commercial aerospace is reflected in the declining dependence of the European industry on government contracts. In the EU government purchases now comprise only 25% of turnover, while in the US the figure is closer to 50%. But this gives the US market greater stability and offers companies such as Boeing the benefit of potentially contrasting and compensating business cycles. In addition the recent Pentagon Dual-Use initiative, as well as programmes such as Mantech, provide extensive funding for projects aimed to facilitate defence/civil synergies (spin-off) as well leveraging commercial technologies for Defence (spin-on). Regarding Dual-Use a key point to grasp is that this does not mean that the commercial business in the US now subsidises defence but rather R&D for commercial technologies now receives more direct support as commercial industry is regarded as the foundation of world class military systems (for further discussion of these important issues, see Lawrence and Dowdall, 1998). The dual-use technology issue will be considered further later in this book.

From Europe's point of view all the recent arguments for rationalisation and greater efficiency support the emergence of Airbus as a military manufacturer. As the EU commission recognises a major advantage for Boeing is the enhanced defence portfolio following the acquisition of McDonnell-Douglas, (European Commission, 1997, p. 5). Synergies and economies of scope across the civil/military divide, noted earlier in this chapter, must be replicated in the EU. In the case of transport aircraft the EU can benefit on the A400M programme by harnessing the latest commercial technology for a defence application. In other words the USA's dual use philosophy can be readily applied for A400M by Europe, with already existing technologies and R&D that has already been paid for.

A400M will make use of existing Airbus expertise and core competencies. On civil programmes technical leadership for Airbus has existed across the whole range of airframe design and systems development. Innovations in wing design, composite materials and avionics systems have created a highly competitive family of aircraft. Arguably the greatest achievement has been in computerised flight management systems and radically new architectures for modular avionics systems. Economies of scope can be attained on A400M by utilising technological advances already achieved by Airbus.

Use of established aerospace technologies, such as the flight management systems which Airbus has developed for the A320, A330 and A340 civil transports gives the A400M an immediate competitive advantage in terms of economies of scope. This advantage is clear in the way that Airbus established a technological lead over Boeing with the introduction of increased automation of flight controls based on the long established expertise of the electronics division at Aerospatiale. This compelled Boeing to respond and develop a radically new avionics suite for the B777, built around the Honeywell AIMS (Aircraft Information Management System). With respect to synergy and dual-use, recent US advances, such as AIMS, show the benefits of joint civil/military development. In the 1980s, US advances in avionics in the following areas were substantially driven by programmes such as Advanced Tactical Aircraft (A12), Advanced Tactical Fighter (F22) and Light Helicopter (RAH-66):

- Glass cockpit
- Two crew cockpits (automation of the flight engineer function)
- Flight management systems

- Digital flight controls and auto-pilot systems
- Area navigation capabilities
- First generation data-link systems
- Warning systems: wind shear, collision avoidance, ground proximity

These military and NASA derived technologies have assisted Boeing in catching up in the field of advanced avionics. But with A400M, Airbus has the opportunity to spin-on its own commercially developed avionics systems into a state-of-the-art military transport. By greater integration of civil and military technologies, elements of the following systems for A400M can migrate from the advanced A340 avionics suite to the military transport application:

- Automatic flight system
- Mission management system
- Electronic instrument and flight warning system
- Navigation system
- Communication system

The significance of the successful migration of these systems from a commercial to military transport cannot be overemphasised.

OFFSET ARRANGEMENTS

However, some analysts would argue that, in areas such as military transport where there are already in existence high quality US-manufactured alternatives, it would be more appropriate from an economic viewpoint to purchase these and, at the same time, negotiate lucrative offset agreements that would inject new employment and income-generating activities into the UK.

However, as an important study of offsets by Martin and Hartley (1995) reveals, such arrangements carry with them a range of potential problems. These include the nature of the offset work provided and the degree to which it represents genuinely new business for recipient companies and countries; the problem of technology transfer on advanced projects and the impact offsets may have, as a result, on the future technological capabilities of a country; the employment dimensions of offset contracts particularly in terms of wage levels and temporary versus permanent employment generated by the work; and the overall impact on a country's defence industrial base of losing specific capabilities to a foreign manufacturer in exchange for offset work which may be (a) less technological in nature, thereby eroding the current and future domestic capability for leading-edge research and development and (b) ultimately susceptible to competition from elsewhere, exposing domestic industry to a possible loss of business in the future which could not then be easily replaced.

THE DUAL-USE STRATEGY

America's growing competitive advantage in aerospace and defence is the result of major industrial rationalisation and to some success with the new dual-use policy and accompanying philosophy. The dual-use strategy has 3 key components:

- Investment in dual use technologies critical to military applications
- Integration of military and commercial production
- Insertion of commercial components into military systems

In a speech in Brussels in November 1997 Paul Kaminski, CEO of Technovation Inc, explained to a European audience the rationale for the new approach:

> 'The bottom line is that we have no choice but to move from separate industrial sectors for defence and commercial markets to an integrated industrial base. Leveraging commercial technological advances to create military advantage is critical to ensuring that our equipment remains the most advanced in the world. The objective is to marry the momentum of a vigorous, productive, and competitive commercial industrial infrastructure with the unique technologies and systems integration capabilities provided by our defence specialists.'

From the point of view of European defence procurement no clearer signal could be given from the world market leaders of how to proceed. Europe can capitalise on the technological and commercial success of Airbus by supporting the creation of the Airbus Military Company and formally launching the A400M programme All the evidence suggests that, in the future, to achieve global market success in key industrial sectors such as aerospace, successful business organisations will require an economic system which contains relatively few sectors which are defence-specific but which operate alongside a wide range of business sectors which contain fully integrated civilian and military production activities.

Within Europe, aerospace is one such sector where the full integration of military and civil technology and production is essential for sustained global success. Gansler (1998) notes that, in the US, the revision of defence procurement to encourage civil-military integration increased the access of the civil sector, under the guise of dual-use developments, to a large share of the approximately $35 billion DoD R&D investments. As a result, US domestic industry is likely to become far more competitive with, ultimately, a reversal of the secular decline in its international technological competitiveness. There are clear lessons for Europe in this US experiment.

In the US, this unification of civil and military aerospace interests, under-pinned by extensive and deep-rooted government research and development programmes, is taking place with remarkable speed. Furthermore, the high profile conversion strategy launched by the Clinton administration in 1993 under the Technology Reinvestment Programme now appears to be operating primarily in the interests of the military sector. The demise of this programme in 1996 and its replacement by the Dual Use Applications Programme appears to have strengthened further the leaching of civil technology developments for military use, rather than the reverse.

Sharper market focus and enhanced production flexibility have enabled the large prime contractors in the US defence/aerospace sector, to implement wide-ranging and accelerating corporate rationalisation. With relatively little real progress in European defence/aerospace industry restructuring, the US appears to have established a clear lead in this corporate and technological transformation.

That is not to say that Europe has neglected the need for industrial restructuring and international collaboration in these critical industries. As noted earlier, since the 1960's, Europe has had experience of a number of trans-national collaborative ventures in the defence/aerospace sector, including 22 in aircraft production, seven in aero-engines and twelve in missiles. However, only 15% of procurement expenditure in France and the UK has been deployed on collaborative ventures and 25% in Germany. The experience of collaborative projects in the defence/aerospace sector across Europe suggests that, for a important reasons, significant excess costs have to be borne by the partners. these include higher administration and organisation costs; costs associated with the allocation of high-technology development work between part-ners sometimes at a suboptimal level; the tendency to duplicate research and development and, in some cases, production work; costs associated with national modifications to a trans-national product; consultation and partner agreement delays; and collaborative project management costs.

Nevertheless, over the last few years, Europe has begun to recognise the need for countervailing power in the defence/aerospace market to counter that of the giant American corporations and the 'new mercantilist' strategy of the US government. Most notably, in 1988, the IEPG instituted an action plan to create a more unified European arms market based on competition, joint ventures and multinational consortia across the European nations. The urgent need for greater integration of European civil and military technologies was emphasised by French Prime Minister, Lionel Jospin, at the Paris Air Show in 1997 : "I consider essential rapprochement between civil and military technology in the aeronautic sector."

The problem for Europe relates to the apparent desire in some countries to retain a 'national champion' approach to the defence/aerospace sector for reasons related to issues of security and national prestige. Only tentative steps towards a genuine merging of resources in these critical sectors across Europe has thus far been considered.

Since it is clearly the case that the unmatched military power of the US also allows it to offer a unique package of security-for-trade deals with overseas customers, the leverage available to the United States through its trade-security linkage puts it at a competitive advantage in this environment. The implications for the European aerospace/defence sector are all too clear. There is a real need for determined and substantial intervention by European governments, both to accelerate the restructuring of these critical sectors and to provide adequate trade support measures to enhance their global competitiveness, in line with US strategic policy.

The consequences and policy implications for the European aerospace/defence sector are transparent. There is a need for a determined and substantial restructuring within the European aerospace sector. However, to be able to offer effective countervailing power to the domination of the US in the global economy, this must be allied with a broader strategy which enables European industry to benefit from the integration of civil and military aerospace. This point will be developed further in Chapter 6.

European companies engaged in the aerospace/defence business must learn the following lesson: in the future, a large quantity of military equipment is going to be sold not just on its technical merits but, increasingly, on the basis of price. In order to thrive in a highly competitive environment, arms manufacturers must focus not only on consolidation but on making significant improvements in operational performance. (Dowdy, 1997, pp. 88–101). The industry is becoming genuinely global over time and if the European aerospace industry is to respond effectively to this emerging trend with its companies competing successfully in a world-wide market, it must be able to maintain design, development and production of a full range of products. If it fails to address this urgent need, European aerospace will become little more than a niche player in an American-dominated global market.

It is only by driving forward the integration of civil and military technologies within European aerospace that such segment champions can be created and the A400M programme allows Europe an excellent opportunity to seize the initiative. The consolidation process within Europe is expected to take the form of trans-national mergers since, as noted, previous instances of European co-operation through joint programmes have tended to generate considerable inefficiencies. The existing European consortia, however, especially the Airbus partnership, represents an appropriate starting point for European aerospace integration. In this context, then, in the broader interests of European industrial restructuring, the addition of a military aerospace dimension to the Airbus portfolio is both an imperative strategically in terms of potential European global power projection and essential in terms of enhancing European commercial competitiveness. The A400M programme offers Europe precisely the kind of project which would enable the European aerospace industry to secure the synergic advantages available to US competitors.

POLITICAL DIMENSIONS

To some extent, the tardiness of a genuine restructuring of Europe's defence industrial base reflects a similar air of caution observed more widely in trans-European debate on a common foreign and/or security policy (despite its exposition as a stated objective of the Maastricht Treaty (Title V, Article J.4) as well as in areas such as defence procurement reform. So far, trans-European government involvement in the restructuring of the defence industrial base has been limited to modest attempts to support collaborative European projects.

Within the Western European Union (WEU), the formation of the Western European Armaments Group (WEAG) represents one such step, relaunched in 1993 as an initiative for a bilateral arrangement between France and Germany (but with increasing interest and involvement by Britain and Italy as the more ambitious elements of its perceived role are scaled down). At the same time, the establishment of the European Defence Industries Group (EDIG) to focus more effectively the joint lobbying on the European Commission (EC) in Brussels by leading defence companies suggests that industry too is keen to pursue a more focused European approach to defence procurement and production. The efficacy of EC response, however, to such developments has been hampered by Article 223 of the Treaty of Rome which exempts the defence industries in Europe from regulations concerning competition and monopoly, which so constrain the behaviour of other industries.

At the heart of the single European arms market debate lies a fundamental question about its precise purpose (for fuller discussion of the issue of evolving European security, see Sperling and Kirchner, 1997). One strongly held view is that Europe needs to radically restructure and rationalise its defence industry within the context of a single European arms market in order to match the market power of giant US competitors. In this context, a single European arms market is viewed as a means of both protecting European defence companies and enabling political attention to be focused upon negotiating reciprocal arrangement for EU-US defence market access. Opponents of this view are concerned about the protectionist nature of this strategy and assert that it is likely to encourage additional protection at the national level, thereby delaying further or perhaps even preventing the necessary degree of trans-European industrial restructuring which the development of a high productivity, lower cost, truly competitive defence industrial base in Europe so urgently requires.

The drive towards defence industry consolidation and rationalisation is now under way across Western Europe (see, for example, AECMA, 1997). Driven by the request from the governments of Britain, France and Germany on 9 December, 1997 to defence industry leaders in Europe to produce a swift tripartite blueprint for European defence industry restructuring, the principal 'national champions' concerned (British Aerospace, Aerospatiale and Daimler-Benz) gave their initial response in late March, 1998. The principles then established were that the ultimate aim would be to create one single company, comprising all core business and owning wholly all of its assets. It would be formed by a series of mergers, rather than joint ventures. It would operate to strictly commercial principles, designed to maximise shareholder value and to open up sources of external finance. It would be managed by a single unified management structure and would have a structure combining a headquarters with business clusters and national divisions. At this stage, it was envisaged by most analysts that what became known as the EADC (European Aerospace and Defence

Company) would be formed around British Aerospace, Dasa, Aerospatiale/Matra, Casa and Saab, once some problematic obstacles had been eliminated.

The initial response included a demand that European governments would seek to resolve some issues regarding the future harmonisation of defence procurement requirements, the provision of long-term stable funding, as well as a range of legal, fiscal and political support matters.

In practice, however, what we are currently observing across Europe is a classic example of strategic gamesmanship being displayed by the key companies involved. As one would expect in a market situation, given the assumptions of rational behaviour and either a profit maximisation or market share maximisation objective at the corproate level, the interests of each individual company will dominate the process of restrucuring rather than the desire of governments within Europe for the rapid emergence of a single powerful European defence entity. A battle for market leadership is therefore being conducted not just between Europe and the US but within Europe itself. (See Gummett (1996) for further discussion of these issues).

RECENT DEVELOPMENTS IN EUROPEAN DEFENCE RESTRUCTURING

Recent developments in the European defence/aerospace industry restructuring saga provide clear evidence of the internal European battle for market dominance that is taking place (for an excellent analysis of European defence industry restructuring, see Guay, 1988). Right up until the end of 1998, the process of European aerospace consolidation appeared relatively straightforward, if somewhat problematic. The key players from the UK and Germany, British Aerospace and Dasa (formed in 1991 from the takeover by Daimler-Benz of Telefunken, Dornier, MBB and MTU and now themselves being transformed into a new company through a £55 billion takeover of the US car manufacturer, Chrysler announced in May, 1998) seeemd to be forging a £14 billion merger which would create Europe's largest aerospace and defence group and the third largest in the world. In fact, plans for such an Anglo-German aerospace alliance date back to the late 1980's but, in the past, had always foundered.

To be truly European, of course, the French aerospace sector would eventually have to be incorporated but negotiations here had been delayed and disrupted by fundamental disagreement at the political level about the necessity to privatise Aerospatiale before a genuine market-based merger could become feasible. At the same time, France was proceding with its own 'national champion' strategy with the planned merger of Aerospatiale and the Matra defence electronics arm of Lagardere. While France was therefore excluded from the initial Anglo-German planned merger, the eventual acceptance of the privatisation requirement by the French suggested that a fusion of the newly merged enterprise with French aerospace interests would follow in due course. The Anglo-German corporate merger would, it was expected, leave British Aerospace shareholders with about 65% of the new company and also give it management control.

By integrating production and marketing of aircraft such as the Eurofighter (Typhoon) and the Airbus civil aircraft range, the merged enterprise expected to make annual cost savings in the range £250m to £300m.. Analysts expected the merged enterprise to then take a major stake in Casa, the Spanish aerospace group which, together with British Aerospace's 35% stake in Saab of Sweden and negotiations for a similar stake in Alenia of Italy, would begin to create a more genuine European aerospace entity. To reduce the degree of concern in France at the Anglo-German merger, Dasa's space business was expected to be excluded from the BAe merger and then linked with the Aerospatiale/Matra merger and with Matra's UK joint venture partner, GEC. Coincidently, in the defence electronics sector, GEC was itself considering a possible merger with Thomson-CSF of France or, alternatively, an American group.

Then, in January, 1999, the entire European restructuring process fundamentally and abruptly changed. British Aerospace suddenly announced that it had acquired the Marconi electronics division of GEC for £7.8 billion, creating at a stroke Europe's largest defence company and the third largest in the world. Indeed, the newly-created BAE Systems become the world's second largest defence company if only sales of weapon systems are taken into account. BAE Systems expect the full benefits from the merger to take 3 years to accrue. British Aerospace view the acquisition as the first step in creating a pan-European aerospace/defence entity but, inevitably in the circumstances, other European companies and governments expressed grave concern at the creation of what is effectively a British 'national champion' rather than a cross-border merger that they feel would have better served the European purpose. Some analysts argued that a BAe-Daimler-Chrysler merger followed by a Thomson CSF-GEC Marconi merger, resulting in an eventual link up between the two newly merged entities would have made better economic and market sense from a European perspective.

This example provides a good illustration of the way in which market adjustment takes place in reality with outcomes that do not always serve the broader interests set by government. British Aerospace, a long-standing proponent of European consolidation in aerospace and defence as the best means to avoid key capabilities slipping into the hands of American competitors, ultimately had to protect its own core business. Acquiring the defence electronics capabilities of Marconi now strengthens their chances of winning prime contracts in their home market as the UK MoD procurement reforms put greater stress on industry taking responsibility for contract management.

Interestingly, the BAe-GEC Marconi deal means that if the UK MoD really want genuine competition in contract tendering in future, there will be many instances where BAE Systems are the only UK contender, so all competition will have to be from foreign competitiors. Furthermore, analysts believe that once the threat to sell Marconi to the US company, Lockheed Martin, was seen as a serious possibility, British Aerospace was left with no option but to acquire it themselves or risk a major erosion of their business opportunities through competition from an American competitor 'wrapped up in the Union Jack'.

Defence industries, unlike most of those in the civil sector, have yet to realise the challenge of and the economic benefits to be derived from globalisation. The modern defence industrial enterprise has evolved from a kind of hybrid company, where defence product innovation and new technology diversification took place side by side, into a systems integrator, frequently sub-contracting manufacture to other parts of the defence supply matrix. To survive and prosper in the global market, such companies need to be able to access a wide range of national markets, offer a broad range of military products and services and operate as a global entity, capable of searching the world to source the best inputs in terms of cost and quality to meet the demands of procurement-reforming governments worldwide.

In the modern defence business, the only viable route to success is for prime contractors to develop into large systems integrators, whether in aircraft, naval vessels, armoured vehicles, missiles or electronics. Such companies have to be able to control the whole contract for defence equipment and need the potential to compete on the global stage in almost every area of the defence market. BAE Systems now emerge as the only British company likely to win prime contracts for a range of defence products from aircraft carriers to combat aircraft. Marconi complements the production range of BAe with interests in shipbuilding, sonar, radar, avionics, missiles and munitions. Marconi brings expertise in areas such as the AS-90 howitzer for the UK army and the 155mm howitzer for the US army. Of equal importance are the synergies between military and civil production that are key to the great success off American aerospace companies. For example, Marconi's 'head-up displays', widely used on combat aircraft, can be transferred to a similar function in BAe's civil aircraft business.

The new venture has a significant global market already with annual sales in the UK exceeding £2 billion, in the US exceeding £2 billion, in the Middle East exceeding £4 billion, in the Asia Pacific region exceeding £1 billion, and elsewhere exceeding £2 billion. The acquisition of Marconi allows BAe to further strengthen its market position in the electronics sector, following additional recent purchases of a stake in STN Atlas of Germany and the takeover of Plessey from Siemens. The capture of US electronics company Tracor by Marconi in 1997 made it the world's 6th largest electronics company. Marconi also owns VSEL and is therefore now one of only two remaining UK shipbuilders for military vessels. Through its acquisitions and international operations, BAe now has considerable global reach with 5,500 employees working in Saudi Arabia, 2,500 in Australia, 3,000 in Sweden, 3,500 in Germany, 4,000 in Italy, 4,500 in France, 70,000 in the UK and 18,300 in the US.

POSTSCRIPT

Following the completion of this book, Daimler-Chrysler Aerospace and Aerospatiale Matra announced that, in response to the BAe-Marconi Electronics Systems merger, they intended to merge their own aerospace and defence business interests in order to establish the European Aeronautics Defence and Space company. This decision terminates for the moment the process of wider European defence integration since it effectively excludes the major British player from the new trans- European corporation. After delays obtaining approval for the BAe-Marconi merger from the European Union and from the US authorities, the new entity BAE Systems commenced operations on 30 November, 1999. The complexity of the European defence industry rationalisation and restructuring process continued to increase when BAE Systems made clear in November 1999 that their next probable strategic move would be to seek a merger with one of the key US aerospace/defence companies—either Boeing, Lockheed Martin, Raytheon or, if recent speculation is correct, Northrop Grumman. This followed an announcement by the US Department of Defence that BAE Systems, given its new pro°le and spread of business interests and operational locations, would in future be 'treated as American'.

Since the announcement of the formation of the new European Aeronautics Defence and Space company, CASA of Spain and Alenia of Italy have expressed their intention to join. These developments seem to suggest that the prospects for the creation of a genuine European defence industrial base which fully incorporates key British players have now receded signi°cantly, although joint projects involving the British continue to develop. Indeed, BAE Systems has strong joint venture European links established with Thomson-CSF and Lagardere in France, Alenia in Italy, Daimler-Chrysler in Germany and Saab in Sweden. Furthermore, the European partners in Airbus Industrie (BAE Systems, Daimler-Chrysler, Aerospatiale Matra and Casa) continue to share a common goal of rapid restructuring to reduce costs and enhance their joint competitive edge against Boeing of the US in the large civil aircraft market. The recent decision by the British government to support the A3XX project merely adds to the urgent necessity of resolving the current trans-European 'merger war'. If this cannot be achieved, it may be that engagement in trans-Atlantic mergers in the aerospace/defence industry come to represent the only really viable business option for European players for the future. What happens next will be crucial for the future of the European aerospace/defence industry, its key players and supplier base and this will form the basis for discussion in the remainder of the chapter. In many ways, as far as the European aerospace and defence sector is concerned, the end game is yet to come.

MARKET RESPONSE AND THE KEY PLAYERS

As we approach the next crucial phase in the restructuring of the European aerospace industry, the role and aspirations of each of the major companies, individually, in their respective partnerships and influenced by government, will determine the nature and timing of the eventual outcome. This section of Chapter 3 therefore concludes with a brief review of the key European market players at the time of writing.

FRANCE

Aerospatiale Matra

Aerospatiale Matra made its debut as a merged entity at the 43rd Paris Air Show in 1999. Following intense pressure from their UK and German partners in the Airbus consortium, the new combination of Aerospatiale (formerly a key component of the French dirigiste industrial and economic policy) and Matra (the high-technology element of private sector Lagardere) has emerged as the major force in French aerospace. The new company has a 1998 turnover of $13.3 billion, making it Europe's second largest aerospace company behind British Aerospace/GEC Marconi and the fifth largest in the world. While primarily a civil aerospace company, it has considerable defence interests including helicopter design and production (within Eurocopter), missiles, some in its own right as well as others in partnership with BAe Dynamics, Daimler Chrysler, Alenia and Thomson-CSF (including Aster, Apache, Meteor, Trigat and Vesta, a new platform for ramjet-powered missiles). Some 52% of the new company will be owned by the private sector with the French government holding a 48% interest which is scheduled to decline in the future. Aerospatiale Matra also own over 45% of Dassault Aviation, following the reallocation of the government's share of ownership to Aerospatiale in the partial privatisation of French aerospace in late 1998.

Dassault Aviation

Dassault remain a major player in the design, development and manufacture of fighter aircraft with other interests in the business jet market. In 1998, turnover exceeded $3 billion and the company's principal products include the Mirage 2000, a major export market success, and the Rafale, which is soon to enter production. In a joint venture with British Aerospace, Dassault has established a new entity European Aerosystems Ltd which will develop enabling systems for future generations of combat aircraft.

Eurocopter

This Franco-German joint venture was established in 1992 with Aerospatiale holding the controlling share (60%) and DASA of Germany (40%). Eurocopter is the largest manufacturer of helicopters in the world and, in addition, takes some 40% of the global helicopter market. In 1998, its turnover approximated $2 billion. On the military side, Eurocopter manufactures and will soon supply the Cougar, the Tiger attack helicopter and the NH90 transport/naval helicopter.

Snecma

Snecma is the world's fourth largest aero-engine manufacturer in its own right and operates as a partner in the world's most successful engine manufacturing consortium. The company recently acquired the TI group's stake in Messier-Dowty, making it the world leader in the supply of landing gear. Through its Hispano-Suiza division, Snecma is also world leader in power transmissions and, through Messier-Bugati, ranks among the world's top suppliers of braking systems, wheels and brakes. Turnover in 1998 exceeded $4.7 billion.

BRITAIN

British Aerospace-GEC Marconi

Assuming approval from the competition regulators is achieved as expected, BAeGEC Marconi will emerge as Europe's largest aerospace company and most significant airframe manufacturer. It will also rank third in the world as a defence company ahead of the US competitor, Raytheon. Turnover in 1998 amounted to some $8 billion. On the defence side of its business, the company has a 33% stake in the Eurofighter Typhoon and produces the Harrier and Hawk trainer while it also owns 50% of the third largest missile producer in the world, (Matra BAe Dynamics). BAeGEC is also Europe's largest radar and electronics integrated company with a range of products including radar, sonar, missile controls and naval ships. The company also holds a 35% stake in Sweden's Saab AB; has purchased the UK/Australia divisions of Siemens Plessey and has acquired control of the BAeSEMA joint venture. At present, negotiations are reported to be taking place with Alenia of Italy on possible joint ventures in missiles, defence electronics, aero-structures and assembly.

Rolls-Royce

Rolls-Royce is Europe's largest producer of aero-engines and ranks second or third behind Pratt & Whitney and General Electric of the United States, depending on the basis of comparison. Turnover in 1998 exceeded $7m. The company has a very large stake in the global civil aero-engine market and on the military side produces the EJ200 engine for the Eurofighter Typhoon, the Pegasus engine for the AV-8

Harrier, the RB199 for the Tornado, the Adour engine (with Turbomeca) for the Hawk and Jaguar, the AE 2100 engine for the C130-J. In addition, the company produces a wide range of engines for military helicopters including the AE 1107 engine for the V-22 Osprey, the RTM 322 engine for the EH101, the MTR 390 for tiger, the T800 (with AlliedSignal) for the Comanche and the Gem for Lynx. In 1990, a trans-European strategic partnership was established with the formation of Anglo-German BMW Rolls-Royce and, in 1995, the company made a successful move into the US market with the acquisition of the Allison Engine Company.

Westland-Agusta
A major helicopter supplier in its own right, producing the Super Lynx, the WAH-64 Apache and the Sea King, Westland, in partnership with Agusta of Italy, emerge as the second largest helicopter manufacturer in the world with EH101 as their major joint product. Combined turnover in 1998 exceeded $2 billion.

GERMANY

DaimlerChrysler Aerospace (DASA)
DASA is the third largest aerospace company in Europe after BAe-GEC Marconi and Aerospatiale Matra with turnover in 1998 exceeding $9 billion. As well as being a key partner in the Airbus Industrie consortium, on the military side of its business the company is involved in Eurofighter Typhoon production, engine programmes including the EJ200 and V2500, holds a 40% stake in the Eurocopter consortium, and also manufactures light combat and trainer aircraft.

The company developed initially through the merger of Dornier, Messerschmitt-Boelkow-Blohm (MBB), Motorem-und Turbinen-Union (MTU) and Telefunken Systemtechnik and, in 1998, merged with the aerospace interests of the US company, Chrysler.

ITALY

Alenia
Alenia is a key player in the European aerospace industry, operating as a major partner in a range of pan-European projects, both military and civil. The company holds a 20% stake in the Eurofighter Typhoon programme and helps manufacture the AMX tactical support and

reconnaisance aircraft, Tornado and Falcon. At present, the Italian government holds a 60% stake in Alenia's parent company, Finmeccanica and plans to sell its shareholding by June 2000. Interest has been expressed publicly in establishing a closer working relationship with BAe-GEC Marconi.

SPAIN

Casa

Casa is considered to be the world leader in the manufacture of light and medium military transport aircraft and plays a strategic role in European aerospace as a partner in a number of key projects, including the Airbus Industrie consortium and the Airbus Military Company. Turnover in 1998 exceeded $1 billion. The company carries out production and assembly work on the Eurofighter Typhoon, the C-101 ground attack jet trainer, and military transports including the C-212-400, the CN-235-300, and the C-295. Casa also carries out limited production work for the F-18. In June 1999, in the latest step towards European aerospace consolidation, Casa announced that it was merging with DaimlerChrysler Aerospace of Germany.

Key suppliers

In addition to this array of major players in the restructuring of the European aerospace industry, a further group of companies (principally first-tier supply chain specialists) will play a strategic part in the reconstruction process. These include:

Lucas Aerospace-TRW

Lucas-TRW is recognised as a major world supplier of integrated flight controls, driveshaft hydraulics and other subsystems. Following takeover by TRW, Lucas has become a new division within TRW Aerospace and Information Systems.

Sagem

Sagem is the European leader in tactical unmanned aviation vehicle manufacture; in fighter avionics retrofit programmes; in helicopter flight control systems; in optronics; and I inertial navigation and guidance. Beyond Europe, it also ranks second or third in the world in all these areas, except helicopter flight control systems where Sagem is the top global supplier.

Thomson-CSF

Thomson-CSF is the largest defence electronics business in Europe with 1998 turnover of almost $7 billion. Its key role in the defence electronics market has been strengthened in the last three years by a range of acquisitions including: African Defence Systems; Sextant Avionique; Pilkington Optronics; Siemens Defence (Norway); Shorts Missile Systems and Thorn EMI. During 1999, Thomson-CSF has reorganised into eight key business groups with sharper market focus. The company lost its bid to acquire GEC Marconi to British Aerospace.

The lesson from the merger and restructuring process taking place on both sides of the Atlantic is that the adjustment of the aerospace/defence market in response to the evolving post-Cold War business environment is neither smooth nor necessarily rapid. What has emerged is a complex process of change in which the pursuit of self-interest (either at the corporate or national political level) stimulates actions and reactions on the parts of the key players which, certainly in the short to medium term, can send out false market signals and delays full market adjustment. Instead of a swift restoration of equilibrium in the market through the interplay of free market forces with minimal adjustment costs, the process is proving to be both costly and the source of considerable dis-equilibrium. Governments have become involved, not through policies to facilitate a peace dividend, but to encourage and even, in the case of the U.S, to subsidise the adjustment process. As a result, a significant proportion of what might have been the peace dividend is actually being consumed in helping the market attain some kind of acceptable outcome. It is perhaps somewhat ironic that national governments, pledged to a policy of competition and enhanced value-for-money in defence procurement should be assisting the defence industry to become less competitive at the national or trans-national level.

THE KEY QUESTIONS

At this stage of the process of European restructuring, then, a number of critical questions appear on the agenda for the next stage of European aerospace and defence consolidation which governments and large corporations across Europe will have to answer. They include:

What should be the structure, organisation and membership of the European defence industrial base?

How can the problems of government involvement in some national defence industries be overcome in the move towards a unified, rationalised European defence industrial base?

What is the appropriate degree of co-operation in the defence market between countries and between companies—who will lead and why?

Which critical technologies within Europe should then be maintained and developed and what are the implications of this?

What is the appropriate strategy regarding issues of juste retour and offsets?

What role, if any, should there be for current of future involvement of US defence and aerospace companies in the European restructuring process?

How can genuine cost-effective defence procurement be pursued where, following complete consolidation and rationalisation of the defence industry, governments in the US or in Europe are faced with virtual monopoly suppliers, without opening up the market fully to transatlantic competitors?

For the aerospace industry, in particular, answers are required urgently. Future global aerospace markets can only be accessed fully by an integrated European company, covering all aspects of the market, which can draw on synergies in technical competence, offer critical system integration attributes, expand from existing core business into potentially profitable new areas such as unmanned military aircraft and reusable space vehicles, realise economies of scale and scope and develop a sufficiently wide civil and military product range to be able to smooth out uneven cash flow caused by the cyclical nature of the business. In short, the complexity of modern aerospace technology, the requirements of integrated systems and, consequently, the extremely high financial expenditure and risk demand a highly integrated European aerospace industry, with or without direct US involvement.

GROUND RULES FOR EUROPEAN AEROSPACE RESTRUCTURING

In the process of European integration, to achieve an outcome that will establish a European integrated company as a major world player, a number of key ground rules need to be observed. First, whatever form the integration takes and whichever companies it involves, the result of integration must be to sharpen the competitiveness and enhance the profitability of the companies involved. Second, to ensure that the emerging company is genuinely viable in the private sector market, all companies engaged in the integration process should be privately owned. Third, the aim of European-wide consolidation should be to establish powerful aerospace and defence industrial cores by harnessing the capabilities and expertise of major European companies, supplementing these cores as required with the addition of others.

Next, to avoid unnecessary conflicts of interest between the integrated company and national governments, where industrial sectors involved in the integration process cross national boundaries, thereby raising questions of national sovereignty, care will be needed to establish an appropriately balanced but still optimal distribution of key roles, such as single sourcing activities and the creation of centres of competence and excellence. Again, it will be essential to construct the European aerospace and defence 'champion' on the basis of genuine partnerships and not by market-domination strategies. Finally, if the outcome is to be genuinely optimal, in the end 'membership' of the group pursuing integration cannot be restricted only to European players. Although the European element must be the dominant part, the newly emerging company formed by consolidation should permit cooperation (or even further consolidation) with interested transatlantic or other partners.

Over the next few years, probably in a spasmodic and somewhat haphazard way, market forces will drive Europe's aerospace and defence industry towards consolidation, with or without the direct involvement of American companies. In the end, the market will impose an outcome on the industry and take its toll of those companies unable to respond quickly or strategically to its demands. Whether such market adjustment can simultaneously release sufficient resources over time to provide a meaningful and sustainable peace dividend is, however, another question. It may be that, when the restructuring game is finally played out, the dividend to be extracted from the 'outbreak of peace' may have to be measured more in terms of ensuring European corporate survival in the global defence market (with all its attendant costs) rather than in terms of genuine enhanced social welfare or civil market competitive edge.

CONCLUSION

Bischak (1997) suggests that there are four principal conclusions to be drawn from the approaches adopted by US prime defence contractors to the post-Cold War business environment in the 1990's. First, the evidence suggests that the route to successful diversification and conversion requires the establishment of:

> 'a clear corporate strategy for increasing commercial sales, developing commercial products, commercializing, where possible, defence technologies, and rapidly shedding excess defence capacity.'

Secondly, attempts to commercialize corporate business activities were:

> 'clearly influenced by civilian federal investments in new technologies such as alternative transportation, environmental remediation, telecommunications, and modernization of the air traffic control system.'

Thirdly, as a result of the process of merger and rationalisation in the US defence industry, the market structure of each major sector of that industry has become increasingly oligopolistic in nature. In the case of most weapon production, just two or three firms remain in the industry in the US. Bischak makes the important point that:

> 'Curiously, federal policy to subsidise defence industry consolidation may have produced one of the least efficient market structures for the defence industry since oligopoly suppliers tend to hold more excess capacity than a monoply market or competitive market... doubly curious, despite the avowed commitment of the Clinton Administration to promote commercial-military integration through its dual-use policy, there is little evidence that the dedicated defence giants emerging from this consolidation process are any more capable of performing such integration.'

Finally, Bischak observes that :

> 'Those firms which have remained in the defence industry have become much larger, more specialised weapon systems integrators pitted against their remaining rivals to deliver the most sophisticated next generation of weaponry... Thus, the Pentagon has found a replacement for the technological competition of the arms race with an oligopoly rivalry among the science-based defence firms dedicated to supplying the most advanced weaponry possible.'

Perhaps ironically, then, the drive towards a more competitive defence supply industry in the US, set against the background of the substantial and sustained decline in defence expenditure, has resulted in an even more highly concentrated and defence-focused industry in which dual-use technology, one of the important steps in delivering a peace dividend, has scarcely yet been addressed. Based on current evidence, the European defence industry seems to be moving in the same direction.

In this chapter, the process of market adjustment as it affects and is influenced by the prime defence contractors has been explored, with a particular focus on the aerospace sector where market adjustment has been most intense. However, while critically important in setting both the pace and extent of market adjustment, prime contractors represent but one element of the defence supply industry. In the new global business environment, for the prime contractors to achieve their desired market goals, they have to depend upon a much larger number of companies located in the supply chain serving the defence industry and it is to this important sub-structure of the defence sector that we now turn our attention.

REFERENCES

AECMA, (1997), *Aerospace Industry Restructuring: the AECMA View,* Report from the European Association of Aerospace Industries Restructuring Working Group, September.

Anthony I., (1995), Defence Industrial Restructuring in Europe, *Defence and Peace Economics,* Vol. 6, pp. 185–205.

Augustine N., (1997), Reshaping an Industry: Lockheed Martin's Survival Story, *Harvard Business Review,* May-June, pp. 83–94.

Bischak G., (1997), *Demobilisation from the Cold War 1990–1996:Lessons for Forging a New Conversion Policy,* Bonn International Center for Conversion.

Braddon D. L., Dowdall P. G., and Kendry A. P., (1996), Organisational Reform, Market Testing and Defence, in Braddon D. L. and Foster D., *Privatization: Themes and Perspectives,* Dartmouth.

Borderching T. E., Pommerehne W. W., and Schneider F., (1982) *Comparing the Efficiency of Private and Public Production: Evidence from Five Countries,* Zeitschrift fur Nationalokonomie, Supplementum 2.

Buchanan J. M., (1978), *The Economics of Politics,* Institute of Economic Affairs, London.

Confederation of British Industry (southwest), (1993), *Positioned For Recovery?* A report prepared for the CBI (southwest) by a team from Coopers Lybrand and the Research Unit in Defence Economics at the University of the West of England.

Cypher J. M., (1982), Ideological Hegemony and Modern Militarism: The Origins and Limits of Military Keynesianism, *Economic Forum,* Vol. 13, Summer, pp. 1–20.

DiFillipo A., (1991), How the Military-Serving Firm Differs from the Rest, *Briefing Paper 10,* March, National Commission for Economic Conversion and Disarmament, Washington D.C.

Dowdy J. J., 'Winners and Losers in the Arms Industry Downturn', *Foreign Policy,* 1997, Summer.

Dunne J. P., (1993), The Changing Military Industrial Complex in the UK, *Defence Economics,* Vol. 4.

Dussauge P. and Garrette B., 'Industrial Alliances in Aerospace and Defence: An Empirical Study of Strategic and Organizational Patterns', *Defence Economics,* Vol. 4, pp. 45–62.

Gansler J., (1988), Military and Industrial Co-operation in a Transformed, Nato-Wide Competitive Market, XVth International NATO Workshop on Political-Military Decision Making, Vienna, 22 June.

Guay T. R., (1998), *At Arm's Length: The European Union and Europe's Defence Industry,* Macmillan Press Limited.

Gummett P., (1996), The Future of the European Armaments Capability, *Briefing Paper No. 5,* University of Manchester, July.

Gummett P., (1996), National Preferences, International Imperatives and the European Defence Industry, in Gummett P., (ed) *Globalisation and Public Policy*, Edward Elgar.

Hartley K., (1996), Defence Industries Adjusting to Change, *Defence and Peace Economics*, Vol. 7, pp. 169–184.

Hartley K., (1998), *The Strategic Defence Review: An Economist's View*, 5th Annual CESER Lecture, May, Centre for Social and Economic Research, University of the West of England, Bristol.

Hartley K. and Martin S., (1993), Evaluating Collaborative Programmes, *Defence Economics*, Vol. 4, pp. 195–211.

Kaminski P., (1997), taken from a speech presented in Brussels, November.

Kovacic W. E. and Smallwood D. E., (1994), Competition Policy, Rivalries and Defence Industry Consolidation, *Journal of Economic Perspectives*, Vol. 8, No. 4, Fall, pp. 91–110.

Lawrence P. K., and Braddon D. L., (1998) *FLA—The Strategic Case*, Aerospace Research Group, University of the West of England, Bristol.

Lawrence P. K. and Dowdall P. G., (1998), *Strategic Trade in Commercial-Class Aircraft: Europe. v. America*, Royal Institute of International Affairs, Discussion Paper 78.

Lock P., and Vob W., (1994), The German Arms Industry in a European Context: A Study in Successful Downsizing, *Defence and Peace Economics*, Vol. 5, pp. 341–348.

Mandel R., (1994), The Transformation of the American Defence Industry: Corporate Perceptions and Preferences, *Armed Forces and Society*, Vol. 20, No. 2, Winter, pp. 175–197.

Markusen A., (1997), Understanding American Defence Industry Mergers, *Rutgers PRIE Working Paper No. 247*, May.

Millward R., (1982), The Comparative Performance of Public and Private Ownership, in Rolls E., *The Mixed Economy*, Macmillan, London.

National Economic Development Council, (1991), *Diversifying from Defence: Case Studies and Management Guidelines*, NEDC, London.

Oden M., Markusen A., Flaming D., Feldman J., Raffel J., and Hill C., (1996), *From Managing Growth to Reversing Decline: Aerospace and the Southern California Economy in the Post -Cold War Era*, Rutgers University Project on Regional and Industrial Economics, New Brunswick, N.J.

Oden M., (1997), Cashing-in, Cashing-out and Converting: Restructuring of the Defence Industrial Base in the 1990s, in Markusen A. and Costigan S. (eds), *Arming the Future: A Defence Industry for the 21st Century*.

Sandler T. and Cauley J., (1975), On the Economic Theory of Alliances, *Journal of Conflict Resolution*, Vol. 19, No. 2, pp. 330–348.

Sandler T. and Murdoch J. C., (1990), Nash-Cournot or Lindahl Behaviour? An Empirical Test for the Nato Allies, *Quarterly Journal of Economics*, Vol. 105, No. 4, pp. 875–894.

Sears M., (1998) The Future for Aerospace Defence Manufacturing: Collaboration or Competition? *Financial Times World Aerospace and Air Transport Conference*, 3–4 September.

Seiglie C., (1992), Determinants of Military Expenditure, in Isard W. and Anderton C. H., (eds), *Economics of Arms Reduction and the Peace Process*, Elsevier B.V.

Skons E., Internationalization of the West European Arms Industry, paper prepared for the Conference on Globalization of Military Industry and Arms Trade, Middlesex University Business School, London, 19–20 September.

Sperling J. and Kirchner E., (1997), *Recasting the European Order*, Manchester University Press.

Steinberg J. B., (1992) The Transformation of the European Defence Industry, *Rand Report*, R-4141-ACQ.

Strategic Defence Review, (1998), Ministry of Defence.

Taylor T., (1993), West European Defence Industrial Issues for the 1990s, *Defence Economics*, Vol. 4.

Tulloch G., (1976), *The Vote Motive*, Institute of Economic Affairs, London.

Tyson L. D., (1992) Who's Bashing Whom?, Institute for International Economics, Washington D.C.

Uttley M., (1993), Contracting-Out and Market-Testing in the UK Defence Sector: Theory, Evidence and Issues, *Public Money and Management*, Januiary-March, pp. 55–60.

Walker W. and Willett S., (1993), Restructuring the European Defence Industrial Base, *Defence Economics*, Vol. 4, pp. 141–160.

Chapter 4

BARRIERS TO CHANGE: THE SUPPLY MATRIX DIMENSION

INTRODUCTION

To translate the opportunity presented by the end of the Cold War into a genuine, substantial and lasting peace dividend without significant government intervention requires that all parts of the defence supply market are able to adjust in a smooth and rapid manner to the new business environment and that the resources released from military production can be efficiently re-employed in civil production. For most of the 1990s, we have witnessed that market adjustment process at work and it is here that the real nature of the market and its capacity to adjust flexibly and optimally as required can be best observed. Having explored in the previous chapter how the prime contractors in the defence industry have addressed the adjustments required in their market behaviour, this chapter and Chapter 6 delve more deeply into the supply and technology base of the defence industry, focusing again on how the market handles such crucial economic determinants. In this chapter, the supply chain (or, perhaps, more accurately, the supply matrix) that now crucially underpins the business success of the prime defence contractors is considered and the post-Cold War market experience of suppliers is examined.

At the outset, it must be acknowledged that this is a relatively under-researched area of the economic analysis of the defence industry, yet one which is critical to our understanding of the transmission effects of defence expenditure changes through the economy and, consequently, how and why the market responds as it does. Much of the initial UK-based research work in the area of defence industry supply chains was conducted by the Research Unit in Defence Economics at the University of the West of England (UWE) in Bristol[1], based upon structured face-to-face interviews with senior defence industry executives from both prime and supplier companies, together with a survey of some 120 companies in the defence supply network. Additional

---

[1]   The author wishes to acknowledge in particular the major contributions of Paul Dowdall, Senior Research Fellow, Research Unit in Defence Economics, UWE, Bristol to the research conducted on the supply chain issue reported in this chapter.

important research has been conducted by the Centre for Defence Economics at the University of York in partnership with the Research Unit in Defence Economics at UWE, Bristol and colleagues at Cranfield University under the government Value of Defence to the Economy initiative. Currently, the Research Unit in Defence Economics is extending its supply matrix analysis, working in partnership with the government's new Centre of Expertise in Aerospace and Defence (see Chapter 7), located at Business Link West (South Gloucestershire). This chapter draws upon and extends the relevant findings of this work and also incorporates the findings of other recent contributions to the literature.

In the last chapter, the response of the prime contractors in the defence industry to the changes consequent upon the 'outbreak of peace' were identified and analysed. In general, those remaining in the defence supply market were seeking to sharpen their business profile and performance through rationalisation measures, designed to enhance productivity, and to restructure through the pursuit of appropriate mergers, take-overs, strategic alliances, 'teaming' arrangements and so forth. Their central goal has been to improve their competitive edge in the market in order to retain and possibly expand their share of a smaller and changing defence market and they are constantly seeking opportunities through their supply chains to achieve it. In much of the literature on corporate adjustment to defence expenditure contraction, reference is frequently made to the existence of a supplier base and on occasions such references have been extended to include some notion of the importance of these suppliers. Hooper and Buck (1990), referring to research on the UK's replacement main battle tank, Challenger II, touched upon some of the issues, commenting:

> 'In addition, the large companies are dependent on a network of subcontractors and suppliers, many of whom are also highly specialised'.

Without question, the major defence contractors provide the business opportunities and economic life-support system for a vast number of smaller sub-contractors and suppliers, especially in engineering. Both primes and their supply companies have faced a difficult and uncertain future as they responded to the challenge of a real decline in national and international defence budgets in the 1990s. Indeed, such is the nature of the defence industry and its supply chain, being highly concentrated at the regional level often with significant clustering of companies around a major prime contractor, that some analysts consider that the multiplier effect of such clustered companies joint activities might be structural in nature and much bigger than conventional multipliers.

For example, the major post-Cold War defence cuts had a much greater than expected impact on parts of California with the Los Angeles area, for instance, losing over 20 per cent of all jobs lost in the US in the early 1990s, principally due to defence clustering and the scale of defence cuts. Studies also suggest that the employment loss associated with defence cuts is considerably greater than that associated with defence spending increases in a particular area. This lack of symmetry and the perceived clustering effect suggest both that there may be something inherently different about regional impact of defence expenditure cuts that cannot be picked up by conventional multiplier or input-output analysis and that prime-subcontractor relationships may be inherently stronger and economically more significant than has traditionally been suggested, especially at the level of the regional economy (for a fuller discussion of these ideas, see Cohen and Garcia, 1994).

Certainly a very large number of smaller and medium-sized enterprises, which depend critically upon chains of subcontracts to the prime defence contractors for most of their business, frequently do not have the resources, expertise or capabilities to conduct international business themselves and may not be prepared for or have much experience of foreign competition. The drive towards European integration among the primes and the potential for US involvement in some aspects of the European defence business will be viewed by the subcontract sector with concern, fearing a consequent loss of business without the capacity to compete effectively in the market. While, in general, American small- and medium-sized enterprises in the defence industry specialise in specific military technologies and depend on government-financed sub-contracts for most of their income, smaller companies in the European defence industrial base tend to focus on relatively narrow product lines, often depending on older dual-use technologies, and in general depend on local customers for most of their business. Historically, international collaboration sometimes leads to a reduction in business for these firms since it often means that local primes end up using foreign subcontractors while local subcontractors capture little work from foreign primes.

In a declining market, it is natural for established trading relationships to undergo both rapid and fundamental change. As a result, the existing supply chain linkages in the defence sector have and will become strained and new linkages (and associated new business opportunities) will evolve over time. This is especially likely when, as in the case of the defence market in the early years of the 1990s, the arduous process of virtually complete industrial restructuring has been accompanied by a deep and prolonged international economic recession. Clearly, these developments will have a significant impact upon business prospects in traditionally stable defence markets and require fundamental change in corporate strategy within the prime contractors operating in the defence sector.

For such fundamental change to proceed smoothly and rapidly, the revolution taking place in the prime contractors requires a major transformation of their supply base. A central feature of the emerging corporate strategies at the prime contractor level in the defence industry is a fundamental re-evaluation of their purchasing process (and, consequently, the supply chain relationships implied by that process). The drive towards an optimum purchasing strategy which can deliver reduced costs together with enhanced flexibility will, without question, intensify the pressures upon the supply chain.

What are the key elements of this 'optimum purchasing strategy'? What characteristics will ensure that a supplier remains attractive to a prime defence contractor both now and in the future? A 1994 survey by Ingersol Engineers Limited of suppliers and sub-contractors in the aerospace industry of the UK, US, Australia, France, Germany and China among others provides a guide. The six most crucial supplier characteristics in order of importance were identified as: strict adherence to delivery and schedule; an established quality track record; the low price of supplier's products; financial soundness; more comprehensive system packages; and quick response to schedule changes. Among characteristics considered quite important were: technology leadership of the supplier; the ability to share development risk; manufacturing facilities; and culture and working practices. The message was clear. The critical requirements for successful suppliers are:

1. Reliable delivery performance indicated by good adherence to delivery and schedule and quick response to schedule changes.
2. A track record of capability, indicated particularly by an established quality track record, financial soundness and, to a much lesser extent, an established reputation in their market.
3. Low cost—relating to both products and spares.

The survey also found that some other issues relating to products, partnerships and relationships were also seen as very important and closer working relationships emerged as the route forward, becoming more important over time.

The focus of the required revolution in the supplier base of the defence industry then will be on minimising cost, offering rapid response to changing market demands, improving external relations via partnership arrangements with suppliers and customers, and enhancing customer service in terms of delivery, quality and service.

Although there are a significant number of very large, first-tier suppliers in the supply chain of the defence industry, some of whom become key players themselves, by far the majority of such companies are small and medium-sized enterprises. These companies frequently specialise in one or two specific production activities or specialist business functions and are often led by a relatively small management team with limited resources, who are faced with constant day-to-day pressure to ensure that the business survives and usually lack the internal capacity for longer-term strategic development or the relevant marketing skills to help move their business away from defence-dependency.

As is the case for most manufacturing industries, large defence contractors require flexible and responsive suppliers and sub-contractors who are willing and able both to work in close partnership with them but can also share in the burden of financing the technology developments that are so vital to their future business potential. Unless supplier companies can aspire to the highest standards in their production then it is unlikely that the main prime contractors will succeed with their business development plans. Indeed, for many prime contractors it is primarily through managing more efficiently their business relationships with supply companies that they now intend to secure and maintain competitive advantage in the market. The competitive advantage benefits accessible through the pursuit of both lean production and lean enterprise (Womack and Jones, 1994) apply therefore not only to defence prime contractors but, crucially, to their supplier companies as well.

Furthermore, implementing systems to ensure the greater flexibility of suppliers is now a key component of the process of corporate adjustment and restructuring being conducted by most prime defence contractors. Some of these recognise that their very survival in the market as part of the defence industrial base depends upon the success of this strategy. The results of research in the UK, however, suggests that this required flexibility may be seriously constrained by a number of inhibiting barriers to effective market adjustment, delaying and disrupting a smooth and rapid transition to the needs of the post-Cold War environment in the defence industry.

SUPPLIER FLEXIBILITY

The discussion of the 'flexible firm' and more generally, the issue of 'flexible specialisation' originated in the literature of industrial sociology. The analysis has concentrated more on the individual organisation and less on the industrial system and supply matrix that supports the individual firm. For the defence industry, as it comes to terms with both the end of the Cold War and the requirements of an uncertain and constantly evolving 'new world order', the analysis must shift from the flexible firm to that of the flexible supply network and recognise the important changes taking place within this sector in the US and Western Europe in particular. Just at the time when defence expenditure globally was peaking in the mid-1980s (and years before the 'outbreak of peace' between the superpowers became a reality) analysts were drawing attention to important changes taking place in the industrial systems of North America and Western Europe. In particular, these changes related to a relative decline in the importance of Fordist mass production and a remarkable expansion of manufacturing activities based on highly flexible technological and organisational structures.

At the heart of what was perceived to be a kind of new industrial revolution was the 'lean production' phenomenon in manufacturing. By employing lean production techniques, pioneered by Toyota, companies could enhance their performance by eliminating various stages in production, combining the remaining stages in a continuous flow, redirecting labour into cross-functional teams, and pressing for constant improvement. Womack and Jones (1994) suggest that, by employing lean production techniques, companies can:

'develop, produce and distribute products with half or less of the human effort, space, tools, time and overall expense. They can also become vastly more flexible and responsive to customer desires.'

While supplier flexibility has become an important feature of many manufacturing industries in the last 15 years, it is only more recently that recognition of the value of that flexibility has spread to the defence industry. In many ways, then, the defence supply network is at last coming to terms with a manufacturing revolution that swept through other industries some years ago.

Defence-specific factors have clearly impacted upon this supply network in recent years, both directly and indirectly, principally through changes in the level and/or direction of defence expenditure and through changes in the tendering and defence procurement processes of governments. These changes in procurement have taken the industry away from 'cost-plus' towards 'fixed- or firm-price' competition. In addition, however, the impact of lean production as part of what is known as the 'Post-Fordist Production Paradigm' has also been considerable (for further discussion, see Latham, 1995; and Womack and Jones, 1996).

While the Fordist approach brought scientific management principles into the automated assembly line and focused the division of labour on to mass markets, it also tended to fragment work and increased the deskilling process. The Fordist approach also introduced the flow line principle of assembly work whereby the movement of parts through the factory is achieved as much as possible by machines and depended less on the movement of people. As a result, assembly line workers tend to become dependent on the machines they work with while their work rate is effectively controlled by managers and supervisors.

The advent of post-Fordist manufacturing processes in many industries in recent years represents a fundamental change. Post-Fordism has characteristics which include flexible specialisation and manufacturing systems and job enrichment schemes, facilitated in turn by developments in new technology. Computer-based design and manufacture systems permit greater flexibility through programming and are more adaptable, as well as having shorter set up times. Collaborative practices within and between workers, management and designers also become more significant. As a result, post-Fordism tends to create a more varied workforce with a fusion of different skills; varied work patterns, and a commitment to quality work, self-discipline and more autonomous decision-making, allowing a decentralisation of responsibility for continuous production. The concept of flexible specialisation therefore entails creating a manufacturing design, development and production system which can react quickly and appropriately to increasingly differentiated customer demands, generating as a result the potential for lower cost, higher productivity and enhanced quality production. Flexible specialisation also allows the construction, often temporary in nature, of a 'virtual firm', drawing together a number of organisations into an entity for the specific purpose of delivering a particular project or design, development or production programme.

The last decade has witnessed the remarkable explosion of so-called 'network organisations' which diverge from the more traditional centrally co-ordinated, multi-level corporate hierarchies and move instead toward flexible corporate structures which are less pyramid-like and more flexible and multi-dimensional. While such networks have proved to be generally successful in the dynamic global competitive environment of modern business, some analysts have raised questions about their longer term viability (for further discussion of networks and hierarchies in modern business organisations, see Thomson et al., 1991). In the modern manufacturing environment in which production processes matter much more than product, such improvements in how goods are produced will be critical in the drive to secure competitive advantage in the market.

DEFENCE CUTS AND THE SUPPLY CHAIN: THE EVIDENCE

In May, 1991, the Research Unit in Defence Economics at The University of the West of England, Bristol, published a report entitled 'The Impact of Reduced Military Expenditure on the Economy of southwest England' (Braddon et al., 1991). Amongst its main findings concerning the corporate impact of post-Cold War defence expenditure cuts was the potential vulnerability of suppliers and subcontractors in the defence industry supply chain. Concern about the possible degenerative and damaging influence that changes in the level and direction of defence expenditure may have upon these defence industry supply chain, led to a further programme of research being conducted by the UWE team, supported by the Department of Trade and Industry in the UK.

Globally, companies are moving away from the polar models of competitive multi-sourcing and vertical integration, towards a new middle ground which involves alternative forms of vertical relationships and arrangements. From this area of study emerges the notion of vertical quasi-integration or quasi-vertical integration (QVI) (Douma and Schreuder, 1991). In the UK, this has been given considerable prominence and forms the basis for the 'Partnership Sourcing' approach to industrial relationships, much promoted in the 1990s by the Department of Trade and Industry, the Confederation of British

Industry, the Bank of England, the Institute of Directors and the Department of Employment through the establishment of 'Partnership Sourcing Limited', London, (Partnership Sourcing Ltd, 1991) which was specifically designed to promote the concept of Partnership Sourcing more widely. In the supporting documentation, the Department of Trade and Industry (1992) states

> 'Partnership Sourcing is the adoption of a deeper and more co-operative relationship between companies and their suppliers ... A long term relationship can produce significant improvements in performance—providing opportunities for total cost reductions.'

In addition to the partnership sourcing initiative, associated moves toward Total Quality Management, Just-in-Time production, Flexible Manufacturing Systems, Vendor Certification, Supply Chain Management etc. are all now increasingly observed across the UK manufacturing base with similar objectives being pursued in other countries (see, for example, Dowdall and Braddon, 1994).

Faced with the urgent need to adapt rapidly and appropriately to changes in the level and direction of defence expenditure and seeking to gain competitive advantage from the move towards new forms of vertical relationship in the post-Fordist era), the defence supplier wishing to survive and prosper must respond. However, what may be defined as the most effective course of action for one player to pursue in the defence supply industry may not be appropriate for the survival of other members of the supply network, thereby putting at risk the capacity of the market to respond to change in the most effective way. So significant are the barriers to change in the defence industry that, without a systemic view of the matrix of interdependencies that form the defence supply network, analysis of individual corporate survival and the functioning of the market for defence goods would be incomplete.

Prime defence contractors, then, whether targeting greater defence market share, diversifying out of defence, collaborating, exporting, cost-cutting, or indeed pursuing whatever combination and permutation of generic strategies and strategic options is deemed most relevant, have come to recognise that the degree to which it will prove ultimately successful will depend on the flexibility and capabilities of their supply base. The survival of an efficient and resilient base of suppliers and sub-contractors is crucial therefore for the longer term viability of the major defence contractors they serve as they, in turn, confront the emerging opportunities and threats in an increasingly competitive global market.

SUPPLY CHAIN STRUCTURE

The prime defence contractors provide a kind of life-support mechanism for the supplier base, demanding from them a surprisingly wide range of goods and services, often requiring inputs and services from companies that would not normally consider themselves to be suppliers to the defence industry at all. It is vitally important to appreciate that, while a few of these companies supply only the defence industry and no other sector of the economy, most of these supplier organisations are multi-faceted with a wide array of existing and potential customers beyond defence For example, studying the supply chain of a major military engine contractor, the UWE Bristol study revealed at least 16 market sectors beyond defence and military aerospace in which defence supply companies in the first-tier of the supply network perceived themselves to operate. The research identified first-tier market sectors which included hydraulics, telecommunications, nuclear power, public utilities, medical/bio-medical, food processing, power generation, automobiles, printing, construction, oil, polymers, doors, office equipment, steel and textiles, providing a good illustration of the breadth of the supply network.

In turn, these first-tier suppliers will derive their own supply requirements from companies located in lower tiers of the network or from each other. As demand flows down through the supply network, its requirements spread into a much wider range of industries, which the research suggests include and extremely broad range of production and service activities including pumps, plastics, fluid connectors, metals, gas turbines, rubber, financial services, components, coolers, valves, forging, catering, foundry, castings, wax, printing, coatings, construction, filtration equipment, consumables, oil, mechanical and electrical engineering, energy, polymers, test equipment, tools, computer software, titanium, bearings, laser cutting, alloys, compressors, condensers, health & safety, HVAC refrigeration, controls, motors, fabrication, paint, plating, carbon composites, naval products, chemicals and publishing.

For the major defence companies and their principal suppliers engaged in these supply activity areas, the new business pressures of the 1990s meant that existing transactional alliances would necessarily undergo fundamental change. Corporate success or failure would now be a function of the degree to which these sectors of the economy can both perceive the need for change and have the capacity to accommodate change through enhanced corporate flexibility of both individual companies and, perhaps more critically, the entire supply network itself. Awareness of changing market requirements and the capability to respond appropriately would now be essential at all levels of the supply chain or network in the defence industry.

Attempts to describe the nature and structure of supply chains previously have tended to take a tierage approach as shown below in Diagram 1.

This traditional view of supply chains as comprising essentially a pyramid structure of discrete tiers tends to disguise, however, the particular degree of intra- and inter-tier dependency which the UWE, Bristol research reveals as central to the defence supply sector. The Bristol research study made the complex, interwoven nature of the supplier base clear and confirmed that many suppliers operated simultaneously in several supply chains emanating from different defence contractors; on occasions as first tier suppliers, on others as second or lower tier suppliers. For example, company X could be a first tier supplier in two or more chains; a second or third tier supplier in several others for different customers; and, simultaneously, be supplying one or more other sub-contractors/suppliers for the same or different customers.

Consequently, the traditional supply 'chain' concept of 'tierage', while still relevant, needs to go through a process of metamorphosis,

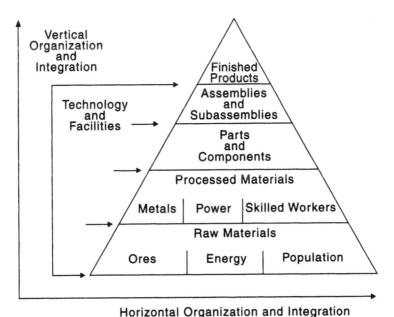

Diagram 1. Original Tierage Structure of Supply Chains.

conceptually, into an extremely intricate and inter-dependent supply 'network' or perhaps 'matrix' (see Diagram 2). Even then, this somewhat complex picture of business relationships that emerges within the defence industrial base is probably but a pale reflection of the true nature of the inter-locking relationships that exist across the industry, once we expand the customer base of first-tier defence suppliers to include all of the major defence contractors they supply.

This is not simply a matter of definition or conceptual depiction. The complex inter-weaving of the supply network has major implications for the process of market adjustment in defence supply and, particularly, for the resilience and flexibility of the defence industry supply base as it attempts to accommodate the shock of declining defence expenditure.

For many large defence contractors, whether or not they are currently engaged in downsizing their defence business, the survival of an efficient, flexible and viable supply network remains of critical importance. As the changes inspired by the 'outbreak of peace' contribute to a fundamental restructuring of the entire defence industry, the danger exists that its supply base fails to respond as required and drags down both the constituent companies and the market performance of the prime contractors they serve. In such a set of circumstances, the outcome of market-driven restructuring in the defence industry- and more widely for the whole economy—is likely to be the attainment of a sub-optimal equilibrium or, at worst, the persistence of damaging dis-equilibrium.

SUPPLIER RATIONALISATION AND ENHANCED PERFORMANCE

Those companies that wished to remain active in the defence supply industry during such a period of intense and unprecedented change had little choice but to assume organisational structures and strategies appropriate to an increasingly dynamic marketplace. Internal structures, systems, managerial style, the technology employed and the needs, values and abilities of employees had to be reviewed to ensure 'good fit' with the evolving external business environment.

As discussed in the previous chapter, having gone through a very painful period of rationalisation themselves, the prime contractors are now realising a significant part of the necessary flexibility required in their business operations through the modification of their supply and sub-contract arrangements and relationships. Faced with falling orders for defence goods, decision-makers in the prime contractors will attempt to pass on the burden of adjustment to reduced business through lower sub-contract orders, the squeezing of margins on those orders given out and by requiring extended credit terms from supply companies. At the same time, as they attempt to win back the desired share of a smaller market, prime contractors will be expecting their key suppliers to be both sharpening their own business performance and substantially cutting costs, while helping the primes meet their technology objectives and sharing the associated funding and risk burden. Against this background of intensifying business pressures, the ability of the defence industry supply network and its individual constituent companies to withstand these problems becomes an issue of considerable concern.

The crucial point here from a market analysis perspective is the extent to which defence firms (and indeed the entire supply network) can survive, relatively intact, as a result of these unprecedented market changes and this will depend critically upon the ease with which companies at all tiers or levels of the network can adjust, smoothly and rapidly, to their new economic environment. In future, suppliers to major defence contractors can expect to be judged more strictly on their performance with respect to cost profiles, delivery capabilities, and the capacity to guarantee organisational flexibility to assist their major customers meet the evolving requirements of the market.

To help overcome the uncertainty created by continuous supply chain restructuring, many major defence companies have now developed long-term purchasing relationships with key members of the supply network, which effectively involves placing long-term contracts with a single, reliable source of supply. This will provide the supply company with a substantial guaranteed business contract but one which, inevitably, will carry with it the requirement for that supply company to deliver effective cost reduction.

One of the main consequences of this approach—and one widely noted across the industry by the mid-1990s—has been the trend for prime defence contractors to reduce the number of companies included in their supplier lists but to also extend the list geographically, both nationally and internationally, in order to 'search the world' for low cost, high quality supply. Major global defence companies are now seeking the smallest viable number of preferred suppliers for all the main components and products they purchase and are attempting to form close partnerships with them. In the case of British Aerospace, for example, by the early 1990s, this had led to a major reduction in the number of suppliers which once stood at over 4,000 companies. By the early 1990s, more than 80% of that business was being sourced with 50 preferred suppliers, with some 70% of product bought in (which in turn was planned to reach 90% eventually).

This represents a true revolution in buyer-seller linkages within the defence industry and is one which continues apace in the late 1990s. Furthermore, as the major defence companies move increasingly towards the 'globalisation' of their business (whether by merger and acquisition; joint ventures or other forms of international collaboration as outlined in the previous chapter), there will emerge a new set of purchasing requirements for companies in the principal tiers of the supply network to absorb and deliver. Again, to the extent that innovation and high technology remain the key to retaining a competitive edge in the defence market, the ability of suppliers and sub-contractors to bear a greater proportion of the risks and costs associated with research and development will be critical for survival and success in the market.

As a result, small- and medium-sized enterprises wishing to retain or initiate business with the prime contractors must, in the future, improve their technological capabilities and attract the appropriate employee skill profile to ensure they meet the supply requirements of these world-class companies (for further discussion, see Hayes and Pisano, 1994; and Scott et al., 1996). For those suppliers and sub-contractors which remain on the supplier list of the prime contractors and which survive the transition, distinct benefits may accrue in the form of increased orders and the attainment of a more consistent, predictable and relatively stable business environment. Those suppliers who fail to make the grade will have no choice but to contract, seek alternative markets or even terminate their operations.

Even for the survivors, the high degree of specialisation often necessary to succeed in a niche market left them more vulnerable than ever to over-reliance on a sole customer, market or, indeed, product. This dependence—in the context of a very volatile and uncertain future defence market—must be considered high-risk business scenario especially as, in the late 1990s, a further phase of supply network restructuring is imminent and, once again, large defence companies plan to shed a significant number of their current suppliers. While explicable in terms of future market projections and the need to continually demand ever greater productivity performance from their suppliers, renewed supply chain contraction now appears somewhat surprising in the light of recent problems besetting the defence (and especially the aerospace) industry. Prime contractors in both the US and Europe have found difficulty at times in finding sufficient suppliers to meet current demand. There is a feeling frequently expressed by senior executives of many defence prime contractors that their original supply base was cut back too severely in the immediate post-Cold War period with the consequence that several important supply sources have since gone out of business and are not available, therefore, when needed.

Those suppliers able and willing to secure a 'preferred' supplier or 'partnership' relationship with a major defence contractor have, in turn, had to bear the burden of corporate adaptation to meet their partner's requirements. In particular, such favoured suppliers will have to guarantee their ability to meet specific delivery and quality performance targets and, simultaneously, achieve significant price reduction over time through enhanced efficiency. This requires significant changes in terms of behaviour and attitude from both the buyer and the supplier, with both needing to become better acquainted with each other's business. The evolving relationship will only be successful if the buyer and seller can operate together on the basis of shared aims, implicit trust, full co-operation, a joint effort to problem-solve and a complete recognition of their mutual inter-dependency for survival and business success.

This 'co-makership' approach—a term attributed to the Phillips Group to identify this new buyer-seller relationship—clearly raises issues of potential vertical collusion between 'partners' or 'preferred suppliers' and the 'parent' company. It also raises the potential problem that, in the new industrial order, the development of the 'co-makership' approach and associated supplier development activities suggests that the buying firm has no option but to assist suppliers fulfil their required production, cost and quality objectives, even though this activity may be to the advantage of a competitor.

It is important, therefore, to recognise that the process of intensifying supplier linkages within the defence industry supply network, while undoubtedly generating positive economic benefits, will also carry with it significant potential costs. In particular, the costs of actually initiating a partnership, the potential for loss of intellectual property rights due to the 'openness' of such partnerships; and the costs encountered in attempting to manage the changes to be anticipated in introducing such a new business arrangement appear significant. Such costs, of course, have to be borne by companies, both primes and suppliers, at a time when the market is scarcely moving in their favour (for further discussion, see Miles and Snow, 1992).

In the new business relationships that emerge, the focus of attention will shift from contract price towards cost and profit. As the Department of Trade and Industry put it in 1992, 'the whole approach is characterised by market price minus rather than supplier cost plus.' If such industrial supplier-prime partnerships are to become successful long-term relationships, prime contractors will have appreciate the need for their key supply partners to be profitable to protect their viability and in order to maintain levels of investment commensurate with the maintenance of high quality output at the lowest possible cost. With primes resisting price increases for their supplies, the implication must be that, to achieve an acceptable margin of profitability without increasing price, suppliers have no choice but to reduce their costs. At the same time, to achieve and secure high standards in supplier performance, the prime contractors will demand the application of rigorous quality and delivery performance ratings as effective organisational monitoring mechanisms. DTI (1992) notes that:

> 'In its ultimate form the approach starts with a target market price for sales success of the product and target profits for buyer and seller. Both parties then seek to achieve the cost, quality and other improvements needed to hit these targets. Partners work together, sharing information and ideas; often with suppliers involved as members of the design team from the start. Suppliers are selected and assessed on their potential as long term partners. Price, quality and delivery performance still form part of the assessment, but other factors such as the suppliers' quality systems and approach to quality, their ability to plan and project manage change, to continuously improve— their whole management philosophy—can often carry more weight.'

This evolving relationship between the major defence companies and their principal suppliers in the first tier of the supply network has perceived benefits, well-documented for other industrial sectors (Anderson and Narus, 1991, pp. 95–113). In particular, the process of supplier approval via advanced business monitoring techniques confers financial stability and certainty upon the relationship. For both partners, prime contractors vetting ensures that product quality standards and delivery schedule requirements will be satisfied and that the supplier/subcontractor operates in a more stable business environment.

THE BARRIERS TO CHANGE

This book is primarily concerned with identifying and exploring crucial elements of defence market adjustment to declining military expenditure in the pursuit of a peace dividend route to enhanced prosperity. During the course of the UWE, Bristol research programme on the adjustment process of defence industry supply base, a number of 'barriers to change' were highlighted which appear likely to impede the smooth and rapid market response required for the attainment of the peace dividend.

At one level, where a defence supply company considers a diversification strategy, the barrier may actually be the perceived costs and, perhaps, the fear of leaving an industry. As Ponsford and Kendry note:

> 'Barriers to exit (from the defence industry) are considerable and include inexperience in commercial marketing; emphasis on product rather than process innovations; a hierarchy of skills and a technological orientation determined by the weapons-system acquisition process; a production structure defined by large-scale systems integration and protected markets through government procurement.'

More particularly, seven specific 'barriers' stand out as potentially serious obstacles to successful market-based transition and, therefore, call into question the efficacy of the market system at the supplier level, unaided, to deliver a meaningful peace dividend. These seven barriers to change include: asset specificity; financial constraints; managerial and cultural inertia; exclusivity of buyer-seller relationships and intellectual property rights; the apparent likelihood of congestion of 'escape routes'; and information gaps, including what might be termed 'problem recognition inability', and the possibility of evolving defence industry market structure generating demand for government-led anti-trust action. It is argued that these factors represent significant barriers to change and result in a combination of market imperfections that call into question the ability of market forces to act effectively as the co-ordinating mechanism within the defence industry supply network.

ASSET SPECIFICITY

Douma and Schreuder in 1991 defined asset specificity as follows:

> 'An asset is transactions specific if it cannot be redeployed to an alternative use without a significant reduction in the value of the asset. Asset specificity may refer to physical or to human assets.'

Clearly, then, the attainment of the required flexibility, necessary to ensure survival for the defence firm, will vary according to the extent of the organisation's degree of asset or resource specificity. For many of the defence contractors interviewed by the research team, the nature of the market they serve and the products and services they bring to that market, necessitate specialisation in terms of both factor inputs and many of the production processes. Plant and machinery used in the development, production and testing areas are commonly very specialised (e.g. very high tolerance levels that are specific to the defence industry and its associated quality standards). Similarly, personnel employed by defence contractors are often specialists in techniques appropriate to designing, manufacturing, and testing activities within defence firms. This specialisation in human capital permeates the commercial functions as well in, for example, contract negotiation, procurement and, for those supply companies able to afford them, marketing departments, which are commonly populated by defence industry specialists—indeed, the research team found that often the staff in these departments are ex-military personnel.

In other resource areas the degree of asset specificity is less significant. While some defence contractors occupy land and buildings that are specialised e.g. dockyards, the majority of organisations interviewed by the research team do not. Similarly, the administrative and finance sections were not found to be significantly defence specific. The research showed clearly that for certain defence contractors, high levels of asset specificity constitute a significant barrier to change and effectively close some 'escape routes' completely. For many defence contractors, asset specificity means that the frequently advocated conversion to civilian production route is simply not an economically viable option.

However, one of the potentially beneficial consequences of high asset specificity is that it encourages companies in the industry to form close, stable links and thereby reduce the potential for damage that might arise from the combative conduct prevalent in traditional 'adversarial' buyer-seller relationships. Asset specificity in defence firms, then, is both encouraging the growth of these intermediate relationships that exist somewhere between the organisation and the market, but at the same time such specificity can retard organisational flexibility so necessary in accommodating the change the defence market is experiencing. Clearly the role of new technology is central here. Advanced manufacturing techniques, such as Flexible Manufacturing Systems (FMS) and Computer Integrated Manufacture (CIM), can greatly reduce the degree of asset specificity and enhance corporate flexibility. The cost of introducing such systems may, however, be prohibitive, particularly where supply companies confront a declining market and find that their access to the required business capital diminishes accordingly.

FINANCIAL LIMITATIONS

Given the scale and pace of change in the defence industry and the degree of corporate strategic adjustment required, it is difficult to see how suppliers and sub-contractors who wish to reduce their defence-dependency are going to be able to finance the transition to a less defence-orientated mode of operation. For an interesting assessment of the financial condition of defence companies in the mid-1990s, see Bowlin, (1995). As the defence market declines, the major defence contractors will be compelled to reduce their orders from the supply companies and may have to extend credit arrangements with suppliers, generating a potential cash flow problem further down the supply chain. In the UK, recent legislation allowing small and medium-sized enterprises to charge interest significantly above base rate on invoices that have not been paid on time may help to ease the cash flow problem to some extent. For those that remain entrenched in the defence market, it has already been noted that major defence companies are expecting their key suppliers to both upgrade their supply performance in a number of critical areas and bear an increasing proportion of the costs and risks associated with research and development expenditure in the future.

It is difficult to see how some supply companies, already suffering damage through their high degree of defence-dependency, are going to be persuaded that it is worth bearing the risks of increasing that dependence when confronted with the prospects of uncertain returns in a declining market. The UWE, Bristol survey findings revealed considerable concern among supply companies in lower tiers of the network about the difficulty of persuading financiers of the merits of the required investment and the requisite commitment by these financiers to what is perceived to be a long period of adjustment in an environment of high risk and uncertainty.

The significance of the financial dimension of supply chain rigidity is accentuated by the observation that one of the key strategies to be adopted by major defence contractors in order to maximise their competitive position in the future defence market will be to seek risk-sharing investment projects with key 'partner' suppliers and sub-contractors. As Ponsford and Kendry have noted:

> 'In seeking a balance between the demands of hierarchy and market—the signature tune of the new economics of organisation—the development of 'partnership sourcing' implies a move to quasi-vertical integration in production, enabling the prime contractor to offload some of the costs of the new production environment to second- and lower-tier firms.'

In such a situation, it must be debatable whether many of these lower tier firms will find themselves in a position to afford the changes necessary for them to enter into partnership sourcing arrangements.

MANAGERIAL AND CULTURAL INERTIA

As discussed above, one aspect of asset specificity within defence companies is the specialised nature of some of their human capital. More particularly here, however, the focus is on management's role as either a facilitator or inhibitor of change. As previously stated, many key personnel working in departments within defence contractors that have direct contact with domestic or overseas military procurement officials were formerly employed by the military or the ministry/department of defence. In selling to traditional markets, this was an undeniably wise approach since such personnel, as well as having the requisite practical skills to perform the job well, can also bring to bear an ability to empathise with the other party in the transaction process as a result of shared experiences and familiarity with 'protocol'.

In the new environment, however, particularly where a company may be seeking to diversify or convert its production from defence to civil markets, these very same personnel may themselves constitute a significant barrier to change for the defence firm as it explores the various options available to it when planning future strategy.

The reorientation of production to meet the needs of alternative, non-military markets requires an expertise all of its own and is likely to require appropriately skilled and experienced personnel to deliver successful transition. Some existing personnel, often in senior positions within the company, may not have the appropriate skills nor, indeed, the required breadth of vision, to effect such a strategy.

Additionally, at a less individual level, defence firms themselves often develop an organisational culture quite distinct from that of non-defence firms. The origins of many of the cultural traits can be traced to the pricing mechanism that dominated the industry for so long—that of cost-plus pricing. Although the cost-plus environment of defence manufacture has long since been eroded by governments pursuing value-for-money in public spending, this long-standing original pricing approach, coupled with an environment of relatively short production runs and the requirement to deliver leading edge technologies, engendered a culture that still exists and which is quite different to that of the non-defence world, constituting a significant barrier to change for defence manufacturing firms. Porter (1985) refers to two generic strategies open to an organisation seeking to achieve or maintain competitive advantage, namely, the 'lowest-cost producer' strategy and the 'product differentiation' strategy. Despite a decade and a half of procurement reform, the culture that still seems to be widespread in defence firms is not one which naturally focuses upon lowest cost as a primary target. If Porter is correct, this severely restricts the range of strategic options available to the defence firm as it tries to adjust under market pressures to accommodate the changing business environment.

EXCLUSIVITY OF BUYER-SELLER RELATIONSHIPS AND INTELLECTUAL PROPERTY RIGHTS

From the discussion above, it appears that small and medium-sized enterprises that wish to remain in the lower tiers of the defence industry supply network will have little option but to attempt to secure a 'partnership' or 'preferred supplier' relationship with a major defence contractor. Having achieved this status and the concomitant benefit of apparent market security (and borne the costs of attaining such status, for example achieving ISO and BS quality ratings in the UK), the company may well experience problems in securing similar arrangements with other potential partners. The issue of the 'leaching' of intellectual property rights to an existing competitor through a supplier linkage becomes particularly significant where one company becomes involved in contractual arrangements with more than one major partner.

Furthermore, a downstream organisation (or principal) in an open, trusting partnership relationship may also fear opportunistic behaviour on the part of a supplier as highlighted by Thoburn and Takashima (1993) reporting evidence from extensive field research:

> 'Some British principals, however, especially in electronics, still fear transferring technology to sub-contractors in case those sub-contractors subsequently set up as rivals.'

Reliance on just one business partner, however successful, can create a degree of dependence which, in the event of business failure or decline at the higher level, would also put the supplier out of business. A number of UWE Bristol survey respondents indicated to the research team that, having to choose between these two approaches, 'partnerships plus dependence' against a wider array of supply links without formal partnerships, the latter would be preferred as it would enhance the potential for market access across a wider range of business areas and remove at least some of the critical problem of over-dependence from which many companies surveyed had already suffered.

CONGESTION OF 'ESCAPE ROUTES'

For the market mechanism to provide a smooth and rapid resolution of the problems for defence supply companies emanating from declining defence expenditure and enable resources to be quickly and effectively transferred from defence to civil production, many of the suppliers will themselves have to seek urgently new market opportunities, within or without defence.

There are three main strategic options available, one or more of which they may decide to include within their evolving corporate strategies. First, companies may attempt to replace lost domestic defence business with enhanced defence export sales. Secondly, there is the increasing opportunity to establish trans-national joint ventures, strategic alliances and other forms of international collaboration. In essence, this is an extension to the partnership approach outlined earlier, except that in this instance different forms of industrial partnership are considered with a much wider geographic focus. Finally, in an attempt to insulate themselves as far as possible from the contractionary consequences of a declining defence market, companies may attempt to access new non-defence customers through a strategy of diversification.

In this respect, the suppliers will be following the pattern set by the prime defence contractors, discussed in the last chapter, most of whom are pursuing similar examples of such strategies, increasingly on a global stage. Increasing the export of defence goods is, however, increasingly difficult at supplier level. International arms sales are usually secured by the large corporations, frequently assisted by government, and suppliers have tended to simply follow their large customers in such circumstances. Some smaller defence industry suppliers do transact a large proportion of their business in the international market directly and certainly, in the last few years, the US prime contractors (especially aerospace companies such as Boeing and Lockheed Martin) have shown much greater interest in working with European suppliers. In part, this reflects the need to seek out new and reliable, quality suppliers as, in the deep recession of the early 1990s, many such companies perished with the contraction in their market. There is some evidence that those smaller US defence supply companies that survived the rigours of market conditions in the 1990s have enjoyed considerable success (Defense News, 1998, p. 20), enhancing their attractiveness as potential industrial partners to the prime contractors.

In the future, it is unlikely that defence markets around the world will ever regain the buoyancy of the peak years of the Cold War and, at reduced levels of demand, will move more towards highly versatile, durable, easily maintained and competitively priced equipment with upgrade capabilities. Supplier companies that can redirect their products and services to meet the needs of this evolving market will survive the transition and may, indeed, achieve growth in market share. For the majority of companies, however, diversification and conversion opportunities may offer the only realistic opportunity for survival. The issue of diversification and conversion, as well as the research, development and technological dimensions associated with such strategies, will be addressed more fully in the next chapter. However, a few points are relevant here.

In the UWE Bristol study, post-Cold War corporate strategies of a sample of 60 first-tier suppliers located in the highly defence-dependent southwest region of the UK were analysed. The results suggested that as many as 75% had already diversified into non-defence markets by 1992 or were attempting to do so. Many of these companies found great difficulty in accessing new markets, with the greatest degree of success apparently enjoyed where the market shift was one of 'pseudo-diversification' into an activity area closely related to the defence sector. Perhaps the most obvious alternative market being explored here is civil aerospace but others included new markets in supplying coastguard operations and land-based power generation.

At one level, it appears that the problem with achieving successful diversification has much to do with the difficulty of transferring resources and systems within organisations and also with the issue of the potential clash of 'cultures' as personnel and plant are redeployed from military to civilian production. At another level, however, the issue of market 'credibility' becomes significant. For some companies, diversification only appeared possible into areas of 'proven expertise' which effectively meant limiting new market search to 'diversification on the periphery' of the defence business.

Most defence supply companies are likely to confront similar challenges in this respect in the future and, as this process continues and expands to include most other defence contractors pursuing similar business search patterns, the 'periphery' is likely to become somewhat congested. Market saturation will, inevitably, mean that some new entrants will not secure the alternative business they require and, furthermore, will be driven into new, relatively unexplored and high risk areas of activity—or, alternatively, will have no choice but to drastically contract their operations.

INFORMATION GAPS AND THE RECOGNITION OF A PROBLEM

The power and potency of market forces in bringing about an appropriate reallocation of resources, smoothly and rapidly, away from the declining defence sector and into activities which take advantage of emerging market opportunities, critically depends upon the quantity and quality of information available to key decision-makers. For the market to work perfectly it is necessary that 'the price mechanism is a perfect channel of information to all parties interested in transacting' (Douma and Schreuder, 1991). At the most fundamental level, for the market to work efficiently, all the players in the game have to be fully aware of the likely impact of reduced defence expenditure upon their business activities and, therefore, of the urgent necessity of revisions to corporate strategy.

The UWE Bristol survey of defence industry suppliers found that, among the defence supplier companies interviewed, such market awareness was by no means as extensive as may be imagined. The conclusion must be that the potential for a market-clearing process being able to resolve the transition from a Cold War economy is and will be severely constrained. Furthermore, the dis-equilibrium that may result will have an unavoidable impact upon the capacity of the defence firm in the future to function effectively, especially in a national context.

The research found that many companies in the defence supply network, especially those located in the lower tiers, while aware of the existing and impending decline in defence expenditure, were frequently unaware of the extent of their own defence exposure. For some companies surveyed in the early 1990s, the impact of declining defence expenditure appeared to be a somewhat remote issue and of little direct strategic significance for themselves. As a result, it can be argued that decision-makers in these firms may form more optimistic expectations of their future business and conduct corporate strategy accordingly than is warranted by the reality of the situation. The outcome may be a much sharper, cumulative and unanticipated decline in demand for their output than they expect, thereby limiting their capacity to plan for and absorb such a negative shock.

There is considerable evidence that, in the lower tiers of the defence industry supply network, recognition by defence firms of the end market for the products of their immediate customers is quite limited. Many companies operating as third and fourth tier suppliers to the defence industry seem genuinely unaware that their products or services were part of the output of the defence industry, since their concern as a quality supplier is only with the company they are dealing with, usually in the next highest tier of the supply network.

The UWE Bristol research proved to be quite revealing in this respect. From survey interviews conducted with senior executives of 120 suppliers to a major UK defence company, against the background of the early 1990s UK defence cuts, it was noted that only 30% of companies in the second tier and beyond expected a reduction in their business from supply chain customers, failing to recognise that many of them were located directly in the supply chains of not one, but several, major defence companies. Even more striking, members of the research team were often asked, during these survey interviews, why the company was included in the survey since: 'we have nothing to do with defence'. Surprisingly, confronted with a hypothetical reduction in business of 50% from their first-tier defence supply customer, almost 90% of second- and lower-tier companies surveyed anticipated little impact on their business. As their customer base was explored in more detail during the survey interviews, it became apparent that such lower-tier companies, in fact, were unknown to themselves part of different supply chains leading to a considerable number of major defence contractors. The attitude and approach of these survey respondents to the survey itself then changed significantly as a result of this 'problem recognition' with a much enhanced willingness to participate.

At this point, serious concern was usually expressed by senior managers participating in the survey as the prospect of a sudden, simultaneous reduction in demand from a number of different defence-related end-customers was noted, with its potentially devastating (and perhaps catastrophic) consequences for the company. Furthermore, the research revealed that a great many companies located in the lower tiers of the defence supply network not only supplied, indirectly, a significant number of major defence contractors, so increasing their exposure to defence cuts, but they also supplied other first tier suppliers across a number of inter-locking supply chains. For many supplier companies, their unrecognised exposure to cumulative reductions in demand from established defence contractors were, in fact, extremely high and, uninformed and therefore ill-prepared to respond effectively, such companies rapidly became financially vulnerable. It was precisely for this kind of reason that so many small and medium-sized enterprises, engaged in defence supply, ceased trading during the 1990s, having been devastated by a market downturn that few had accurately predicted or even anticipated.

The diagram below illustrates the point and is based upon a real-world survey-based situation. It indicates how a company in the defence industry supply network may be adversely affected in several ways simultaneously and rapidly as a result of the interdependencies of that network, possibly leading to cumulative collapse.

In Diagram 2 below, a situation is illustrated in which Company A's exposure to defence contraction may, in reality, be far greater than it perceives. Company A may deal directly with the Ministry of Defence in which case it will experience direct impact from reduced orders from the government. It may also be a first tier supplier in the supply

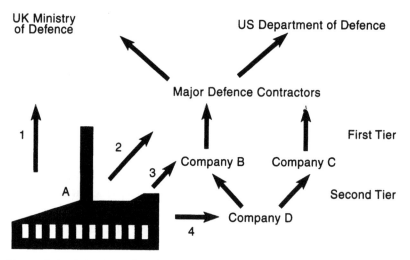

Diagram 2. Supply Matrix Interdependencies.

chain of a major defence contractor where, again, the direct effects of reduced orders will be obvious.

However, Company A may also appear lower down in the supply chain of another defence sub-contractor, Company B, which is itself experiencing the impact of reduced military expenditure and, therefore, possibly reducing its orders from its own suppliers.

As defence spending declines and prime contractors reduce their market demands, this will set in motion a 'chain reaction' of reduced demand. The process is complicated further by the fact that Company A also supplies Company D which appears in the supply chain of another defence sub-contractor/supplier, Company C. At this level, it is quite unlikely that Company A would envisage any connection with defence expenditure in its dealings with Company D and may be totally unaware of the defence-dependent nature of the relationship between Company D and the two first-tier suppliers, Company B and Company C.

It is critically important to recognise that this somewhat complex supply matrix actually understates significantly the true complexity of 'real world' inter-locking supply network relationships. Once we expand the customer base of these network companies to include all of the defence contractors they supply, the degree of interdependency becomes both more acute and yet also perhaps less apparent to any small company by itself, operating in its own market niche.

What can we conclude from this? The complex inter-dependency of the defence industry supply matrix clearly has implications for the economic impact of defence cuts on the industry in general and specific companies within it. Many companies will be far more exposed to declining defence expenditure than they anticipate and will be likely to pick up and respond to 'false signals' in the marketplace. Recent improvements in information flow to major defence contractors from government in the UK about the future trend in defence expenditure over time may appear to offer suppliers the necessary time and scope for adjusting their businesses gradually towards a new market equilibrium. However, the degree to which such enhanced information then flows down the supply chain to lower tier suppliers is questionable and the research suggests that supplier inter-dependency may, in some instances, lead to a decline in business appearing extremely rapidly and from several different directions at once. As a result, there will undoubtedly be casualties amongst defence supply network companies in this swift and unexpected market adjustment, the consequences of which may fundamentally change the nature, scope and efficiency of the network itself and of the firms contained within it. As in so many instances, the market mechanism certainly operates, fundamentally changing the economic outcome, but in this instance does so to the detriment of the industry, particularly at the level of small-and medium-sized enterprises, eroding both the current prosperity and future prospects of this critically important sector upon which so much of the potential for generating a real future peace dividend depends.

ANTI-TRUST ACTIONS

In the discussion above about barriers to change in the defence industry supplier base, those considered so far are essentially endogenous to the defence firm or supply network. Other barriers exist, however, that may be imposed on the defence firm or supply network from outside. Such barriers could include national and trans-national government policies which focus upon (a) the macro-economy (through defence budgets and macroeconomic climate), (b) regional policy (reversing industrial decline or limiting regional expansion) and (c) industrial policy (accelerative or decelerative; targeted at a firm or an industry/sector) or competition policy.

In particular, it is competition policy which might introduce new barriers to change that would limit the degree to which the defence supply market can respond as required. The very partnership arrangements highlighted above (and supported for the most part in the 1990s by government) which offer suppliers a possible 'teaming' solution to their difficulties inevitably raise concern of a restrictive practice/anti-trust nature.

Kay (1991), referring to the industry-wide migration towards new intermediate forms of vertical relationships, commented that 'many of these vertical relationships are viewed with considerable suspicion by anti-trust and regulatory authorities, as is vertical integration in general'. If the partnership arrangement is viewed as a deliberate distortion of the market, essentially representing a kind of 'vertical collusion', then the potential for legislation in this area must increase and therefore curtail, once more, the list of available strategies open to defence firms in the future.

If the motivation behind what has been called 'quasi-vertical integration' is increased security in, or enhanced control of, the market environment, upstream integration by one major company (effectively locking in its suppliers) can put competitors at a competitive disadvantage as their choice of suppliers is then reduced. Of even greater concern to anti-trust legislators, such a development could result in the competitor having to buy inputs off the upstream part of the new quasi-vertically integrated firm. Where upstream quasi-vertical integration allows one contractor to consume all of an essential or important input the market will be fundamentally distorted and, similarly, for downstream integration with distributive outlets.

Such examples of partnership integration raise questions about the degree to which a particular market may or may not be contestable, given that such arrangements confront competitors with very effective entry barriers. Firms considering entering markets where essential input suppliers and sub-contractors are already tied into exclusive partnership sourcing arrangements can only hope to compete effectively if they, themselves, can operate on similar terms i.e. as integrated or quasi-integrated organisations. This necessity both stimulates and perpetuates oligopolistic behaviour and clearly further concentrates market power, leading to more market failure.

In the transition to the post-Cold War economy and the possible attainment of a peace dividend, the impact of changing market conditions upon companies operating in the supplier base of the defence industry and their response—will play a significant part in determining the outcome. In the highly competitive, cost-conscious world of defence manufacturing in the late 1990s, the degree of success or failure of the defence firm now critically depends upon the success or failure of the supporting upstream supply network.

Corporate flexibility emerges as the key issue, not just flexibility at the level of the individual firm but for the entire network. Within the network, each company's strategic planning must take into account the flexibility of the surrounding network, particularly the upstream section. The survival of each company will often be affected by the survival of others in the network, especially those upstream and, in turn, will affect the survival of others, especially those downstream. In essence, then, we have a 'matrix of interdependencies' in the defence industry and the survival of such a matrix in a declining defence market will inevitably be a function of it's flexibility.

As we have seen, however, the paradox is that this flexibility is diminished by the nature of the matrix itself and by the fact that the market is in decline. In summary, then, this essential flexibility—the key to successful market adjustment—is inhibited in the contracting defence industry by:

i) existing high levels of asset specificity, heightened even further by the emergence of new forms of quasi-vertical relationships which encourage specialisation and thereby create additional asset specificity.

ii) Declining orders intensify pressure upon suppliers and sub-contractors and act as incentives for them to accept increased risk-sharing in the emerging new buyer-seller relationships while, at the same time, reducing the financial ability of these companies to invest in processes and technologies that will provide them with the flexibility they require.

iii) the existence of particular, deep-rooted organisational cultures that have developed over time in the defence industry which inhibit change.

iv) the emergence of 'partnership sourcing', quasi-vertical integration or single sourcing corporate strategies which directly suppress flexibility through exclusivity and may raise concerns about the leaching of intellectual property rights.

v) the congestion of 'escape routes' as many defence industry suppliers seek to expand their business opportunities beyond the defence market and do so in similar market niches at the same time. Such congestion certainly constrains flexibility through the effective shortening of the list of strategic options.

vi) information flows and perceived market signals may be far from perfect in this complex matrix; as a result, many company responses are likely to be misjudged or simply inadequate. The potential for a sub-optimal market outcome is consequently increased significantly.

vii) the evolving matrix relationships may be viewed suspiciously by anti-trust legislators which, if they become subject to anti-trust/restrictive practice legislation, again potentially shortens the list of available strategic options.

It should be clear from the above discussion that economic analysts are only just beginning to understand the real nature of supply chain inter-dependencies and their significance for the future of the defence industry. The events of the last few years have focused attention at last on a much-neglected area for research. Indeed, as Bingaman noted:

> 'One of our great failings in the last several years has been that the DoD has never seen itself as needing the kind of in- depth understanding of industrial base that we clearly do need at this stage of our history. We cannot just shut down many weapon systems, many production lines, and plan to reconstitute that capability down the road if we don't even know what the capability was to start with.'

Such an 'in-depth understanding of the industrial base' is unlikely to flow from existing theoretical frameworks which remain largely trapped by neo-classical terminology, models and rhetoric and much greater emphasis in the future needs to be placed upon a better understanding of the flexible network in the defence supply industry. This is particularly important as the failure to capture adequately the diffusion effects of the subcontract and supply network on defence spending at the regional level has often invalidated attempts to forecast regional impact. The tendency to focus principally on prime contractors in analysing defence industry response to change and to omit such a significant supplier network response may serve to create a false impression of the actual situation. Lovering (1993) commented, for example that:

> 'Official estimates of the geographical distribution of the defence industry relate only to a third of estimated total employment in the defence industry, omitting sub-contractors, suppliers, and non-equipment producers. this overstates the bias towards southern England, although it has been ignored in most commentaries.'

Despite recent contraction in global defence expenditure, the defence industry continues to play an important strategic role in the regional economies of many nations. This role can only be maintained if the supplier base and its technological capabilities remain relatively intact and receive support to enable it to undergo a smooth and rapid transformation to the requirements of the new business environment. Such support may include innovations in facilitating access to long-term investment and a more constructive exchange of information within and between different tiers of the supply network and with government.

Without such support (particularly from government with respect to the need to preserve a range of critical technologies during the contraction of the defence industry), the supply chain is likely to experience rapid and uncoordinated fragmentation with serious economic consequences, especially at the regional level. As Lovering noted in 1993:

> 'the dismantling of the Cold War industrial order is precipitating massive job losses without leading to equivalent gains in non-military sectors ... More fundamentally, the contraction of the defence industry is not simply a matter of the industry modernising itself, cutting down on excess capacity and reducing waste. The restructuring is leading to concentration, internationalisation, commodification, and a change in the articulation of the defence sector with the rest of the economy.'

However, as is made clear in a new study of the defence/aerospace supplier base of the southwest region of the UK published in 1999, for those companies remaining as suppliers to the defence industry, their dependency and vulnerability appears as great as ever. In this study, a large number of companies in the aerospace and defence industry supply chain in the southwest region have been surveyed to identify areas of strength and weakness which exist in skills, accreditations and certifications; technical resources, products and services and establish their current dependency on the defence/aerospace primes The study was undertaken by a partnership between Business Link West (South Gloucestershire), the Research Unit in Defence Economics at the University of the West of England, Bristol, the Regional Supply Office, the West of England Aerospace Forum and the Defence Contractors Network. Business Link West, through WESTEC (the Western Training and Enterprise Council), bid for and won support from the European Social Fund, Objective 4 for this research project.

A detailed questionnaire was distributed to 350 supplier companies in the southwest region with 91 companies returning the questionnaire. This satisfactory response rate of 26% is in line with most postal questionnaires. Of the 91 respondents, 69 companies provided complete information, while the remaining 22 companies provided varying levels of response.

The survey revealed that:

i) More than three-fifths of companies responding to the survey depend upon the aerospace/defence business for more than 30% of their annual turnover. This both underlines the continuing significance of the aerospace/defence sector to the region's economy and serves to highlight the potential vulnerability of the region and its constituent companies to the changing fortunes of this sector.

ii) Interestingly, more than three-fifths of the survey companies were involved in the export market, with two-fifths exporting within Europe and one quarter exporting to the USA.

iii) Almost all survey companies had achieved ISO and/or BS qualifications while very few had achieved TS 157 or FAR qualifications, implying that over the last few years, a considerable effort has been made by suppliers to meet he increasing quality and other demands of their customers.

iv) Both regionally and nationally, the survey responses indicated a significant degree of supplier dependency, with numerous examples of companies sharing the same supplier. There was also limited sample evidence of critical suppliers appearing in the supply lists of more than one company.

v) Both at the regional and national level, similarly, survey responses indicated that several companies supplied one or more of the same customers. The survey revealed that one South West customer had as many as 24 of the surveyed companies in their supply list.

vi) Critically, the survey revealed that, of the sample, as many as 29 companies depended upon one key customer or supplier for more than 30% of their annual turnover or procurement spend. 18 of these were in the two lowest turnover categories, underlining again their potential vulnerability.

vii) The survey provided limited evidence of the existence of co-operative links in the South West region with approximately one-fifth of respondents indicating involvement in such initiatives.

viii) Analysing the materials used in the region's aerospace/defence production suggested the versatility of the supply chain in the variety of materials processed, often by the same company. Similarly, analysing regional capabilities emphasised the wide range of specialist skills and facilities within the region. Finally, analysing regional aerospace/defence product suppliers revealed an emphasis towards mechanical engineering skills, especially in, for example, hydraulics, engine system parts, airframe components, fastenings and tooling.

The evaluation of responses to the southwest region aerospace/defence supply chain mapping initiative indicates the need for regional support in this sector. In particular, regional support is required with a view to enhancing business performance in the supply chain through up-skilling and awareness training to improve the opportunities available to small and medium-sized enterprises.

CONCLUSION

The revolution sweeping through the defence industry supply chain is now a global phenomenon and one which poses both significant opportunities and considerable threats to the supplier base of the industry. While out-sourcing by prime contractors has grown dramatically over the last decade, these same companies are cutting drastically the number of smaller and medium-sized enterprises that will operate in future in their supply chains, while extending their geographic catchment area for suppliers on a global scale. Prime contractors are now seeking partnership arrangements with key suppliers who can deliver the quality and technological edge they require to compete in international markets. In the shake-out of the defence industry supply chain, many small- and medium-sized enterprises which formerly enjoyed a close business relationship with the prime contractors will perish, and those which survive will have to confront the challenges of greater dependency on both the primes and the industry itself in the future.

Perhaps more than any other element of economic transformation following the end of the Cold War, what ultimately happens to the supply matrix underpinning the defence prime contractors will be critical to the successful outcome of their strategies for defence market success or, as we will explore in Chapter 5, for conversion to alternative markets. In many respects, the revolution in the supply base of the defence industry has scarcely commenced and the companies engaged in this sector will ignore these new challenges and opportunities at their peril.

REFERENCES

Anderson and Narus, (1991), Partnering as a Focused Market Strategy, *California Management Review*, Spring 1991, pp. 95–112.

Bingaman J., cited in Jane's Defence Weekly, 20th March 1993.

Bowlin W. F., (1995), A Note on the Financial Condition of Defence Contractors, *Defence and Peace Economics*, Vol. 6, pp. 295–304.

Braddon D. L., (1996), The Regional Dimension of Defence Economics: An Introduction, *Defence and Peace Economics*, Vol. 7.

Braddon D. L., Cullen P., Dowdall P. G. and Kendry A. P., (1991), The Impact of Reduced Military Expenditure on the Economy of southwest England, Research Unit in Defence Economics Report, Bristol Polytechnic HEC, May.

Braddon D. L., Dowdall P. G., Kendry A. P. and Reay S., (1992), Defence Procurement and the Defence Industry Supply Chain, Research Unit in Defence Economics Report, Bristol Polytechnic HEC, March.

Braddon D. L. and Dowdall P. G., (1996), 'Flexible Networks and the Restructuring of the Regional Defence Industrial Base: The Case of southwest England', *Defence and Peace Economics*, Vol. 7.

Cohen S. S. and Garcia C. E., (1994), California's Missile Gap, *California Management Review*, Vol. 37, No. 1, Fall

Department of Trade and Industry, (1992), *Managing in the '90s*, DTI, London.

Douma S. and Schreuder H., (1992), *Economic Approaches to Organisations*, Prentice Hall International.

Dowdall P. G. and Braddon D. L., (1994), Puppets and Partners: The Defence Industry Supply Chain in Perspective, in Latham A. and Hooper N., (eds), *The Future of the Defence Firm*, Dordrecht.

Hayes R. H. and Pisano G. P., (1994), Beyond World-Class: The New Manufacturing Strategy, *Harvard Business Review*, January-February.

Hooper N. and Buck D., (1990), Defence Industries and Equipment Procurement Options, in Kirby S. and Hooper N. (eds) *The Cost of Peace: Assessing Europe's Security Options*, Harwood Academic Publishers, Chapter 6, pp. 107–140.

Kay J. A., (1991), Managing Relationships with Customers and Suppliers: Law, Economics and Strategy, *Business Strategy Review*, Spring.

Latham A.,(1995), The Structural Transformation of the US Defence Firm: Changes in Manufacturing Technology, Production Process, and Principles of Corporate Organisation, in (eds.) Latham A. and Hooper N., *The Future of the Defence Firm: New Challenges, New Directions*, NATO ASI Series, Kluwer Academic Publishers.

Lovering J., (1993), Restructuring the British Defence Industrial Base After the Cold War: Institutional and Geographical Perspectives, *Defence Economics*, Vol. 4., pp. 123–139.

Miles R. E. and Snow C. C., (1992), Causes of Failure in Network Organisations, *California Management Review*, Summer, pp. 53–72.

Partnership Sourcing, (1991), *Partnership Sourcing*, Text Matters.

Ponsford D. and Kendry A. P., (1992), Technology Transfer and Defence Diversification in the Southwest Region, *Proceedings of the Technology Transfer Society*, 17th Annual Meeting Proceedings.

Porter M., (1985), *Competitive Advantage*, The Free Press.

Scott P., Jones B., Bromley A., and Bolton B., (1996), Enhancing Technology and Skills in Small- and Medium-sized Manufacturing Firms: Problems and Prospects, *International Small Business Journal*, April-June, pp. 85–99.

Thoburn J. T. and Takashima M., (1993), Improving British Industrial Performance: Lessons from Japanese Sub-Contracting, *National Westminster Bank Quarterly Review*, February.

Thomson G., Frances J., Levacic R., and Mitchell J., (1991), *Markets, Hierarchies and Networks: The Co-ordination of Social Life*, Sage Publications, London, for the Open University.

Womack J. P. and Jones D. T., (1994), From Lean Production to the Lean Enterprise, *Harvard Business Review*, March-April, pp. 93–103.

Womack J. P. and Jones D. T., (1996), *Lean Thinking: Banish Waste and Create Wealth in Your Corporation*, Simon and Schuster.

Chapter 5

DELAYING THE DIVIDEND: THE CONVERSION CONUNDRUM

INTRODUCTION

In the initial wave of optimism that followed the end of the Cold War at the beginning of the decade of the 1990s, there were heightened expectations of a peace dividend to be attained from the process of disarmament that would surely follow. With a much-reduced demand for military output, a significant proportion of the vast expenditure which had, for so many decades, been absorbed by the resource-hungry military industrial complex could now be redirected to more socially-desirable purposes. In particular, public and political expectations were high concerning the potential for improved public services (education, health, welfare) and for enhanced private civil sector development, especially for civil research and development which, it was argued, had previously been 'crowded out' by high levels of defence expenditure.

The scale of the task confronting such a dividend in alleviating human suffering and acting as a catalyst for human betterment was immense but significant improvements in the global human condition was thought to be possible even with a relatively modest peace dividend. Conversion and diversification of military production facilities and labour force skills to meet the emerging opportunities of civil markets in the post-Cold War global economy was imperative, yet the track record of such resource transfers in the past had hardly been notable for success. This chapter explores the 'conversion conundrum', defines the relevant concepts and examines past experience of attempts to pursue a successful conversion strategy. Initially focusing upon corporate conversion in the West, the chapter then turns to an examination of the conversion process in Russia and considers the obstacles to success in that context. Finally, the issue of military base conversion is explored and the evidence for successful resource transfer in this sector evaluated.

CONVERSION AND DIVERSIFICATION

If the end of the Cold War is to prove to be the catalyst that triggers off a genuine and lasting peace dividend, previously high levels of military expenditure, production and employment will need to be transformed, rapidly and smoothly, into a range of new wealth-generating civil production and employment opportunities, sufficient to absorb the displaced labour and attract new capital investment. In a perfect world, this would mean that those people currently working to research, develop, produce and, when required, use military weapons would cease those activities to a degree commensurate with the decline in demand for their services and immediately switch their labour into alternative wealth-generating activities, employing existing plant and equipment in doing so. Economic dislocation would be avoided, income loss would be minimal and the world would certainly be a more peaceful and perhaps prosperous place.

With a few notable exceptions, however, evidence suggests that attempts to achieve both conversion and diversification from defence-dependency have either ended as complete and very expensive failures or, where they have enjoyed some success, have failed to generate wealth and employment equivalent to that lost through defence sector contraction (see, for example, Blong et al., 1992). In the imperfect world that surrounds us, labour and capital resources do not switch easily between alternative uses, although modern manufacturing techniques are beginning to move the process of production in that direction. The central problem in switching resources out of the defence sector into alternative activities is that, as Sandler and Hartley (1995, p. 284) emphasise, such:

> 'Proposals for direct conversion often ignore the costs involved in discovering and entering new civil markets. Similarly, the fact that resources are valuable in the defence sector does not guarantee their marketability elsewhere in the economy.'

The immediate result of reduced military expenditure is employment loss and it will depend upon the effectiveness of the market and/or the policies put in place by government and their efficacy as to the extent and duration of this employment loss (see Richards, 1991). Nor is it simply a matter of converting the productive assets of the defence industry into generating a peace dividend, however measured. In the context of both the national and regional economy, significant reductions in defence expenditure not only adversely affect defence production and employment in the industrial sector but may also have a damaging impact where military bases either contract or close. For specific communities, where high levels of defence-dependency include local economic reliance on both defence companies and military bases, the conversion and diversification routes to securing a peace dividend may depend on both rapidly accessing alternative industrial market opportunities and, particularly in rural areas, finding appropriate uses for redundant military facilities. Pianta (1990) noted the importance of the variety of institutional actors and policy tools in assisting a specific country such as Italy with conversion and argued strongly for the development of a national conversion strategy. This chapter will explore the vital role of conversion in securing a real and lasting peace dividend.

For decades, economists have explored the potential for economic conversion and/or diversification, both at the plant and community level and, indeed, there have been many instances when conversion strategies were pursued by governments, particularly after the two world wars. Sandler and Hartley (1995) note, for example, the award by the UK government of prefabricated housing building contracts to defence companies after 1945. Some of these companies had also had civil market interests before the war (such as motor vehicle production) and were able to return to these activities almost immediately.

At that time, in the US as well as the UK, diversification and conversion were particularly difficult to achieve as defence companies tended to be highly specialised. Over the ensuing decades, however, a number of defence companies pursued expansionary policies, often taking them into civil markets through acquisition strategies, broadening the base of their production.

Despite their undoubted technological prowess (and even though government support was available), the fact that many of these attempts at corporate diversification ended in comparative failure illustrates the nature of the diversification/conversion problem only too clearly. Sandler and Hartley (1995) refer to a classic example of such failure regarding the Boeing-Vertol company and its plans to switch resources from military transport helicopters to light rail vehicle production after the Vietnam war. Technical problems relating to doors, emergency and maintenance systems and derailment eventually led to Boeing facing a $40 million legal settlement and ultimately leaving the market.

DEFINITIONS

DeGrasse has defined economic conversion as a:

> 'process of adjusting to reductions in defence procurement that involves advanced planning to reuse, for non-military purposes, a substantial percentage of the resources currently deployed for defence production.'

DeGrasse (1987) separates the conversion and diversification dimensions, however, noting that:

> 'it is particularly important to distinguish conversion from corporate diversification, a widely-used business strategy for reducing a firm's reliance on one market or customer. Diversification, an approach for acquiring other firms or developing a new business over an extended time period, does not necessarily involve re-employing people or facilities made redundant by cuts in defence procurement.'

Dumas (1991), similarly, distinguishes between three basic policy approaches in addressing the economic dislocation caused by declining defence expenditure; namely: economic conversion, diversification and community adjustment. Economic conversion is the most thorough approach, involving the retraining and reorientation of defence workers, together with the restructuring of organisations which serve the military sector in order to produce civilian goods and services efficiently. Dumas makes the point that only conversion attempts to:

> 'recoup the largest part of the enormous investment that society has made in the skills of workers that are the labour force and in the facilities and the equipment that are the capital of the military sector.'

For Dumas, diversification 'seeks to minimise the economic stress of transition by reducing economic dependence on the flow of military dollars'. Of critical importance, however, is Dumas's contention that: 'where major military firms have tried to diversify by producing civilian products in their military division without the kind of retraining and restructuring that is at the heart of economic conversion, the results have been disastrous both for the companies and their customers'. (For an interesting discussion of the diversification issue, see Markides, 1997).

The third approach, community adjustment:

> 'involves the provision of financial and other assistance to military-dependent cities and towns to help them over the problems created by base closings, loss of contracts by local military producers, or the need to reintegrate large numbers of discharged military personnel into the local economy.'

Dumas concludes by noting that, of these three approaches, neither community adjustment nor diversification deals directly with the needs of displaced defence employees as they attempt to 'redirect and reshape their skills in preparation for re-employment in efficient civilian economic activity'.

CONVERSION, DIVERSIFICATION AND THE MARKET

Whereas neo-classical economics informs us that the invisible hand of market forces will guide the conversion process most efficiently, a different view is taken by Aeroe (1993) who adopts an approach to conversion which blends together organisational economics and strategy literature. From these two approaches, a firm can be perceived as a function of its core skills and the strategic alliances in which it is involved. Furthermore, technological innovation cannot then be perceived as autonomous or as structurally determined but should be seen as a result of the interaction between the various actors involved including, in the case of the defence sector, government defence ministries and politicians. In the theoretical perspective of conversion developed by Aeroe, the market does not exist a priori but is perceived to be a social institution, maintained and developed by the actors involved with this institution.

One of the significant problems confronting companies as they seek to diversify or convert their production activities is the need to establish a new set of business relationships, both with purchasers and suppliers. In this sense, accessing the market can become an obstacle to a smooth and rapid transition from military to civil production. The new market which a company seeks to enter either already exists or must be created; in either case, the crucial requirements for successful entry are precisely the establishment of these relationships (and the trust that goes with them) and the exchange of relevant information which enables the market to operate efficiently. In taking on the challenge of new market entry, opportunistic entrants will have to recognise, and be able to challenge effectively, existing buyer-seller relationships which may, over the years, have generated a kind of mutual inter-dependency, especially where complex products for major customers are involved.

Consequently, constraints on conversion do not just relate to individual firms but must also be examined in the context of entire production systems, including inter-firm linkages within and between various industrial sectors. This latter perspective is relevant because defence systems include components from a vast range of industries and, as we observed in Chapter 4, incorporate many small and medium-sized enterprises in several tiers or strata of the supply matrix.

Some analysts define conversion to include a wide variety of reactions and strategies not restricted to single firms or factories. Conversion can then be seen as a refocusing from military to civil production through the adaptation of existing military technology, capital and labour force skills—in essence, organic development into new areas of production and markets.

This definition is more all-embracing in that it covers a broader base for the conversion process (technology, capital, skills) and is concerned with the processes associated with production as well as with the product itself. Consequently, the conversion process should not be viewed as simply a plant-by-plant process, in which the existing defence production system is transformed into a civil production system, as suggested by Melman. Conversion may actually necessitate the creation of many new organisational forms and strategies in order to allow successful access to new markets, including extending the scope of production at existing plants to plant closure with subsequent resource reallocation.

In some cases, cost-effective conversion solutions might be rejected or delayed by the application of political power and obstructive socio-cultural norms. Clearly, in considering the success of conversion ventures or in constructing a theoretical framework for successful conversion strategies, not only must economic factors be included but also the range of socio-cultural and political factors need to be incorporated. Chan (1995, p. 53) emphasises this point:

> '...the prospects for a peace dividend in the aftermath of the Cold War are clouded by political incentives and economic interests that may oppose or retard significant military retrenchment. Moreover, the resource savings from any military retrenchment may not necessarily be reallocated fully and efficiently to produce gains in civilian production and productivity. Any such gains are apt to take some time to materialise, whereas the political costs and socio-economic disruption caused by lower military expenditures are likely to be felt more immediately.'

For conversion to be successful, it must maintain or improve firms' competitive advantage in the civil market and, consequently, market demand must drive the process of conversion rather than it being simply the result of existing technological capabilities and configuration of the defence firms. The important point here is that defence technological capabilities are not necessarily those which will give the firm the greatest competitive advantage in civil markets, except perhaps where dual-use technologies can be effectively exploited to facilitate the transition (for further discussion, see OTA, 1993).

It follows that the process of conversion could be assisted by the establishment, at community and/or national level, of facilitating institutions, designed to create an appropriate infrastructure to smooth the conversion process, both with respect to economic and social impacts (for further discussion of the conversion-community-human development issue, see BICC, 1998). Such institutions could be given a remit to seek out and identify new economic opportunities and potential national and global markets, provide or support appropriate employee retraining, and pursue other means of enhancing the prosperity of the region in which the conversion process is being carried out. It is here that there may be a clear role for government to lend their support to the process of dual-use technology development, offering strong military/civil synergies, as a means of stimulating the conversion process and releasing a substantial peace dividend.

In the US, where the conversion issue has been more vigorously pursued (BICC, 1997), it is important to note that it is not only the DoD that influences military technology, dual-use developments and the defence industrial base but also NASA. In 1993, NASA's 6 Regional Technology Transfer Centres were chosen to establish the Technology Access for Product Innovation programme (TAP-IN). TAP-IN was specifically developed to assist companies in accessing and utilising defence-related technologies emanating from the DoD and NASA and also to aid defence-dependent companies access new markets. Between 1993 and 1996, TAP-IN provided assistance on over 6,000 occasions to companies entering new markets and launching new products. TAP-IN also helped companies such as Century Aerospace develop commercial uses for defence technologies, in this case a single engine business turbo jet based on a military design. This is precisely the kind of facilitating institution, mentioned above, that can help drive forward the conversion process and stimulate dual-use solutions. Additionally, in the US, the conversion process remains high up on the political agenda and, in regions where defence cuts have severe economic impact, considerable efforts are made to explore the potential for remedial action at the local and state level (see, for example, ECD, 1991).

A number of other definitions of conversion, economic conversion, re-conversion and also diversification have been specified by economists over the years. (For further details and for a useful analytical framework for both resource reallocation and conversion, see Sandler and Hartley, 1995, pp. 291–293.)

Smith and Smith (1992) highlight the difficulty associated with both diversification and conversion strategies:

'Diversification reduces a company's dependence on defence by acquisition or organic growth of non-defence operations. Diversification in the face of declining demand is difficult enough, the tobacco firms failed repeatedly despite their high cash flows. Conversion ... is yet more difficult ... given the nature of military production the major constraint is managerial capacity to change: the ability to create an alternative culture.'

EARLY EXPERIENCE

By far the most important experience of defence expenditure contraction and associated attempts at conversion and diversification occurred in the late 1940's. In the UK, some 7.8 million people were released from the defence-industrial sector (4.3 million from the armed forces) with unemployment increasing from 1% in 1945 to 5% in 1946, then falling again to 1.8% in 1948. In the US, defence expenditure declined by 80% after 1945, with some 9 million people released from military service (14% of the labour force). Military-producing companies attempted to adjust to this rapid and substantial change by diversifying into the civil sector. Most projects were abandoned as either unsuccessful or of marginal value and, in some cases, were sold off to other companies with appropriate market focus and expertise. Ultimately, the emergence of renewed military demands for the Korean War in the early 1950's helped to preserve these defence-dependent firms. Among the conversion/diversification strategies pursued at the time, the most successful proved to be the moves by military aerospace companies into the civil commercial and executive aircraft markets, such success being attributed principally to their familiarity with appropriate areas of technology and market requirements and behaviour.

Another, largely unsuccessful US attempt to convert from military production occurred after the Korean War. In this instance, however, the need for successful transition was diminished, given that a much smaller proportion of the US economy was harnessed to the war effort.

Despite the massive arms build-up in the West during the Reagan-Thatcher years, defence producers were aware that the increase in the defence budget was not sustainable in the longer term, necessitating further consideration of conversion and diversification opportunities. Given government commitments in many nations to reducing public expenditure as a proportion of GDP, intensified, in turn, after the end of the Cold War, by political and public perceptions and expectations of a peace dividend, conversion strategies rose into prominence once again.

In 1984, a report commissioned by the Swedish government (Thorson, 1984), based upon the experiences of Swedish defence suppliers, identified five factors which could affect an organisation's ability to convert. These factors included:

a) the degree of a company's defence business dependence;
b) its military export dependency;
c) corporate research and development intensity;
d) the degree of military specialisation; and:
e) profitability levels.

In general, the report concluded that companies with high research and development intensity and profitability but low levels of defence market- and defence export-dependence would find an easier path to conversion.

OBSTACLES

During the early 1990's, as the real implications of the end of the Cold War began to materialise, strategies for conversion and diversification were given added emphasis by major defence companies. Evidence (Braddon et al., 1991) suggests that, in the early 1990s, defence supply companies were actively exploring the whole range of their business activities, looking for civil market applications and opportunities. Compared with the market with which they were familiar, these companies viewed the civil market as being 'overcrowded and highly competitive' with 'lower margins and smaller profits'. Access to the civil market could only be achieved effectively through 'evolution not revolution', making use of 'directly applicable technology' and also some transferable 'business and financial abilities'.

It is important to note that, for those companies operating within the supply network of the defence industry (who are not prime but rather sub-contractors and suppliers) the potential for increasing business in the civil market is usually enhanced. Most of these companies already operate in civil markets, have a less specialised skill base and corporate culture than the primes, and may more easily be able to switch resources smoothly and effectively from the military to the civil side of their operations. Evidence suggests that such transition, while far from easy, can be achieved. In the 1991 Bristol study, for example, one sub-contractor operating in the aerospace sector considered itself to be too aerospace-dependent, since some 60% of its business was related to this market, half of which was military in origin. Through a combination of 'good planning and good luck', the aerospace contribution to company turnover was reduced to just 30% over 5 years, only 5% of which was military in nature.

However, for both prime contractors and for their suppliers, conversion and diversification opportunities have sometimes been constrained by the fact that such companies are often just one division within a much larger, more diverse organisation or conglomerate. Strategic policy, therefore, is regularly determined at a level beyond their direct influence and, as a result, division or plant run-down, closure or divestment were often more likely to emerge as strategies rather than the conversion or diversification option.

The restructuring and conversion of the defence industrial base in Western nations has both necessitated a significant reduction in military productive capacity and generated a considerable under-utilisation of the high-cost resources previously deployed to military production (Kennaway, 1993). In pursuing the conversion or diversification objective and initiating or expanding civil operations, the major defence contractors have to overcome the damaging legacy of the past. As key (and often quasi-monopolistic) suppliers to a near-monopsonist government purchaser, such companies enjoyed a secure market position, locked into a cosy relationship with a customer for whom cost was rarely a significant constraint and product quality and specification was all important.

Despite the 'value-for-money' reforms implemented in defence procurement during the 1980's, the major defence contractors remain high cost and high price suppliers; an inevitable outcome given the technical and security requirements they have to meet. As Brauer and Marlin (1992) comment:

> 'The issue of conversion involves not only just what is produced, but also the corporate culture and customary approach to business of military-oriented industries, which often differs dramatically from a more free-market environment.'

The issue of corporate culture in the defence supply sector is critical in understanding both attitude and strategy towards restructuring. As Smith and Smith (1992) noted:

> 'there are certain common, though not universal or unchanging, patterns in the corporate cultures of defence companies. These operate both at the formal level of explicit goals, procedures and systems and at the informal level of the norms, attitudes, values, styles and skills that predominate. The

goals of the defence companies are heavily product oriented and technology driven. ...Time horizons are long ... so rapid response to fast moving markets is not a priority. Innovations are radical rather than continuous. ... cost minimisation is rarely a primary goal of the defence culture ... they have little need to understand more diffuse markets, tend to be tolerant of bureaucracy and delay, and are heavily rule driven.'

There are several key characteristics which distinguish military markets from perfectly competitive, free-market models. For military markets, these include: the existence of a powerful single purchaser; the involvement of very few suppliers at the prime contractor level; and a focus upon a limited range of very expensive, technologically-advanced products, with prices set through detailed and protracted negotiation, although increasingly subject to competitive tendering in recent years. Unlike the more competitive market environment (and despite the drive towards competitive tendering and market testing in the defence sector of some countries such as the UK, new military firms rarely enter the market and old firms rarely exit.

The difficulty experienced by many prime defence contractors in pursuing an effective transition to the civil market is exacerbated by the specialist and sometimes non-transferable skill base of a large part of their labour force. Other important barriers to exit from the defence supply market include the burden of very high, 'government-imposed', overhead costs; the prevalence of very specialised capital equipment unsuitable for alternative use; the concentration of highly specialised labour operating with limited concern for cost minimisation; the necessity of lobbying for, rather than the marketing of, defence products; a business focus which allows little opportunity to gain expertise in market research; a long-standing supply relationship with the government which often limits the attainment of commercial, competitive experience among senior managers; and constrained access to the capital markets. As a result, as they attempt to come to terms with the business pressures of the competitive, commercial sector, many military companies find difficulty in functioning effectively in a market-driven environment (see, for example, National Governors Association, 1992; Gansler, 1995).

Despite their relevance to the problem of industrial adjustment to a post-Cold War world, these issues are hardly new. In a similar vein, several important hurdles confronted by defence-dependent companies in their pursuit of effective conversion and/or diversification were identified in a mid-1960's study by the Denver Research Institute.

These obstacles included:

- reluctance to accept the financial risks
- insufficient commitment by senior management
- design and quality control problems with new products
- market research, pricing and after-sales service problems
- the difference in civil and military production control.

These long-standing problems of industrial adjustment in the defence sector serve to emphasise the enormous challenge posed by the decline in defence budgets, particularly for those regions and companies heavily dependent on military expenditure, and the complex and difficult issues to be confronted by governments attempting to engender a real peace dividend, directly through policy or indirectly through the market (see Aeroe, 1993 for a fuller discussion of some of these issues). It is a challenge that many—if not most—defence-focused producers have found immensely difficult to address successfully. Indeed, examples of genuinely successful and long-lasting penetration of civil markets, generating employment, income and profit levels equal to, or better than, those enjoyed in the defence sector, are few and far between.

Successful transition to civil markets has been made but usually at the cost of reduced total turnover and employment. As Norman Augustine, Chief Executive Officer of the Martin Marietta Corporation, commented in 1993:

> 'In past periods of defence reductions, the canonical solution for the defence industry has been to diversify away from defence. We tried making buses, canoes, banjos, pagers—even coffins. The best I can say is that our record was unblemished by success. Defence conversion does not consist of training unemployed aerospace workers to be unemployed automobile workers.'

SUCCESSFUL CONVERSION

To achieve a successful conversion strategy, Markusen (1997) noted that companies have to become more entrepreneurial internally, creating new groups to permit cross-over of expertise. She cites the case of Boeing which has consistently excelled in both civilian and military markets, aided by internal mobility practices which allow personnel to move easily between civilian and military sectors of production. While highlighting some examples of conversion success, Markusen comments that her research work for the Regional and Industrial Economics Project at Rutgers University confirms that, even with successful conversion strategies, both large and small companies are usually unable to recoup the full amount of business lost from defence cutbacks, particularly in the transitional years, although they do 'cushion the blows'.

Markusen (1997) suggests that the move into markets outside defence business often requires the catalyst of some kind of management 'shock', often through the acquisition of new or younger management from an external organisation. Most critical of all is the acquisition of management with civil marketing skills and experience which may have to be accessed by partner arrangements with other companies already operating extensively in civil markets. Greater cost-awareness and enhanced efficiency in production are also essential for successful conversion strategies as, in many cases, is securing a new source of bridging finance where retained earnings are insufficient to cover the costs of the conversion process.

Challenging conventional wisdom on the efficacy of markets to restore equilibrium, Markusen indicates that there have also been many examples of successful government intervention which have served to facilitate the conversion process, especially where the assistance from government has been at the regional or local level. Technical assistance with business plans and accessing support from external consultancy organisations has proved valuable and she cites evidence that, in particular, the availability of regionally-based revolving loan funds has enabled many companies to survive the two to five year time period before conversion strategies reach fruition. Table 10 below summarises some examples where corporate strategies of diversification over the last 2 decades have proved relatively successful. Table 11, similarly, notes successful attempts with conversion strategies.

While there is no real theoretical background to economic conversion or diversification (Udis, 1987), the theory of transactions costs, advanced by Ronald Coase, help to define why an organisation expands or changes its strategy. The theory advances the idea that strategy is developed on the basis of economising on transactions costs, which Williamson (1981) describes as the economic equivalent to friction on mechanical systems. In 1981, Panzar and Willig proposed the concept of economies of scope, which describes cost savings to be obtained from the scope of an organisation's operations, in a multi-product environment, rather than economies of scale, which can be applied to the size-related benefits gained from concentration upon an individual product. Hannah and Williamson (1990) provide a review of recent contributions to the literature which spell out the importance of scope and scale economies. Teece (1980), however, suggests that scope economies do not provide the necessary or sufficient condition for cost savings to be achieved through the merger of specialised firms. He sees only two inputs of value in achieving scope economies, namely knowledge/know-how and specialised indivisible physical assets, to enable multi-product firms to evolve. Teece argues that:

> 'diversification based on scope economics does not represent abandonment of specialisation economies in favour of amorphous growth. Rather, it represents a movement from extending through a product range to extension of a capability in response to competitive guidelines.'

For sub-contractors to the defence industry, the rationale for conversion and the process by which it is implemented tends to be rather different from that of the primes. The strategic over-view of small and medium-sized enterprises operating in the defence industry will be determined mainly by two factors—the regional environment which sets the 'culture for innovation' and includes labour skill and capital availability; and also the information provided to them by the prime contractors with whom they contract.

This second factor is likely to be very important in determining the degree to which sub-contractors feel it to be necessary or wise to pursue a conversion strategy. While the acquisition of such information is relatively easy for a large sub-contractor, working in close liaison with a prime, the further removed from the prime the sub-contractor happens to be, the more difficult it will be to pick up implicit or explicit signals in time to react (Oakey, James and Watt, 1998). Where the sub-contractor manufactures or supplies a product which has a wide range of applications, conversion capability will be higher. Alternative customers will relatively easily fill the gap in business created by reductions in demand from a defence prime. Where, however, the sub-contractor offers a specialised product or sub-assembly designed specifically for a defence prime contractor, alternative customers are likely to be few in number and early action to diversify or convert the business will be essential for survival. As Oakey et al. suggest:

> 'the impression created by the survey firms is not of very high-technology enterprises strongly engaged in the provision of sophisticated input material

TABLE 10 EXAMPLES OF SUCCESSFUL DIVERSIFICATION STRATEGIES

British Aerospace Enterprises, UK	Established in 1987 with remit to innovate. Fairly independent, it could draw on BAe resources and had main Board access. Set up several successful ventures, sometimes located out of BAe control.
The Dowty Group (now Messier Dowty), UK	Reduced defence-dependency from 52% to 33% over six years; divested mining technology business; major success in developing solid state Lithium batteries which offer high power to size/weight ratio.
GEC Marconi, UK	Successfully entered the market for TV satellite dishes and receivers, utilising previous experience in military communications. Joint venture with Amstrad which gave it required market expertise and outlet access.
Babcock Thorn, UK	Diversifying from their management role at the Rosyth Naval Dockyard in Scotland, the company have made several successful moves into the civil market including: refurbishment contracts for London Underground railway carriages, construction of a cutter for HM Customs and excise and hull construction for a Tricat Ferry.
English Electric Valve in partnership with the former Royal Signals and Radar Establishment, UK	Successfully develped new market for thermal imager cameras which have been sold to fire brigades worldwide.
GEC Sensors, UK	Developed new sensors for fast food chains to monitor the quality of cooking oil.
Ferranti International, UK	Developed a new market in the application of military sonars for fish farms.
Martin Marietta Corporation, USA	In 1990, developed 'Peace Dividend' strategy where diversification would be funded from consolidation of corporate position in the defence markets. Became more competitive in the defence sector, principally by merger and takeovers, and expanded into new civil markets including energy, postal services and civil aviation. Merged with Lockheed in 1994.
Rocky Flats, USA	Premier plutonium trigger weapons production facility in Colorado. the end of the Cold War terminated weapons production at rocky Flats. Followed diversification strategy from 1992 and moved into environmental restoration and hazardous materials waste management.
Racal, UK	Developed very successful Vodaphone cellular telecommunications business; only profitable arm of business in 1990. Joint venture with Honeywell (offering marketing and support in the US) on civil aircraft communications. Separated telecom, security and defence businesses in 1990.

Source: Voss A., Converting the Defence Industry—Have we the Political Will?, Oxford Research Group, February 1992.

TABLE 11: EXAMPLES OF SUCCESSFUL CONVERSION STRATEGIES

Fail-Safe Corporation, US	Sub-contractor on the SDI programme. From 1987, designed and developed a board-level computer which operates within other computers and claims the capacity to repair them internally for as much as 20 to 30 years. Applications have been in the emergency shut down systems in the oil industry. Aided in the successful conversion strategy by a Small Business Innovation Research contract from the US Government.
Spreewerk, Luebben, Germany	Developed new market in fertiliser, extracted as a by-product from the process used to destroy over 20,000 mortar and rocket shells.
France-Conversia, France	Consortium of 19 French armaments companies (including Aerospatiale, Alcatel, Dassault, Eurocopter, Matra, Snecma, Thomson-CSF and GIAT) formed in 1994 to seek market opportunities from the conversion of military industries to civil production in the former Warsaw Pact nations.
AM General, Indiana, US	Successfully converted the military jeep known as the Humvee into the civilian-orientated AM General Hummer, a recreation/sports vehicle.
Frisby Airborne Hydraulics, US	Originally 90% defence-dependent, by 1992 Frisby were only 20% dependent without a single redundancy among their staff. Helped by the fact that it was a small company; that it had the ability to deliver a revolution in cultural attitude; and that it moved towards participative management and employee involvement in the conversion process.

Source: Voss A. (op cit); Networker, Newsletter Issue No. 8 of the Arms Conversion Project, March / April, 1994; and Fortune, October 2, 1995.

for hub high technology main defence contractors. Indeed, the general trend in most survey firms was for defence work to provide a useful contribution to their overall level of sales.'

CONVERSION IN RUSSIA

To resolve both the deepening economic crisis and to address the changing requirements of the post-Cold War world, Russia had little choice but to attempt a radical down-sizing of the defence sector and a rapid expansion of civil production through a conversion strategy (Cooper, 1991). In 1994, the Economist Intelligence Unit reported:

'In defence, as in most other industries, the collapse of the Soviet Union in late 1991 was followed by a chaotic period when factories were left to their own devices. Many stood idle or went bankrupt. Arms production shrank by two-thirds.'

The accuracy and interpretation of Russian military and economic data has always had to be treated with extreme caution. However, all the available evidence suggests that the Russian defence industry, in particular, has suffered a more severe contraction than that of the West although, given the right conditions, the potential scope for conversion could be considerably greater.

Estimates suggest that in the first two years alone after the end of the Cold War, Russian tank production had almost halved (from 1,300 to 675); artillery production had fallen from 1900 new weapons to just 450; military aircraft production had declined from over 600 to just 170; and submarine and surface ships output had decreased from 20 to 8 vessels only.

Immediately afterwards, estimates by Novecon, the Moscow-hased economics agency, suggest that defence production in Russia fell by a massive 33.4 per cent in 1993. More worrying, there was evidence that the performance of those companies which had enthusiastically pursued Mikhail Gorbachev's *konversiya* strategy, switching resources into civil rather than military goods, fared even worse with a decline in production in 1993 of some 35.6 per cent. In part, this reflected the coincident decline in consumer demand for goods, especially for commodities such as tape recorders, video equipment and vacuum cleaners—the very products on which the success of konversiya depended.

Throughout 1994, the position of the Russian military-industrial complex, according to Viktor Glukhikh, the then chairman of the Russian state Committee for the Defence Industries, 'remained critical' with only sufficient funding available at one point during that year to finance the construction of just 17 aircraft and 7 per cent of their naval requirements. During 1994, estimates suggest that the Russian defence ministry cut its orders for new equipment by an unprecedented 67 per cent. By that stage, using Western accounting principles, some 70 per cent of all Russian defence industrial plants would have been declared insolvent. During the period May 1993 to May 1994 alone, Russian military employment declined by some 16 per cent, with hidden unemployment in this sector exceeding 30 per cent.

Of even greater significance, and potentially damaging for long-run economic recovery, Izyumov et al. suggest that the decline of the Russian military-industrial complex was then beginning to have a deleterious effect upon skills:

'The qualification and technological potential of the defence complex is decreasing rapidly. Some enterprises are already unable to produce the complicated, high-tech articles they had previously manufactured. Some even lack the skills to produce spare parts for the weapons they had previously sold.'

Traditionally, the principal symbol of the economic power and potential of the arms industries in the FSU was the formidable success achieved in the global arms market. Earnings from arms exports, although notoriously suspect, have undoubtedly fallen catastrophically during the 1990s. Against a possibly optimistic estimate of US$20 billion for the value of the Soviet Union's annual arms exports in the mid-1980s, Rosvooruzheniye (the Russian arms exports agency established in 1993) estimates arms export sales for 1995 will amount to some US$2.5 billion, although this level is some 40 per cent higher than that of the 1994 low point.

Despite the problems constantly encountered with economic growth, it is important to note that the process of defence conversion has been actively pursued by the governments of both the FSU and, more recently, Russia, for several years. The conversion programme was formally launched by President Gorbachev in December, 1988. Under President Yeltsin, the strategy continues with somewhat mixed results. As Cooper (1993) noted:

'The new Russian government inherited a Soviet defence conversion policy, but in circumstances of acute budget stringency lacked resources to implement it. To a considerable extent, defence enterprises were left to their own devices. Some have shown remarkable initiative in finding foreign partners and organising new civilian production; others have been paralysed, capable only of begging for state budget support or credit on preferential terms.'

Transforming the most successful and politically powerful sector of the Russian economy was always going to be an essential but formidable challenge, confronting a wide range of critical economic and political issues (Barry, 1994, pp. 419–427; Bernstein, 1994, pp. 117–126; BICC, 1995). The defence sector has always had a priority claim on managerial, labour and material resources. It differed from other sectors of the economy in that it could offer employees incentives in terms of higher salaries, bonuses and fringe benefits and was the only part of the economy to face genuine international competition through the arms race. The gap between research, innovation and eventual production that has been damaging to the civil sector of the economy is not a feature of the military sector.

Unfortunately, these strengths have, in the past, been offset to some extent by the absence of incentives to economise on the use of capital, labour and material inputs in military production. Given its critical strategic role within the economy (see Weickhart, 1986; Adomeit and Agursky, 1978), now significantly reduced, and its unquestioned political influence, it seems certain that the military-industrial complex in Russia will remain a key player in facilitating or, perhaps, obstructing the process of overall economic transformation

For example, Leitenberg noted that:

> 'the fruits of the conversion efforts over the past three years must be seen as extremely discouraging. Yet it is important to emphasise that the lack of progress is attributable not to technical obstacles, but to political, bureaucratic and managerial ones.'

A further problem confronting the conversion strategy in Russia in the late 1990's is that the precipitate decline in military expenditure has impacted adversely upon the scientific community with a large number of defence scientists and engineers leaving the country to work abroad, both denying the Russian economy the benefit of their skills and expertise and also increasing the fear of global proliferation of nuclear technology. Cooper also makes the critical point that:

> 'the defence complex is itself a principal actor in the unfolding drama of Soviet development in post-communist times. It has the power and influence to undermine progress towards a market, mixed economy ...Decisions adopted during recent years have also put the defence industry into a position where it can determine the success or failure of efforts to improve the living standards of Soviet citizens.'

Without substantially greater involvement by Western companies, financial agencies and international institutions in facilitating the transition of the Russian economy in the future, the evidence of the last five years suggests that deep and sustained economic instability in the Russian Federation will the inevitable and, ultimately self-destructive price of peace (see Braddon, 1996, for a fuller discussion).

By far the most important systemic change required in the transformation of the Russian economy is the rapid and smooth reallocation of resources from the military to the civil sector. Critically, in this process, for a genuine and long-lasting economic recovery to take place in Russia and in similar transition economies, resources must be channelled by rapid and smooth market adjustment from the defence sector into the production of goods and services required by both the domestic consumer and particularly the global market (see Braddon, 1997, for a fuller discussion). However, the evidence from the early 1990s in Russia suggested that, far from a rapid and smooth transition, conversion was always perceived as a much longer-term and far more broad ranging process than usually envisaged in the West (Vid, 1990).

The military-industrial complex in Russia certainly consumed a vast range of resources that could be released for alternative use, particularly important in an economy where the consumer goods and services requirements of the domestic population are almost unlimited. Furthermore, many Russian military enterprises had been heavily engaged in civil production, yielding both experience of the sectors requiring expansion and suggesting the capacity for exploring and exploiting potential new market opportunities. Furthermore, reduced military expenditure should provide the potential for a substantial 'peace dividend' with which to regenerate sectors of the economy designated as critical components for economic reconstruction and recovery.

Unfortunately, at least in the medium term, the scope for acquiring such a peace dividend appears to be very limited. There are two principal reasons which constrain the immediate acquisition of positive economic gains from declining military expenditure. First, while reductions in defence budgets clearly provide resources that could finance conversion activities, evidence suggests that such resources will be severely eroded (if not fully depleted) by the new costs arising from military contraction, costs which are just as likely to be experienced in Western nations as in Russia.

Following a significant decline in defence expenditure, substantial additional costs are likely to be associated with the decommissioning of weapon systems (especially nuclear); maintenance and safety costs for those weapons taken out of service and held in reserve; environmental recovery costs to make good the damage associated with former defence-related production and military-related activities; and extensive governmental and corporate redundancy costs in terms of income protection, retraining and job creation. Secondly, in the current situation confronting the Russian economy, considerable priority would need to be attached to the policy objective of reducing further the budget deficit. Overall, the scope for economic expansion based upon the notion of a realisable and significant 'peace dividend' must be treated with extreme caution.

RUSSIA'S TWO CONVERSION STRATEGIES

To date, Russia has experimented with two approaches to the conversion of military industry. The 'physical' conversion approach, prominent between 1988 and 1991, aimed to retain some 30 per cent of military production capacity while converting the remainder to civilian production. Successful transition was expected in five to six years or earlier if economic conditions were favourable. Failure with this. approach has been attributed to the 'absence of clear-cut programmes, the wrong choice of priorities and directions of the use of the released potential'.

A second approach—'economic' conversion—utilised the income-generating capacity of the military sector through the arms trade to provide the financial resources to underpin conversion. In this approach, conversion is seen not merely as a transfer of resources from military to civil production but as a process of wider diversification, coincident with simultaneous expansion in both military and civil sectors. The inherent conflict in this approach is best demonstrated by the example of sectors such as aviation and space technology, where the income-generating capacity was high and the conversion process, consequently, was terminated in order to maximise potential earnings from the export market.

During 1992, senior Russian economists and industrialists became increasingly concerned about the poor progress being achieved with defence conversion. Vitaly Shlykov, a defence ministry advisor, demanded an end to the excessive production of armaments in Russia, whether for internal or external customers and argued that: 'reliance on the export of armaments will only deepen the domestic crisis and reduce the prospect of genuine reform'. The enormous financial burden of the conversion process was also made clear in 1992 with estimated costs of 150 billion roubles for a seven year conversion programme affecting 70 per cent of Russia's defence complex being proposed. By the end of 1992, it was estimated that, while defence production at some 600 plants within Russia had declined by almost one-half in the previous two years, the conversion programme had been: 'largely unsuccessful, with only a 9 per cent rise in civilian output. Of the 900,000 workers shifted out of defence work, 300,000 are unemployed'.

Furthermore, the experience with the conversion programme had yielded very few successful transfers of production from military to civil sectors: 'except for ... foreign contracts for various civilian products from formerly military shipyards and various optical products'. Under the twin impacts of declining military budgets and conversion strategies, the structure of the defence sector in Russia changed considerably over the early years of the 1990's. By 1993, over 460 defence plants were undergoing specific conversion to civil production; 21 defence enterprises had been closed; a further 130 were about to be closed down and another 400 defence enterprises were operating on the basis of a reduced working week (for further discussion of the Russian situation in the mid-1990s, see Khanin, 1994).

Under the 1993 Budget, some 250 billion roubles were earmarked for military conversion projects in Russia, coincident with a new approach to the conversion priority. This new approach, designed to avoid a further disintegration in Russia's defence industrial base, transformed conversion efforts from a strategic goal to a more pragmatic approach and ensured that factories that ensure Russia's own armaments supply will be subsidised together with those converted plants producing civilian goods previously imported (for further discussion of the conversion experience of Russia, see Bougrov, 1994).

The deterioration of the Russian economy after 1995 and the growing threat of serious economic and political instability weakened significantly the resolve of Western governments and companies to provide support for Russian economic reconstruction and set back the cause of conversion. To date—and in general—the conversion strategy within Russia has yielded few significant benefits and, with time at a premium, a new approach is clearly required. Both for Russia and, indeed, for the defence-dependent areas of the other economies in transition within Central and Eastern Europe, the process of defence industrial restructuring needs to be fully integrated within the overall process of micro- and macro-economic structural adjustment at the national level (Anthony, 1998; Zukrowska, 1995). Furthermore, the crucial role of research and development in the conversion process in Russia needs to be addressed (BICC, 1997).

MILITARY BASE CONVERSION

For many communities, often in isolated parts of a country, the construction and operation of a major military base in their locality can provide employment opportunities and considerable local income generation. Military bases may therefore confer substantial economic and other benefits upon the local economies in which they operate and their contraction or closure may seriously undermine the economic viability of surrounding communities.

American experience shows that military bases typically form part of the economic core around which services and support employment develops. Cities in the US with military bases tend to have higher ratios of service and support employment to manufacturing and mining employment than was the case with similar cities without military bases.

US evidence suggests that some small isolated communities have a greater economic dependence on military bases than comparably sized communities have upon defence procurement contracts, although, in general, the local economic impact of a base with 1000 personnel is likely to be significantly less than that associated with a defence company employing 1000 personnel. Again, in all communities affected, base run-down and closure during periods of recession will inevitably generate greater economic and political pain than closures taking place in periods of economic stability or expansion.

The regional and localised economic impact of base contraction and closure will depend on several factors. These include:

(a) the nature and size of a base scheduled for contraction or closure and the relevant closure timetable;
(b) the density of bases and the proportion closing within a specific region (a 'clustering' problem which may undermine the critical mass of the regional economy and which may be overlooked in the decision-making process);
(c) base proximity to rural and urban communities and their capacity for economic regeneration;
(d) the potential for retaining part of the operational functions of a base after closure in the form of a 'contractorised enclave';
(e) employment of local civilians on the base; demand for housing for service personnel and their dependents;
(f) demand by military and civilian staff for local services and utilities (especially telecommunications, energy, roads and other transport; security and policing, and education and training);
(g) demand for local businesses to service the base; and:
(h) the business rates and taxes payable to local authorities.

In terms of local economic impact, the incomes and expenditure of military base personnel and their families should be particularly significant since salaries in the armed forces tend to be on a par with or considerably higher than for equivalent employees elsewhere in the public sector. However, to some extent military bases tend to be relatively closed economies with many goods and services provided and consumer internally, thereby diminishing the economic stimulus on the local or regional community. Even that proportion of on-base expenditure which could provide business for local suppliers and contractors (e.g. construction work) will, in many instances, be channelled through central purchasing with implications for the wider economy beyond the region. Clearly, then, the degree to which a military base affects a regional economy will depend crucially upon the proportion of income and expenditure generated that flows into off-base consumption.

REGIONAL MULTIPLIER EFFECTS

The regional multiplier effects of military base operations can also be affected by the age profile of employees. Where a base contains a large number of younger service personnel, the marginal propensity to consume (and therefore the multiplier effect) is likely to be above average. Traditional estimates of regional income multipliers are constructed on the basis of Keynesian linear expenditure equations and this may, indeed, be appropriate for evaluating the impact of a single base closure. However, in a sub-region where several bases are targeted for simultaneous closure, the combined multiplier effect could be non-linear and, consequently, could generate a 'catastrophe' in terms of a disproportionate impact in sub-regional income and employment reduction. Furthermore, US evidence suggests that the consequences for local employment through multiplier impacts of base run-down or closure may be considerably less significant than for a comparable loss of civilian jobs. One study found that whereas the loss of 100 military base jobs led to a further 66 lost jobs in the locality within six months, the loss of 100 civilian jobs led to a further 258 lost jobs over the same time period.

BASE CLOSURES

While the base closure phenomenon has largely been confined to the US in the past, the mid-1990s marked the beginning of a new phase of base closures across Europe and beyond. Most Western governments have announced plans to reduce the number of operational military bases and refocus the activities and strategic role of others. Furthermore, the significant revision in US military strategy following the end of the Cold War has led to a review of US operations in Europe and a consequent decision to implement a wide-ranging programme of European base closures during the next few years. Inevitably, such closures will have a significant economic impact upon the specific localities in Europe where military base closure is implemented. The nations within the European Union most vulnerable to US military withdrawal are: Germany (where 511,000 US troops were stationed in the late 1980's); the UK (70,000); and Italy (33,000). US expenditure on military goods and services at the time revealed the same three countries benefiting most: Germany receiving US$6,384 million; the UK receiving US$1,105 million; and Italy receiving US$585 million.

Military base and military establishment run-down and closure has been a fairly prominent feature of the US since 1961 with around 500 military bases or activities being terminated during the 1970's alone. Even before the end of the Cold War, Congress legislation in 1988 targeted 86 bases for closure and 59 for realignment (either expansion or contraction). While nationally this significant policy decision would affect less than 1% of DoD employment, the regional impact was significantly greater with California, for example, being estimated to lose some 5% of its DoD military employment.

Following the US-Soviet Union agreement in February 1990 to limit non-naval military forces located between the Atlantic and the Ural Mountains to 225,000 on each side, US troop withdrawal and consequent European base rundown and closure was inevitable. The US European Command, in negotiation with European governments, implemented a planned reduction from 217,000 US troops stationed in Europe to 158,000. Consequently, in 1990, the US, as part of the initial phase of a post-Cold War strategic defence review, identified 94 of their military bases and sites in Germany for closure, with a further 14 bases scheduled for a reduced operational role. Similarly, plans were implemented to significantly reduce the number and strategic role of US air bases within Europe. The combined effect of US base closures in Europe and those implemented by European individual governments in response to their own changing domestic military requirements seems certain to focus increasing attention upon the significant regional economic impacts of such contraction.

The analysis of the regional impact has generally taken the form of case studies of individual base and military establishment closures and, occasionally, of the loss of specific elements of the armed forces due to military reorganisation following defence expenditure cuts. Examples of closures in the past which provide good examples of what can be achieved over time from base conversion include:

a)   Larsen Air Force Base, Washington; converted in 1966 to activities including aviation use, industrial development, education facilities and residential development. Among the new activities located at the former base were Grant County Airport and associated airline company offices; Big Bend Community College; the Columbia Basin Job Corps Centre, the McChord Air Base Training Facility, Grant County Housing Authority and various industrial functions.

b)   Craig Air Force Base, Selma, Alabama; converted in 1978 to a similar range of activities including the operation of Craig Field Airport, the Alabama Criminal Justice Training Centre, Wallace Community College, the Department of Correction Guard Training Facility, an elementary school, Craig Golf Course and a range of business enterprises.

c)   Ent Air Force Base, Colorado Springs; converted in 1980 to new uses including athletics training, office facilities and residential development. Some of this former base was acquired for the development of the US Olympic Committee Headquarters, including the national governing bodies for 18 sports.

(Source: Civilian Reuse of Former Military Bases, 1961–1990).

Studies of US military base reuse have produced a number of examples of 'good practice' which have served to facilitate the process of base transition from military to civilian use and have, as a result, enhanced the positive economic benefits resulting from the transfer. Some examples of these 'good practice' guidelines are shown below. (For further analysis of the scope, impact and opportunities associated with military base conversion, see Cunningham and Klemmer, 1995).

a)   In cities where there is a strong need for jobs and housing, closing military bases becomes an opportunity, as long as the cost of restoration and regeneration does not prove prohibitive.

b)   Close involvement of the community in the planning process and continuing to develop local communication as reuse plans are implemented.

c)   Utilising the inherent value of the site, such as proximity to transport routes, presence of wildlife, value as a historic site and proximity to urban areas rather than trying to develop completely new facilities and activities.

d)   Using Conversion and Development Organisations to co-ordinate and facilitate the implementation of the reuse strategy and maximise the opportunities provided by existing military facilities.

e) Securing the backing of private investors for a base reuse project can be the most important part of the implementation of a base conversion strategy.

f) Addressing the problem of base conversion four to five years before its closure permits the initiation of a dialogue between all the parties concerned and a full examination of all the options that may be available for base reuse.

(Source: Network Demilitarised, 1994).

Establishing a consistent methodology for evaluating the regional economic consequences of military base run-downs and closures is a complex task. Experience in the United States, therefore, is invaluable and has demonstrated some of the problems and emphasised the need to evaluate the importance of military base contraction in terms of economic adjustment. US studies of base closures have focused on the economic implications in terms of employment and income loss, with associated multiplier effects, for the local community concerned and the policy requirements to ensure the swift and effective transition of redundant military bases to income- and employment-generating alternative uses.

Unavoidably, decisions on military base contraction or closure do raise important issues in the economics of public choice. Retaining an obsolete military base for reasons of its contribution to the regional economy presents a classic example of concentrated benefits and dispersed costs. Benefits accrue principally to a narrowly defined segment of the population in the affected geographic region while the costs are borne by all citizens. Recognising the potential conflict of interests between regional economic and political actors and the requirements of defence and economic decision-makers on a national level, US experience has shown that it is often necessary to counter parochial views with the creation of a statutory superstructure designed to amend regional perceptions of the marginal cost of base closure to reflect more accurately their opportunity cost.

A final factor determining the economic impact of military base contraction and closure is the degree to which central or local government can be pro-active in providing support and/or compensatory funding to help regenerate local communities. Again, the US experience provides some important lessons.

Following on from the establishment in the US of the Office of Economic Adjustment (OEA) in 1961, the Economic Adjustment

Committee was established in 1970 to help promote non-defence dependent jobs and to assist in the diversification of the local economies of communities affected by base closure. Although a full, objective evaluation of the OEA's activities has yet to be undertaken, such evidence as exists for the period 1961–1990 suggests considerable success in transforming well over 100 former bases with some 158,000 new jobs more than compensating for the loss of 93,000 DOD civilian jobs at the bases. This transformation involved 12 bases being converted into college campuses; 33 bases converted into vocational/technical schools; 75 bases became office and industrial parks; and 42 bases became airports.

In 1990, President Bush signed a statute setting up the Base Closure and Realignment Commission. The remit of this Commission is to review planned base closures and make independent recommendations to the President, designed to identify which bases should close and to generate substantial cost savings in the closure process. For example, since 1988, base closures have had a significant impact on Charleston, South Carolina where more jobs have been lost even than in economically-devastated California. In 1993, the Commission voted to close the Charleston Navy base and Shipyard from 1995. Closure would involve 20,000 redundancies and would cost the regional economy $644 m per annum in lost local expenditure.

The 1991 Defense Authorisation and Appropriations Bill further enhanced government support for communities adversely affected by base closures. The bill offered $200m of aid for defence conversion initiatives in these communities to be co-ordinated by the Economic Adjustment Committee and granted eligibility for economic assistance to communities facing base closure-related job losses of 2,500 within an urban area or a 1% reduction in defence jobs where the total workforce is either 250,000 in urban areas or 100,000 in rural areas.

The academic literature in this field is relatively thin. Among the most substantive recent contributions is Twight, 1990 who contends that this area of the economics of defence is essentially:

'an application of public choice theory to a particular subset of interrelationships the legislative and executive branches of government.'

Twight makes the important point that:

'Retaining an obsolete or inefficient military base presents a classic example of concentrated benefits and dispersed costs. whereas the benefits from sustaining an unneeded or inefficient facility fall squarely upon a narrowly defined segment of the population in the affected geographic region, the costs in terms of reduced military readiness and wasted resources are borne by all citizens. The residents of Limestone, Maine, have no trouble understanding that closure of Loring Air Force Base would mean a direct loss of income to them, but the people in Boise, Idaho, have much less incentive to understand or act on the understanding that keeping Loring AFB open would slightly reduce the military effectiveness of the United States.'

Recognising the potential conflict of interests between regional economic and political actors and the requirements of defence decision-makers nationally, Twight concludes:

'Major base closures or realignments directly involve five powerful interest groups: legislators, constituent groups in affected regions, military leadership, DoD and the public. Each has much to gain or lose from base realignment decisions. To avoid the institutionalisation of parochialism as the prime determinant of base closure policy and practice, we must create a statutory superstructure that shapes the perceived marginal cost of parochially inspired actions to reflect more accurately their opportunity cost, channelling those actions in ways that do not undermine either the military security or the economic prosperity of the nation.'

Although there has been relatively little detailed analysis of military base closure in the mainstream economics literature as yet, there is a growing body of 'real world' case studies that provide us with clear evidence of both the local economic impact of such closure and the ways in which a successful transformation of the local, defence-dependent economy can be pursued. Examples include Braddon et al. (1991), Network Demilitarised (1996), BICC (1996) and BICC (1997b).

CONCLUSION

Conversion and diversification still appear to represent extremely difficult challenges for defence contractors, despite the advent of the high technology, flexible manufacturing system age which should, at least theoretically, have helped facilitate such business transformation. Yet, for defence contractors, large or small, primes or sub-contractors, at one level the conversion process is no different from that facing any firm in any market where a strategic change of direction is required. Every company in every market has to keep up to date with market trends and respond flexibly or perish. The difference in the case of defence companies in the 1990's is that the time available to undertake such strategic change is very limited, the cost could be immense at a time when financial resources are severely constrained and the corporate culture which has served them so well in past decades may no longer be so relevant or so helpful in such a highly competitive global trading environment. The solution to the conversion problem—as indeed to the delivery of a real peace dividend—appears to require a major programme of research exploring both successful and unsuccessful recent attempts to convert from military to civil industry and the kinds of incentives required to encourage conversion success. The aim should be to identify the key features that make such business transition strategies work. Some analysts would suggest, however, that the solution is technological in nature, particularly the wider development and application of dual use technology. It is to the issue of technology enhancement and transfer and to the increasingly problematic trans-Atlantic trade rivalry in such areas that we now turn.

REFERENCES

Adomeit H. and Agursky M., (1978), *The Soviet Military-Industrial Complex and Its Internal Mechanism*, Kingston, Ontario.

Aeroe A., (1993), Technology Management View of Conversion from Defence to Civil Production: Experiences from Southern California, *Technology Analysis and Strategic Management*, Vol. 5, No. 3.

Anthony I., (ed), The Future of the Defence Industries in Central and Eastern Europe, SIPRI Research Report No. 7, 1998, Stockholm International Peace Research Institute.

Augustine N. R., (1993), America at the Crosroads, *RUSI Journal*, June.

Barry M. J., 'Privatization, Conversion and Restructuring in Russia's Military-Industrial Complex: Macroeconomic Implications of a Sector Set Apart', *Comparative Strategy*, 13, 1994, 4,S, Washington D.C..

Bernstein D., Defence Conversion in Russia: Micro and Macro Economic Issues; in Restructuring the Military Industry, China Association for Peaceful Use of Military Industrial Technology, Bejing, 1994.

BICC, (1995), *Conversion of the Defence Industry in Russia and Eastern Europe*, Bonn International Center for Conversion, Report 3, April.

BICC, (1996), *Conversion in Poland: The Defence Industry and Base Redevelopment*, Brief 8, Bonn International Center for Conversion, November.

BICC, (1997a), *Research and Development Conversion in Russia*, Report 10, Bonn International Center for Conversion, May.

BICC, (1997b), *Base Closure and Redevelopment in Central and Eastern Europe*, Report 11, Bonn International Center for Conversion, July.

BICC, (1997c), *US Conversion After the Cold War: 1990–1997*, Brief 9, Bonn International Center for Conversion and the National Commission for Economic Conversion and Disarmament, Washington D.C., July.

BICC, (1998), *Converting Defence Resources to Human Development*, Report 12, Bonn International Center for Conversion, October.

Blong C. K., Lukey C. C., Pasterick E. T., and Sullivan B. E., (1992), *Defence Industrial Conversion: Problems and Prospects*, paper presented at the Nato Defence College Annual Symposium on Armed Forces in a Community of Shared Values, Rome, Italy, April 6–7.

Bougrov E., (1994), Conversion in Transitional Economies: the Case of the Former USSR and Russia, *Defence and Peace Economics*, Vol. 5, Number 2, pp. 153–166.

Braddon D. L., Cullen P., Dowdall P. G. and Kendry A. P., (1991), The Impact of Reduced Military Expenditure on the Economy of southwest England, Research Unit in Defence Economics Report, Bristol Polytechnic HEC, May.

Braddon D. L., Dowdall P. G. and Kendry A. P., (1991), The Economic Consequences of the Closure of a Military Base, Occasional Research Paper, Research Unit in Defence Economics, Bristol Polytechnic HEC, December.

Braddon D. L., (1996), *Economic Instability in Russia: The Price of Peace?*, in Carlton D., Ingram P., and Tenaglia G., (eds) Rising Tension in Eastern Europe and the Former Soviet Union, Dartmouth.

Braddon D. L., (1997), *Dancing on the Edge of the Chasm: The Struggle for Survival in the Former Soviet Union* in Carlton D. and Ingram P., (eds) The Search for Stability in Russia and the Former Soviet Bloc, Ashgate.

Brauer J. and Marlin J. T., (1992), Converting Resources from Military to Non-Military Uses, *Journal of Economic Perspectives*, Fall.

Cooper J., (1991), Military Cuts and Conversion in the Defence Industry, *Soviet Economy*, Vol. 7, Part 2, pp. 121–142.

Cooper J., (1993), The Former Soviet Union and the Successor Republics, in (ed) Wulf H., *Arms Industry Limited*, Oxford University lPress and Stockholm International Peace Research Institute.

Cunningham K. B.nd Klemmer A., (1995), *Restructuring the US Military Bases in Germany: Scope, Impact and Opportunities*, Bonn International Center for Conversion, Bonn.

De Grasse R. J. Jr., (1987), Corporate Diversification and Conversion Experience, in Lynch J. E., *Economic Adjustment and the Conversion of Defence Industries*, Westview Press Inc.

Dumas L., (1991), *The New Economy*, National Commission for Economic Conversion and Disarmament, April-May.

ECD, (1991), *The Los Angeles Regional Hearing: The New American Agenda—Economic Conversion for Jobs, Prosperity and Development*, June 28–29, National Commission for Economic Conversion and Disarmament, Washington D.C..

Economist Intelligence Unit, (1994), EIU Country Report on Russia, 3rd quarter.

Gansler J., (1995), *Defence Conversion: Transforming the Arsenal of Democracy*, The MIT Press.

Hannah L. and Williamson P., (1990), Realising the Potential of Scale and Scope—a Review Article, *Business Strategy Review*, Autumn, pp. 91–97.

Hartley K., (1994), The Economics of Disarmament: An Introduction, *Defence and Peace Economics*, Vol. 5, pp. 83–86.

Herbert J. and De Penanros R., (1996), The Role of the state in French Defence Industry Conversion, *Defence and Peace Economics*, Vol. 7, February.

Izyumov A., Kosals L. and Ryvkin R., (1995), The Russian Military-Industrial Complex: The Shock of Independence, in Di Chiaro III J., (ed.) *Conversion of the Defence Industry in Russia and Eastern Europe*, Proceedings of the BICC/CISAC Workshop on Conversion, April.

Kennaway A., (1993), *Restructuring the Defence Technology and Industrial Base*, Conflict Studies Research Centre, RMA Sandhurst.

Khanin G., (1994), The Economic Situation in Russia, in Rowen H. S., Wolf, C., and Zlotnick J., (eds) *Defence Conversion, Economic Reform and the Outlook for Russian and Ukranian Economies*, London.

Le Nouail M. N. and Sauvin T., (1996), Is Territory a Factor in the Conversion of Military Activities?, *Defence and Peace Economics*, Vol. 7, February.

Leitenberg M., (1992), Non-Conversion in the Former Soviet Union, *The New* Economy, Vol. 3, (2)

Markides C. C., (1997), To Diversify or Not to Diversify, *Harvard Business Review*, November-December, pp. 93–99.

Markusen A., (1997), *Defence Firm Conversion Progress in the United States*, BICC Bulletin No. 4., Ist July.

Melman S., (1985), *The Permanent War Economy*, Touchstone Books, Simon and Schuster, New York.

National Governors Association, (1992), *State Economic Conversion Policies: An Update*, In Brief, Washington D.C., NGA Center for Policy Research, January.

Network Demilitarised, (1994), *The Conversion of Military Sites.*.

Oakey R. P., James A., and Watts T., (1998), Regional Sub-contract Suppliers to Prime Defence Contractors: Evidence of their Performance in Response to Recent Changes in Demand, *Regional Studies*, Vol. 32.1, pp. 17–29.

Office of Economic Adjustment, (1990), *Civilian Reuse of Former Military Bases, 1961–1990*, Washington D.C.

OTA, (1993), *Defence Conversion: Redirecting R&D*, Office of Technology Assessment, Congress of the United States.

Ozhegov A., Rogovskii E., and Iaremenko L., (1991), Conversion of the Defence Industry and Transformation of the Economy of the USSR, *Problems of Economics*, Vol. 34, pp. 79–94.

Panzar J. C. and Willig R. D., (1981), Economies of Scope, *American Economic* Review, Vol. 71, No. 2, May.

Pianta M., (1990), *Conversion of Military Industry to Civilian Production: The Case of Italy*, paper presented at the International Summer School on Global Security, Arms Control and Disarmament, (ISODARCO), Bologna, July 16–26.

Richards P., (1991), Disarmament and Employment, *Defence Economics*, Vol. 2, pp. 295–311.

Sandler T. and Hartley K., (1995), *The Economics of Defence*, Cambridge University Press.

Smith R. and Smith D., (1992) Corporate Strategy, Corporate Culture and Conversion: Adjustment in the Defence Industry, *Business Strategy Review*, Summer.

Teece D. J., (1980), Economies of Scope and the Scope of Enterprise, *Journal of Economic Behaviour and Organisation*, Vol. 1, No. 3, September.

Thorson I., (1984), *In Pursuit of Disarmament: Conversion from Military to Civil Production in Sweden*, Liber Allmanna Folaget, Sweden.

Twight C., (1990), Department of Defence Attempts to Close Military Bases: The Political Economy of Congressional Resistance, in Higgs R. (ed) *Arms, Politics and the Economy*, Holmes and Meier Publishers.

Udis B., (1987), The Challenge to European Industrial Policy: Impacts of Redirected Military Spending, *Westview Special Studies in International Economics*.

Vid L., (1990), Guns into Butter, Soviet Style, *The Bulletin of the Atomic Scientists*, January-February, pp. 16–19.

Voss A. (1992), Converting the Defence Industry–Have we the Political Will?, Oxford Research Group, February.

Weickhart G. C., The Soviet Military-Industrial Complex and Economic Reform, *Soviet Economy*, (2), pp. 193–220.

Williamson O. E., (1981), The Economics of Organisation: The Transaction Cost Approach, *American Journal of Sociology*, Vol. 87, No. 3., November.

Zukrowska, K., (1995), Macro-Politics of the Government and the Arms Industry Sector: the Polish Practice, paper presented at the NACC Seminar on Demilitarization and Disarmament in Transition: Socio-Economic Consequences, Minsk, Belarus, 22–24 March.

Chapter 6

TECHNOLOGY AND TRADE DIMENSIONS

INTRODUCTION

Despite the numerous problems encountered by defence companies and governments in pursuit of effective corporate and community conversion and diversification, ultimately such strategies remain central and critical to the delivery of a real and lasting peace dividend. Perhaps more than ever before, military technology now has a major role to play in ensuring that such strategies are a successful element of post-Cold War economic restructuring as defence procurement continues to change and human and other resources transfer, swiftly and effectively, from military-related application to alternative uses in the civil sector (see Gummett and Walker, 1993, pp. 145–170; and Coopey, Spinardi and Uttley, 1993). In addition, the focus of attention has now moved on to encompass product developments which harness technological advance to enable dual-use applications to military and civil sectors, simultaneously.

Economists have studied the important roles played by research, development and technology in the economy for decades and have often focused attention upon the economic impact of the share of total research and development funding being absorbed by the military as opposed to the commercial sector (see, for example, Buck et al., 1993; Hartley and Singleton, 1990; Thee, 1990; ACOST, 1989; POST, 1991). For decades, there has been a widespread conviction among the critics of defence expenditure that the share of research and development (R&D) resources being devoted to military aims was too high in relation to the share being devoted to civil objectives with damaging economic consequences, particularly in terms of consumer goods market competitiveness. This conviction remained strong over the years despite the remarkable series of inventions (for example, polythene, radar, jet engines, antibiotics, computers and atomic energy) and analytical tools (for example, operations research) which all originated in military research and development but were then transferred very successfully to civil applications (for further discussion of the burden or benefit of military R&D, see Buck and Hartley, 1993).

Three additional factors have served to strengthen this conviction since 1990—the end of the Cold War and with it the removal of the critical need for super-power military edge; the growing opinion that the spin-off of military technology to the benefit of non-military sectors of the economy is no longer as effective as it once was; and the increasingly competitive nature of the global market in consumer goods which has alerted both companies and specific governments (such as the US) to the danger of neglecting the development of their civilian technology base through excessive focus on the military side. Indeed, as will be discussed later in this chapter, growing awareness of this danger has led President Clinton to initiate a new drive for US global economic dominance. This initiative is based upon the recognition that, economic superiority is now arguably more important than military superiority, necessitating a complete strategic review of economic, military and security issues and a focused attempt to blend them together, strategically, in such a way as to maximise America's productivity and global competitive edge (for a UK perspective, see DTI, 1989).

Although the effectiveness of technology transfer from military to civil use may have lost some of its earlier potency in recent years, it remains the case that military research and development (R&D) has been historically, and remains, a potent force in stimulating new technological advance. From 1940, the US military became a major influence driving technology development in the world, both by funding massive R&D expenditure on defence programmes and itself becoming a major customer for high-technology products. After the war, US industry flourished as those new technologies created during the war with military support were applied to the commercial market immediately after the war and commercial spin-off became a key element of economic growth.

In the 1990's, however, there are numerous examples of joint technology development (in aircraft and telecommunications, for instance), founded upon two-way technology exchange between civil and military scientists. In some cases, for example electronics, civil sector developments such as transistors and integrated circuits were eventually commercialised only because the US DoD was a major customer, effectively reducing business risk for these new technological developments.

This chapter explores the technological dimension of military expenditure and examines its links with the successful generation of a peace dividend. The dual-use technology option is considered and the recent attempts by the US to blend economic, trade and military security strategies to create a more competitive US profile in world markets is assessed, together with observations on the European response. The focus here is once again the aerospace industry since it represents perhaps the best and most appropriate current example of the deployment of all of these strategies.

GLOBAL MILITARY RESEARCH AND DEVELOPMENT (R&D)

In the peak years of defence spending, towards the end of the Cold War, global military R&D exceeded $120 billion annually with the US, as noted earlier, leading the Western nations efforts in this field. Indeed, the US contributed some 35% of the global total, creating a situation at the end of the Cold War where, for example, military R&D in the US was approximately five times that devoted to health and twenty times that targeted on the environment. However, such estimates rarely capture the true scale and scope of military R&D expenditure, even in those nations that choose to release reasonably accurate estimates. In the US, for example, during President Reagan's terms of office, it has been estimated that over 20% of the aggregate defence R&D budget was categorised as 'black' (under which classification no data is revealed publicly) while, for the US airforce R&D budget, the estimate was as much as 40%. Given the complexities and sometimes deliberate obfuscation by governments in defining terms such as military, research, and development and the variation in such definitions between countries and over time, the reality of this global resource commitment and its distribution remains a matter for conjecture.

Whatever its true scale, military R&D has played an indispensable part both in driving military capabilities and also, through technology transfer to the commercial sector, has enhanced industrial productivity and competitive edge for many companies and count where such activity is concentrated. At the same time, however, critics would argue that the diversion of such an enormous share of national resources into the defence sector denies crucial investment capital to the commercial sector of the economy and may, simultaneously, erode competitive edge. Furthermore, there is growing evidence more recently that the efficacy of such transferred technology is not what it once had been. The principal reasons for the reduced effectiveness of military technology in transferring beneficially to the commercial sector are argued to be (a) the fact that the technological requirements for some civil goods (particularly in electronics) have now outstripped those of the military sector (so that, in fact, a reverse technology 'spin-on' is actually occurring) and (b) that a significant proportion of military R&D is now involved with such specific and specialised capabilities, delivered at very high cost, that applicability to the civil sector is unlikely.

Some countries devote a high proportion of their aggregate military spending to R&D activities providing at least the potential and resources for budget transfer to support R&D projects in the civil, commercial sector. In the immediate aftermath of the end of the Cold War, for example, France devoted almost 15% of its defence budget to military R&D; Sweden just over 12%; the UK over 10% and the US almost 14% (the single largest investor in military R&D, committing over $40 billion annually in the 1990's to this activity).

At the other extreme, many countries spend little on military R&D and, in turn, cannot expect to benefit directly from any direct peace dividend outcomes from this kind of military-to-civil resource transfer. These include, for example, Belgium (.07%); Italy (2.8%); Norway (1.9%); and Japan (2.5%). For those countries with significant military R&D sectors, then, the opportunity seems to exist for rapid resource reallocation and new wealth-generating investment in the civil sector. Whether this can be achieved through market forces alone, however, is debatable since, as noted in the last chapter, the barriers to the conversion of military R&D are formidable.

First, the transfer of resources from military to civil sectors will be resisted by influential groups who have a vested interest in maintaining high levels of military R&D expenditure, including defence companies, defence ministry personnel and their political masters and the scientists and engineers engaged upon long-term military research programmes who do not wish to change career direction. Given the concentration of military R&D establishments at the regional level in most countries, they will also be supported by regional lobby groups who will not wish to lose the local income-generating activities of the establishments or researchers operating in their communities.

Secondly, an important example of market failure will also tend to obstruct the conversion of military R&D. For market forces to work properly requires that all actors in the market have access to full market information. Particularly in the case of military R&D, this is impossible given the need for high security that is paramount in such activities.

Third, most military R&D and the scientists and engineers engaged upon it have an extremely narrow focus which may not be immediately applicable to the civil market. New technological skills will have to be acquired, together with additional expertise in marketing and in providing customer after-sales service. In essence, this is a cultural dimension and reflects the kind of world in which military R&D has historically functioned. To move rapidly and smoothly into new civil market the R&D requires a degree of organisational and personnel flexibility that is not immediately apparent in considering the usual *modus operandi* of the military R&D sector. It is questionable, to say the least, whether the transfer of key research personnel at high cost would be feasible and the newly emerging civil research areas may choose instead to employ less expensive, younger and more recently trained staff.

Again, the potential for conversion in military R&D is likely to be constrained by macroeconomic factors. Although an economic boom may provide the opportunity for new product development and launch, interest rates tend to be higher at such times implying a financial constraint on access to capital with which to fund the transfer from military to civil activities. Alternatively, in periods of recession, aggregate demand is low and will prove a powerful disincentive to undertaking high risk, high cost conversion into markets that may well be already saturated.

Technically, too, there may be a problem. Military R&D tends to operate frequently in the 'blue skies' area of design and development. These activities are both high cost and high risk and, historically, the cost-plus approach has pervaded the entire culture of the military sector. Such cost and risk profiles are unacceptable in the highly competitive civil marketplace but, as noted earlier, such culture is inherently difficult to reshape over a relatively short period of time.

Furthermore, for scientists and engineers working in military R&D, status, salary levels and working facilities all tend to be significantly higher than they would be in the commercial world, representing a powerful incentive at the personal level towards inertia. That inertia is reinforced by the fact that defence companies and the personnel who work for them are good at what they do and would not necessarily perform as well in a culture and industry alien to them. As the Bristol research team were told forcibly by a senior executive of one leading aerospace/defence company while researching the impact of the post-Cold War defence cuts in the early 1990's: 'if your research conclusions tell us to make lawn-mowers, you will be the last research team to come through these doors!' No doubt such companies could manufacture lawn-mowers and could also provide a useful service researching enhanced lawn-mower efficiency. The fact remains, however, that they could only do so at enormous cost, with a massive reduction in both personnel numbers and income-generation and would still perform less well than those companies already operating in that market niche. There is clearly a limit to the 'avenues of escape' from the military R&D sector and, as a result, most conversion is likely to take place at the periphery of the defence sector into products and markets not entirely dissimilar to those such companies and establishments are used to working with.

In essence then, to convert military R&D to technology areas more focused on civil production requires that R&D resources in terms of expenditure, scientists and research facilities are actually transferable, relatively smoothly and efficiently, from the military sector to the civil sector. The question, then, for all countries with a significant defence sector under pressure from defence cuts is how to simultaneously deliver a substantial peace dividend, maintain leading-edge military power, sharpen global competitive edge in civil consumer markets and make the most effective use of the scarce national resources being devoted to research and development activities. This is as true for the transitional economies (see, for example, Gonchar, 1997) as it is for the market-orientated nations of the West.

MILITARY EXPENDITURE, R&D AND TECHNOLOGICAL CHANGE

By far the most significant contributor to global military R&D expenditure is the United States. At the end of the Cold War, the US accounted for over 30% of total global R&D expenditure and about 40% of global military R&D expenditure. In 1990, for example, the US government committed some $40 billion towards military R&D, just under two-thirds of all government R&D in the US at the time (for further discussion, see Smith, 1985). The potential for a real peace dividend appeared strong, at least on paper, when such expenditure is contrasted with the social expenditure of the US government at the start of this decade, with R&D expenditure for health amounting to just over $8 billion and expenditure on environmental R&D of just under $2 billion.

The prospect of a technological peace dividend, then, appeared to be a strong possibility at the beginning of the current decade. To convert military R&D to technology areas more focused on civil production requires that R&D resources in terms of expenditure, scientists and research facilities are actually transferable, relatively smoothly and efficiently, from the military sector to the civil sector. In addition to the potential benefit to be derived in terms of a technological peace dividend in public goods areas, there should also be an additional potential dividend to be acquired from the stimulus to innovation to produce better consumer products and generate enhanced productivity in the private sector.

In the latter connection, although considerable private investment in R&D is motivated by the expectation of short-term economic returns to the investors, there is scope for government R&D as well; public-sector R&D investments in general, as well as particular R&D skills and equipment located in national laboratories, government research institutes, and government-funded university research centres, can make important contributions to industrial innovation and competitiveness.

Of course, a sensible comparison among categories of R&D spending cannot be based only on the amounts spent, but must take into account the relative opportunities for productive R&D investments and the relative costs of pursuing these. That having been said, it would be difficult for anyone familiar with the US R&D scene to dispute that major R&D needs and opportunities in health, energy, environment, transportation, and agriculture, among other fields, have been neglected mainly because of lack of sufficient funds.

For most of this century, the role of military research and development in fuelling technological change and, through technology transfer, thereby creating competitive advantage in commercial as well as military markets has been profoundly important. Prior to World War I, the military budgets of governments funded the development of wireless, aviation and guidance and control systems. The Army and Navy provided support for the development of automatically piloted aerial torpedo prototypes and flying bombs. The driving force of military expenditure behind technological advance continued apace after 1918. In particular, military-funded construction projects creating systems for the mass production of various military weapons also stimulated rapid and wide-ranging technological changes.

The intense demand pressures on technology during World War II proved a massive stimulus to post-1945 technological advance. In particular, wartime projects initiated three major technological systems that spread world-wide in the following decades. These three critical technological systems were computers, nuclear energy and aerospace. Direct technological benefits accrued to the US in the two decades after 1945 from the legacy of research at wartime laboratories located at MIT, including the critically important development of the Whirlwind digital computer and the radar system employed to defend the US against possible Soviet missile attacks. Furthermore, IBM developed much of its commercial computer hardware, utilising the learning experience of working on the Whirlwind project. From 1968 until 1972, the DoD were responsible for the development and deployment of a national US computer network that formed the basis of what was to become the Internet.

During the 1970s, the global economy began to grow around the advent of new technologies and production processes in which the distinction between civil and military applications became less important. The rapid expansion of world trade was driven mainly by growth in civil markets and, increasingly, the demands of the military sector for leading-edge technical advance no longer dominated technological innovation itself. Both the US and the UK, however, still desired to retain independent capability in high-level military technology development but chose to do so by different mechanisms. The US relies principally upon military programmes to fund the R&D and technology development effort, keeping it separate as far as possible from civil industry. However, increasingly over the last two decades, the symbiosis and synergy between their scientific progress in military and civil sectors in terms of dual-use applications has become more obvious. In contrast, Europe has taken a primarily civil sector-based route to scientific progress through such intra-European initiatives as BRITE (Basic Research in Industrial Technologies for Europe); the Eureka programme; ESPRIT (European Strategic Programmes for Research and Development in Information Technology) and RACE (Research in Advanced Communications and Electronics). Unlike most US defence companies (at least until recently) European prime contractors frequently have large civil sector divisions which, in theory at least, should facilitate the two-way transfer of technology.

In this context, the development of dual-use technology appears to many observers to offer a way out of the dilemma posed by declining military budgets, increasing development costs and intense global competition in civilian markets. The military technology base can benefit from the remarkable scientific advances made in civilian technology—particularly in the sphere of information technology—where today that civilian technology is sometimes more advanced than the military. At the same time, there is scope for the civilian sector to be enhanced technologically by improved access to the military technology base. Furthermore, in the context of the previous chapter, to the extent that technologies developed in the military sector can be identified as dual use, they provide the opportunity for genuine diversification and conversion of military R&D from strictly military ends. It is scarcely surprising that the pursuit of civil/military integration through the development of dual-use technology currently attracts the interest of political decision-makers who envisage its development providing a solution to many of their urgent problems. Gansler (1998) for example, has presented the argument particularly strongly:

> 'Perhaps most essential for the transformation of our defence acquisition practices and industrial structures is the need to bring about far greater civilian/military industrial integration. In many respects, the advanced technology and the production and support processes meet our defence needs can be better satisfied by commercial capability ... The natural trend toward globalisation must be accommodated by greater civil/military integration on an international scale.'

The objective, as Gansler made clear is to create:

> 'a new civil/military partnership, not one in which we become simply the purchasers of commercial products and processes, but a dynamic and vigorous engagement that, through R&D, creates advanced products and systems with common technological bases and that, through the use of flexible manufacturing, allows production of our low-volume defence-unique items on the same lines with high-volume commercial items.'

DELIVERING THE PEACE DIVIDEND? THE DUAL-USE OPTION

Dual-use technologies refer to those technical advances which can be utilised as successfully in the civil as in the military sector. It is generally agreed that the potential for dual-use is most likely in 'generic' technology areas such as information technology, new materials science and process technology. In these areas, there is frequently little fundamental difference observed between civil and military focused R&D.

In the US, as discussed later in this chapter, the Department of Defense has, on occasions, publicly encouraged the development of a dual-use R&D policy in recent years. The Department has started to reduce the number of precise and restrictive military specifications which manufacturers are obliged to meet, a measure now being adopted more widely in the UK under the 'smart procurement' strategy. Maintaining superiority in military R&D remains at the heart of US military strategy in the late 1990's but is now also perceived to be central to a much broader economic strategy for global market dominance. Within the aerospace sector, while there are clear benefits to be derived from dual-use technologies on aircraft and space vehicles, there has been a much longer-term dependence on military R&D funding for its own sake (and, in the US, direct government-financed R&D initiatives).

The US, in particular, has also made a priority of identifying the specific critical technologies that it considers essential to maintain both military and economic power, including: materials synthesis and processing; electronic and photonic materials; ceramics and composites, computer-integrated flexible manufacturing, systems management technologies, micro- and nano-fabrication, software, microelectronics and opto-electronics, high-performance computing and networking, high-definition imaging and displays, sensors and signal processing, data storage and computer simulation, aeronautics and transportation technologies, applied molecular biology and energy technology. Most of these critical technologies have clear dual-use applications and are seen by key agencies in the US as crucial to the preservation of national economic and military strength. For example, the Office of Technology Assessment has depicted the relationship between the technology base and national economic and military power as a tree, where the roots represent generic technologies, the trunk of the tree the critical technology base and the branches are seen as specific military or civil applications of that technology.

In the UK, the Ministry of Defence in 1986 identified a number of important spin-offs from defence research establishments into civil applications, including: new aluminium-lithium alloys, aircraft noise reduction systems and helicopter rotor systems. A UK industrial survey in 1986 indicated that 37 out of 142 defence supply companies questioned had achieved civil spin-off from military R&D work. At around the same time, a study by the Department of Trade and Industry in the UK found that of 40 defence companies (receiving between them over half of the UK's defence procurement budget), 160 product lines had been developed for civil markets, generating a turnover of some £3.2 billion per year and representing about 20% of their civil sales. On the other hand, in 1989, a report by the UK Cabinet's Advisory Council for Science and Technology (ACOST) found that less than 20% of the UK government's military R&D was at that time targeted at technologies where civil spin-off was likely to occur.

One of the great problems encountered by dual-use proponents, particularly in the US, is how to maintain long-term political support for such a strategy. In the United States, for example, while the Department of Defense has given its support to a dual-use strategy and has taken practical steps (i.e. cutting the number of military specifications required in defence goods), Congress has reduced its support for dual-use programs and demanded that the DoD justify their dual-use expenditure only on the basis of military need.

In the United States and in Britain, politicians have tended to be cautious in their support of conversion or diversification strategies. A less cautious and more supportive approach has appeared during the 1990's, however, under the Clinton and Blair administrations. The Clinton administration has focused its conversion strategy on technology reinvestment.

Historically, although the US had few military aircraft during World War I and had lost the advantage gained from the early pioneers of aircraft development to Europe where the German, French and British military had subsidised aircraft and aero-engine design and development, between 1918 and 1939, US aviation technology regained much lost ground and developed rapidly. On the military side, the successful development of bomber and fighter aircraft during the 1920s by Martin, Boeing and Curtiss together with modern aero-engine development drove the industry forward while, as Zienke and Souder (1992) noted:

> 'the growth of civil aviation in the US paced that of military developments ... and the accomplishments of civilian aircraft were translated into superior military designs ... By 1935, the absolute world domination of civil aircraft design by Lockheed, Boeing and Douglas kept US aeronautics in top competitive condition. By 1939, the US ranked perhaps fifth in air power, globally.'

By 1940, US military aircraft had established parity in performance with British military aircraft and Britain had no bomber aircraft comparable to the US B-17, B-24, B-25 and B-26. Perhaps more critically, at about the same time, aero-engine technology transferred to the US from Britain. In 1942, the RAF allowed a Rolls-Royce Merlin 61 engine to be integrated into the US P-51 Mustang fighter. The consequences were dire for British (and European) aviation as this decision both gave the US a superior aircraft to anything the Europeans could offer and, more important, provided US companies such as General Electric, Pratt and Whitney and Westinghouse with jet engine technology transfer, enabling them to rise quickly to the forefront of the industry.

After 1945, the US provided an unrivalled government commitment to R&D in high-performance aircraft, both military and civilian. Government support on this scale inevitably helped establish a competitive leading edge for US companies in the rapidly expanding and lucrative global market for commercial aircraft with the result that the world's airlines had little choice but to purchase aircraft such as the Lockheed Constellation and Boeing 707 and 747 if they wished to remain competitive. The same was true for the military aircraft sector of the aerospace business with the US now dominating global markets for high-performance fighter aircraft, e.g. the F-4, F-5, F-15, F-16, F-111 and C-130J Hercules.

To put the point rather more strongly, the US has gained enhanced global competitive advantage in aerospace (and in critical supporting industries such as avionics and electronics) by providing financial support for the aerospace industry through massive government funding of research and development in the military aerospace sector, implemented through the procurement decisions of the Department of Defense (through, for example, the Defence Advanced Research Projects Agency), the Department of Commerce (through, for example, the Advanced Technology Programme) and NASA (through, for example, the aeronautical research and development programme). While openly supporting a free trade/free market philosophy, in reality the US has implemented a covert strategy of government-financed indirect industrial support which has enabled its aerospace companies, in particular, to become global market leaders. The point is made here not to criticise or challenge such actions, rather to applaud governments that intervene to ensure that the market works in its favour. In the current context, there is much to learn here from the European perspective and it is interesting to note that, during the 1990s, the Clinton administration has once again intensified such action to ensure global market dominance.

The strong commitment to support US aerospace industry by governments over the years has enabled aerospace companies in the US to gain much from important military/civil technology synergies where, often, whole systems developed for the military could be 'spun-off' to civil applications, reducing costs and risks for commercial users (see Alic et al., 1992). To illustrate the point, taking the example of the avionics sector, military technology has migrated to civil aircraft design and production including, for example, data and signal processors, data buses, software elements such as operating systems, and sensors such as infra-red and millimeter wave imagers. These critical technological developments originated in military R&D for the digital avionics systems for the F-15 and F-16 aircraft, reinforced in the 1980's and 1990's by Joint Service initiatives to upgrade avionics for the A 12, F-22 Tactical Aircraft and the RAH-66 Light Helicopter. Again, major military technology developments in satellites, for example, have been refocused to the civil sector with great strategic and commercial impact. The development of satellite technology in the form of the US NAVSTAR Global Positioning System (GPS), for example, has had a commercial impact so significant that it has been described by the Office of Technology Assessment as 'exceeding anything envisioned by the US military' with 'civil applications moving forward at breakneck speed.'

Other examples of civil aerospace projects deriving benefit from military aerospace developments in the US are numerous. For example, Boeing has been helped significantly in its design of large composite structures due to involvement in military programmes, particularly through its role as sub-contractor to Northrop-Grumman on the B-2 'Stealth' bomber programme. Boeing was entrusted with the development of the outboard and aft-centre sections of the B-2 using the latest in advanced composites technology. Similarly, fly-by-light/power-by-wire technology derives from military programmes, in particular that of the Sikorsky UH-60 Black Hawk programme in 1980. Through NASA's AST programme, Boeing received the fly-by-light technology and McDonnell Douglas the power-by-wire elements. The purpose of redirecting these technologies to the civil aerospace sector was to enable US commercial aircraft to access the benefits of full-authority digital computer control. At the same time, there are many instances where products and technologies designed for commercial application have also been able to achieve 'spin-on', that is, higher and longer production runs due to the procurement of large military orders, reducing commercial costs and enhancing competitiveness.

US aerospace manufacturers are often involved in both military and commercial aircraft development and production simultaneously, unlike most of their European counterparts, allowing at least the potential for technology transfer within the organisation and, to some extent, economies of scope. Indeed, at times, the inter-dependency goes even deeper. For example, it is frequently alleged that during the first twenty years of jet production, Boeing was supported by steady profits from its military business, especially the B-52 and Minutemen missile. On the other hand, it is also evident that the technological advances made by commercial aircraft development have helped to reduce military aircraft development costs and commercial contracts also enabled design teams to be kept together during periods of weak military demand. On occasions, the proximity of civil and military aerospace production is remarkable. For example, in one particular instance, work on commercial aircraft (such as the Boeing 737, 757,and 767) and on military aircraft (such as the Black Hawk helicopter and V-22 Osprey Tilt-wing transport) takes place within the same division and even the same engineering group. Again, in Wyman Gordon's forging and casting division, the same employees produce alloy castings for both commercial and military aircraft using the same manufacturing processes and the same equipment. The scope here for the wider application of dual-use technologies and for enhanced military-to-civil conversion is clear indeed.

As technology flow has become more genuinely two-way between military and civil sectors in the US in recent years, it has had a major impact on the nature, organisation and operational behaviour of the defence industry in particular, with the traditional defence industry gradually dissolving into a range of high technology industries where global competitiveness is the over-riding goal (for an excellent discussion of this development, see Scherpenberg, 1997).

For the US and, indeed, for Europe, the fundamental requirement for enhanced commercial success in the aerospace and defence industry must be the greater integration of civil and defence sectors, combining new over-arching systems integration skills and new integrated production technologies to provide the civil sector with enhanced access to leading edge defence research and development while allowing the military sector access to path-breaking civil advances in information technology and microelectronics. In practice, combining the enormous potential of military/civil technology symbiosis with a determined and focused strategy of driving forward dual-use technology development, may well become the mechanism through which the necessary surge of prosperity commensurate with a genuine peace dividend has the best chance of being realised.

DEVELOPMENTS IN THE UNITED STATES

It was noted above that the Clinton administration had reinforced government support for technology development and the restoration of US competitive edge in global markets during the 1990s. The dramatic changes to defence strategy and operational requirements necessitated by the end of the Cold War encouraged the Department of Defense to radically restructure its procurement policy in 1993. Under President Clinton's Acquisition Reform proposals, future technology research contracts would be placed on a competitive basis with those producers dedicated to the pursuit of applicability of that research to both commercial and military aircraft. The intention here was to initiate a new approach to the fostering of dual-use technology, thereby enabling the Department of Defense to gain access to lower cost, leading edge technology that resides in the civil sector of aerospace.

On October 28, 1993, Clinton spelt out the key role of technology policy in the new administration, outlining an array of devices to be employed in the future to support US aerospace producers and ensure their competitiveness in the global market (see US Department of Transportation, 1994). These included: tax incentives for investment in R&D; switching of federal resources towards basic research and civilian technology; the promotion of defence conversion; direct expansion of Federal investment in basic research through agencies such as the National Science Foundation; and the strengthening of collaboration with industry through consortia.

A range of newly created or expanded technology support programmes was also announced including the Department of Defense's Technology Reinvestment Project (TRP); the Department of Commerce's Advanced Technology programme (ATP); and the cross-departmental Co-operative Research and Development Agreements (CRADAs). The critical point here is the long-term nature and multi-sectoral applicability of Federal support for R&D in manufacturing technology, a distinctive characteristic which is not replicated in Europe. For example, the US Department of Commerce has acknowledged that Federal R&D directed towards composite manufacturing research in the automobile industry has successfully migrated to the aerospace industry.

The Technology Reinvestment Project (TRP), formally controlled by DARPA, has the objective of attaining technically superior defence systems at reduced cost, while supporting and sustaining the industrial base on which the Department of Defense depends. Yet, by 1995, critics in Congress were seriously challenging the dual-use nature of TRP, since the technologies being developed seemed to be primarily commercial in application with few military spin-offs. Defence funding, therefore, it was alleged, was being diverted through TRP for commercial gain. This criticism was responsible, in part, for TRP being revised and renamed the Dual-Use Application Programme (DUAP) with an enhanced focus on military applications and a halving of its budget in 1994–95. TRP and DUAP allow the Federal government to provide 50% of the funds required for a particular aerospace project with the remainder being provided by industry.

Among many new and important technology gains acquired by the US commercial aerospace industry from R&D initially funded by the Department of Defense for military purposes are FLASH, the $43m fly-by-light advanced systems hardware project, conducted over 2 years from 1993 which funded a McDonnell Douglas-led team in their attempt to develop components critical to making fly-by-light technology for both military and commercial aircraft. The lead company in this project has acknowledged that the TRP funding enabled it to accomplish the work twice as fast as it could have done without such support. DARPA estimate that FLASH could reduce aircraft weight, on average, by 2,700 kg which, in turn, could improve reliability and maintainability by some 10% while reducing wire count on aircraft by up to 80%. Similarly, another important research programme was VITAL, the vehicle management system integration technology for affordable life-cycle cost project, again led by McDonnell Douglas, with a remit of developing components, interfaces, software and tools necessary to achieve affordable vehicle management systems. The objectives were to produce technology that would meet the requirements of both the military and commercial aerospace markets, extending the useful life of existing aircraft while setting the standard for the next generation. Tested on an F/A-18, VITAL technology has already migrated to commercial applications, playing a significant part in Boeing's Active Aerolastic Wing programme which will probably be employed on three commercial aircraft, the MD-90-40X, the High Speed Civil Transport aircraft and the Future Thin-Winged aircraft. Among other US aerospace suppliers and manufacturers in the

McDonnell Douglas team benefiting from VITAL technology are divisions of Allied Signal, Raytheon, Honeywell, Litton, United Technologies, Lear and Lockheed Martin.

Among many other examples of military-to-civil technology transfer are ALGS, the autonomous landing guidance system, originally developed for the McDonnell Douglas F-15 STOL (Short Take-odd And Landing aircraft); and PMMW, the passive millimetre wave camera project, under which McDonnell Douglas and TRW are developing a sensor that would enhance all-weather flight capabilities for both military and commercial aircraft.

Schemes such as TRP and DUAP represent the formal and visible part of the US government's support programme for R&D in the military and commercial aerospace industry. Additionally, however, there are many other opportunities for US commercial aerospace to derive benefit from the fruits of military-funded R&D work, including the development of an Integrated Composites Centre to electronically integrate the technical and management functions of planning, scheduling and controlling the fabrication of organic matrix composite aircraft components (as developed by McDonnell Douglas for the F-15, F-18 and AV-8B military aircraft and then transferred to the commercial sector, saving an estimated $48 million over the period 1994 to 1999, according to the company); the development of the hybrid laminar flow control programme by the United States Air Force and NASA in 1994 (tested by Boeing on a modified commercial B-757 aircraft with benefits in terms of much reduced wing drag, lower fuel requirements and a significant improvement in operational costs and range); the development of integrated controls and avionics by USAF to enhance fighter aircraft performance (which have since been transferred to US commercial aircraft); and the development of new wire insulation constructions for power and signal applications in aerospace vehicles by USAF for air force and navy aircraft (then applied by Boeing to some of its commercial aircraft).

The Department of Defense also provides support for companies in the supply chain of the US aerospace industry, both military and commercial, through the USAF Small Business Innovative Research programme (SBIR) and the Small Business Technology Transfer Research programme (STTR). Small businesses have, since 1995, been actively encouraged to target rapid commercialisation of their innovative technologies under a Fast Track procedure, involving external funding from private investors.

US aerospace industry R&D also received support from the Advanced Technology Programme (ATP) whereby industry and government share project research and development costs equally and joint ventures are established between small and large companies to develop innovative technology. Estimates suggest that recently Boeing, for example, have received over $50 million annually from ATP support.

Co-operative Research and Development Agreements (CRADAs) provide another kind of government support for US industry with distinct benefits accruing to US aerospace manufacturers. A CRADA is a partnership between a private company and a government facility to research and develop a particular product or innovation through technology transfer to the private commercial sector. CRADA projects benefiting the US aerospace industry in recent years include projects relating to electron beam processing (with Lockheed Martin, Boeing and Northrop Grumman involved in the partnership), enhanced alloys for aircraft parts (involving Boeing); and software development for application on massively parallel computers (involving Hughes, Olin Aerospace and Boeing, the latter employing these super-computer developments in the design of the HSCT aircraft.

Overall, the evidence from the US regarding government support for the enhancement of aerospace design, development and production technology appears to confirm the view of Albrecht et al. that:

> 'There are indications that some US Defense contractors were able to use this lavish support of their defence contracts to pay the learning costs while they introduced CAD and CAM and then moved into the manufacture of high-quality components for civil aerospace.'

In certain instances, however, evidence suggests that some NASA technology developments have migrated to competitor aircraft in Europe before being utilised on US aircraft, giving European aerospace manufacturers the possibility of a temporary and often brief competitive advantage. Examples of this include the development of winglets (used first on Airbus aircraft); the supercritical wing (first employed on the Airbus 320) and engine technology developments, emanating from NASA but utilised first by SNECMA in the high-pressure compressor for the GE-90 engine.

THE EUROPEAN DIMENSION

Within Europe itself, military and civil technology synergies have also been an important feature of the aerospace industry, although on a much smaller scale than in the US. The early aero-engines developed by Rolls-Royce—the Avon, Olympus and Spey—all originated as military aero-engines, although more recent engines have been principally commercial in origin. In addition, SNECMA has benefited from combined civil and military sales of the CFM-56 while GEC of the United Kingdom is developing a heads-up display for use on commercial aircraft. The needed technologies came out of military developments for night flying.

In Europe, however, governments have spent less overall on military aircraft than their US counterparts, such expenditure has been fragmented with individual countries sometimes pursuing 'national champion' production of their own aircraft, and military R&D has also taken a smaller proportion of overall procurement. As a result, there have been fewer opportunities to derive commercial spin-offs from military aircraft development. To some extent, reduced spin-off opportunities are attributable to the fragmented nature of European military procurement with already constrained national defence budgets often being deployed inefficiently on projects which effectively duplicate military R&D, reducing the potential for spin-offs from a more concerted, focused European military R&D strategy.

In France, the aerospace industry is financed primarily by the General Directorate for Armament (DGA) which provides the resources for two-thirds of the industry's research and development with a focus mainly on military aerospace. In the French context, it is important to recognise that the production of military aircraft is an essential part of France's military-industrial complex and has profoundly influenced its structure and organisation.

France commits a larger proportion of domestic R&D to its aerospace sector than the United Kingdom and much more than Japan and Germany, though significantly less than the United States and produces an extensive and expanding range of military and civil products. One important example is the French presence in the civil and military helicopter market. Aerospatiale effectively dominates 30% of the global civil helicopter market and also holds 60% of the capital in GIE Eurocopter, giving it a significant share of the global military helicopter market as well.

Basic research in French aerospace industry is controlled through the National Office for Aerospace Research (ONERA), created in 1946, which operates under the direct authority of the Defence Ministry. ONERA plays an important role in co-ordinating company-based research as well as conducting tests and simulations on their behalf. ONERA distributes the findings of its advanced aerospace research freely to (French) businesses, and encourages them to undertake joint research projects. The organisation effectively leads the transfer of technology between the military and civil aircraft sector.

Since the 1960's, the French government has given strong support to this process of technology transfer from military to civil aerospace, becoming directly involved as a result in major projects such as Concorde, the Airbus consortium and the Ariane space launch vehicle programme. As a result, civil aerospace activity has increased markedly over the years, influenced at government level principally by the National Centre for Space Studies (CNES). In the 1980's, under pressure from the French Defence Ministry, closer ties were established between DGA and CNES and, in 1991, the Delta Committee brought the two government agencies together to ensure close co-operation and technology transfer between military and civil space developments.

Although French aerospace is effectively divided between the military sector (Dassualt) and the civil sector (Aerospatiale), close military/civil links and synergies still exist. Aerospatiale is a significant sub-contractor for Dassault and, as long ago as the late 1970's, the two companies (with the support of the DGA) created a joint research programme to produce composite wings for the Falcon 100 executive transport aircraft.

At another level, the interdependency of military and civil technologies are also crucial for the survival of key French companies. For example, Snecma's role in the Rafale combat aircraft programme is vitally important to its long-term future. Snecma depends critically upon the civil aero-engine market for most of its income but, in doing so, works closely with General Electric in the CFM International consortium. The Rafale programme provides Snecma with leading edge technological developments with which to enhance its competence in key technology areas and prevents it becoming overwhelmed in the consortium by its US partner.

In United Kingdom, too, the government has played a prominent role in supporting the aerospace industry. From government policy for the aerospace sector has been the responsibility of the Procurement Executive of the Ministry of Defence. At the same time, the government retains a joint military and civil R&D base at the Royal Signals and Radar Establishment and at the Aerospace Division of the

Defence Research Agency at Farnborough, as well as with many aerospace firms in the UK.

A substantial proportion of the UK's defence technology development takes place in the defence research establishments, created in 1991 from the amalgamation of four non-nuclear research establishments located in different parts of the country. From 1993, the DRA operated as a trading fund, enabling it to function in a contractor role with the government, conducting its business along commercial lines. With MoD funding in decline, DRA is working more with other clients and is strengthening its connecctions with industry generally and with the academic community. By the end of this year, DRA plans to conduct some 15% of its annual turnover of business with clients from outside the MoD. This should help to increase significantly the proportion of UK R&D which has civil as well as military application, a figure estimated in 1986 by the Advisory Council on Science and Technology at about 20% of aggregate UK R&D.

In 1991, the Parliamentary Office of Science and Technology, reviewing the U.K's conversion history, were unable to identify: 'any example of successful complete conversion in recent years' and a further 1994 study by Ernst and Young, management consultants called in to explore the future of Britain's defence industry found that the only scope for real conversion in UK defence was the aerospace sector with civil capabilities restricting potential development even in that sector.

The Blair administration in 1998 put forward a proposal for a UK Defence Diversification Agency in an effort to encourage commercial exploitation of defence technology and help to generate a technological peace dividend. This approach will be considered further in terms of policy analysis in Chapter 7.

In recent years, particularly since the end of the Cold War, the principal focus for dual-use applications within the defence sector has been in the aerospace industry, where the transfer of technology from military to civil aircraft and, more recently, from civil to military has been a prominent feature.

Indeed, the fusion of military and civil technologies in this industry and the degree to which governments are able to cross-subsidise civil and military aerospace markets from military expenditure has given rise recently to a major transatlantic trade dispute over aircraft subsidies.

DEFENCE AND AEROSPACE RESTRUCTURING: THE TRADE DIMENSION

At the heart of the problem lies the fact that the dominant position of US manufacturers in the global market for commercial airliners has been threatened over the last two decades by the increased market penetration by the European amalgam of aerospace producers, Airbus Industrie. Just over two decades ago, the combined strength of the major US aerospace manufacturers (Boeing, McDonnell Douglas and Lockheed) dominated 95% of the market for commercial jets with the remainder taken by the European companies (British Aerospace, Aerospatiale, Deutsche Aerospace and CASA), working in partnership within the Groupement d'Interet Economique (GIE) of Airbus Industrie.

Over the last two decades, the share taken by US companies has declined to about 60% of the market with Airbus increasing its share to just below 40%, and a 50/50 split of new business between Airbus and Boeing is now a real possibility This remarkable example of market penetration is, however, based upon share of new orders. In terms of actual share of the existing global fleet of airliners, Airbus only controls some 13.5% of the market and it is estimated that, given the life profile of civil aircraft, the Airbus partnership will remain essentially a new market entrant for at least another 30 years.

It is not surprising, therefore, that this new and rapidly-growing market entrant is viewed as a distinct threat to US supremacy in the commercial aircraft market, given earlier US experience in the steel and automobile industries, traditionally strong exporting sectors which, despite import protection measures and powerful domestic lobby groups, by the mid-1980's had seen their comparative and competitive advantage eroded. Consequently, in recent years attention has focused on the aeronautics industry and the strategic behaviour of key players within it, both corporate and governmental (see, for example, Lawrence and Braddon, 1999). In particular, the role of government subsidies, direct and indirect, has come under intense scrutiny especially those involving government funding for military research and development (R&D) which generates positive spin-offs for commercial aerospace and vice-versa.

Even for the US, the clearest voice apparently propounding free trade ideology, the rationale for state involvement in influencing market outcomes was unavoidable. As Kuttner comments:

'If it made pragmatic sense for America in the 1950's and 1960's to preach the freest possible markets, it made far less sense in the 1980's and 1990's

... by 1980, as *laissez-faire* hardened from self-interest into dogma, the world was turning into one big marketplace, outrunning the macroeconomic policies of individual nations.'

While proponents of *laissez-faire* may eschew government intervention as a distortion of the market and likely to generate suboptimal outcomes, many private sector decision-makers believe that firms may make losses or greater-than-normal profits due to systematic reasons beyond simple randomness or luck; systematic reasons that have much to do with industrial policy and the role of the state.

In recent years, therefore, the academic attention of economists, political scientists and business analysts has switched to focus more upon firm-specific aspects of strategic rivalry in the global marketplace. Important contributions from economists to this growing literature include those of Krugman and Lancaster. The analysis here focused upon the mechanisms by which global competitors can secure and sustain critical competitive advantage. Sustainable competitive advantage is argued to flow from four possible sources, namely strategic investment in research and technology; the achievement of economies of scale and scope in the market; the capacity to fully exploit the learning curve and the ownership of intellectual property rights, although in this latter case, there is some evidence that technology transfer can sometimes shift the benefits to other countries and competitors (see, for example, Milburn, 1989). Of these sources of competitive advantage, the first two are arguably the most significant for the defence industry.

For high technology industries that operate within the defence sector but also have a strong civil dimension to their operations, such as aerospace, research and development costs represent a major element of total cost and represent significant business risk. Boeing, for example, invested $2 billion in the design and development of the 747 jet and a further $4.5 billion on the 777 aircraft. The scale of research and development expenditure required in the high technology sector is now such that it represents in practice a major barrier to entry to potential competitors and will usually confer a first-mover advantage for the company that seizes the initiative. The strategic rivalry theory of trade, then, explains trade flows in such industrial sectors by reference to the research and development commitment undertaken by key players in the global trading game. As Griffin and Pustay comment:

> 'Why is the US a large exporter of commercial aircraft? Because Boeing is one of the few firms willing to spend the large sums of money required to develop new aircraft and because Boeing just happens to be head-quartered in the United States.'

The more important questions to ask here, however, is why and how does a company like Boeing find itself in a position to commit the vast funds required for new product development in the high-cost commercial aircraft sector. It is here that government intervention can have a fundamental and powerful impact on the global market outcomes of their key industries.

In the aerospace industry, as with other defence/civil industries, it must be recognised that governments are now inextricably linked with global market success, whether that support is covert (as in the case of the US where, despite: 'an obsession with open markets for American business', it derives indirectly from spin-offs from the government's defence and space budgets and the consequent impact on the pricing, technical quality and profits of the civil aircraft business) or overt (as in the case of launch aid to Airbus Industrie from European governments). Such support can also encompass a wide variety of other forms of intervention including state funding for technology demonstrators, preferential purchasing by governments, export support through licensing, export credit guarantees and state-provided marketing assistance.

A company like Boeing, with a large domestic market for its aircraft and a 'family' of products designed to meet the needs of its commercial airline customers has the potential to extract both scale and scope economies, significantly reduce average costs of production and thus secure a competitive advantage over rivals in the global marketplace.

In the case of the current battle between Boeing and Airbus Industrie for global market share, market structure takes the classic form of a duopoly with both companies competing in the global market. The theory of duopoly tells us that one firm can drive up its profits if it can increase output while convincing its competitor that the increase in output is permanent. If this strategic move is effective, the competitor will be induced to reduce its output. To be fully effective, the strategic move must be credible, that is, the competitor must believe that the increase in output will be maintained, regardless of its response. This is where the role of government can be critical in determining market outcomes. Where a government wishes to ensure that the strategic move made by its domestic company is credible, it can intervene to provide support by introducing an export or production subsidy (possibly by adopting measures which increase the flow of technology from the military to the civil sector or vice versa) which will shift that company's reaction curve in the market outwards, thereby achieving the 'rent-snatching' or 'profit-shifting' outcome desired.

Further support for the economic case for strategic government intervention in the aerospace industry has been presented by Hartley (1995), particularly with respect to critical research and development activities, based upon the industry's high development costs, long-term product development requirements, high risk, delayed returns and unpredictable spin-offs. In such an industry as aerospace, once critical leading-edge systems integration skills have been acquired, government has a role in their preservation and development. As a result, government becomes central to the process of determining the eventual size and market performance of the aerospace industry.

> 'The central question is whether the resources used in the aerospace industry would make a greater contribution to national output (and welfare) if they were used elsewhere in the economy ... a plausible case for state support can be developed based on the dynamic aspects and the technology features of the aerospace industry, namely that it is a high technology, high value-added industry with valuable systems integrator skills and spin-off to the rest of the economy. It is also the type of industry which will contribute to higher living standards and maintain a nation's future competitiveness'.

Following the end of the Cold War and the sharp decline in defence expenditure world-wide, aerospace manufacturers experienced a sudden, significant and prolonged reduction in demand for military aircraft, coincident with a deep economic recession in the major industrial nations which impacted adversely on their civil market business. For a business that has, historically, enjoyed the counter-cyclical 'feather-bedding' of defence expenditure to sustain production and sales through the worst years of economic recession, the harsh economic realities of the post-Cold War world have sharpened concerns about national and corporate competitiveness in the global market. In particular, it intensified concerns among aerospace manufacturers about the degree to which governments can, directly or indirectly, intervene in the aerospace market and influence global trade outcomes in commercial aircraft.

While the United States expresses concern about European aerospace subsidies, principally in the form of launch aid for new aircraft, the European aerospace manufacturers are more concerned about the degree to which massive United States defence budgets underpin research and technology development in US aerospace, thereby providing huge covert subsidies to their industry to ensure it retains it competitive edge in the struggle for global market dominance.

The difficulties associated with attempts to estimate aerospace subsidies both within and between nations are well documented. Bearing in mind data problems, Hartley cites and compares 1992 estimates as a snapshot of state support of aeronautical research and development. Support emanating from the defence ministries of the European governments involved in the Airbus programme amounted to approximately $4 billion compared with well over $7 billion in the US. Traceable government support for civil aerospace amounted to approximately $1.2 billion in the Airbus nations and $3.7 billion in the US.

In total, then, US aerospace subsidies (based upon the limited and questionable data presented in official publications) appear to amount to about twice that of the European governments. The data above, however, omits other aspects of government expenditure on aerospace, particularly the indirect benefit accruing to civil aircraft manufacture from spin-offs from military and space projects, an area in which, it is argued, the US has an established long-term advantage compared with the European manufacturers. Overall, it is suggested that, as a result of these indirect subsidies, US aerospace firms derive a 25% cost advantage over their European rivals. The significance of such indirect subsidies has long been recognised:

'Without the Federal Government, there would simply be no aircraft industry ... no aspect of the industry, including the commercial sector, could exist without the R & D funds provided by the state's purchases of military equipment.'

Tyson confirms the crucial role of US industrial support in the aerospace sector:

'Even before Airbus became a serious market contender, competition between McDonnell Douglas, Lockheed, and Boeing was possible only with substantial US government support for each of them. Overall, government subsidies in the United States and Europe have increased competition and accelerated innovation in the aircraft industry ... it is impossible to conclude that the overall welfare effects of such subsidies have been positive. But there should be no presumption that they have been negative either.'

The scale of US government support for its aerospace companies appears immense, both in terms of contracts awarded and, more particularly, in terms of the scale of R&D funding. In FY1996, for example, Lockheed Martin received contracts worth in excess of $19 billions, McDonnell Douglas over $12 billions and Boeing over $4 billions. In addition, however, Lockheed Martin received more than $5.5 billions in R&D funding, McDonnell Douglas over $1.5 billions and Boeing almost $2 billions.

It is interesting to note furthermore that US aerospace manufacturers benefit not only from state funding within the US but also from the financial commitments made by other governments to co-development of particular aerospace projects. It has been estimated, for example, that the Japanese government committed over $18 millions and the Japanese Development Bank some $1.1 billions to support Japanese involvement in the development of the Boeing 777 aircraft. The use of such 'program partnerships', whereby participants share design and development costs and risks and some sales and marketing was also apparent on the Boeing 767.

In general, over many decades, it can be argued that the US has gained enhanced global competitive advantage in aerospace (and in critical supporting industries such as avionics and electronics) from an apparent commitment to a free trade/free market philosophy which has masked a covert strategy of government-financed indirect industrial support (see Lawrence and Dowdall, (1998) for a fuller discussion of these issues).

STRATEGIC TRADE AND DUOPOLY BEHAVIOUR IN AEROSPACE

It is this fusion of technological leadership and strategic trade policy that, in the late 1990's, appears to offer the potential for global competitive advantage in key industrial sectors, especially defence, aerospace and similar high-technology industries. For those countries with significant military R&D expenditure and governments willing and able to provide political and other support to enhance trade potential, the scope for market success is immense. Indeed, it is in this area that the real economic benefits of the post-Cold War business environment may show themselves, rather than in a conventional kind of peace dividend.

In the defence and aerospace industry, as in many others, it must be recognised that governments are now inextricably linked with global market success, whether that support is *covert* (as in the case of the US where, despite an obsession with open markets for American business, it derives great benefit indirectly from spin-offs from the government's defence and space budgets and the consequent impact on the pricing, technical quality and profits of the civil aircraft business) or *overt* (as in the case of limited and repayable launch aid to Airbus Industrie from European governments). Such support can also encompass a wide variety of other forms of intervention including state funding for technology demonstrators, preferential purchasing by governments, export support through licensing, export credit guarantees and state-provided marketing assistance.

The increasing importance of corporate strategic rivalry and the role of governments in strategic trade management was highlighted by Porter in 1990. The clear conclusion from this analysis was that success in global trade derives from four country-specific *and* firm-specific elements, namely factor conditions, demand conditions, related and supporting industries and the firm's structure, strategy and rivalry position. In essence, this approach is a hybrid which blends classical factor endowment theory (with the additional insights of Heckscher, 1949, Ohlin, 1933, and Leontief, 1968) with modern corporate game-theoretic approaches. In this model of global trade, governments unavoidably play a critical role in creating an environment that can either help or hinder a company's global position.

The focus here is on key high technology industries such as aerospace, where relatively limited global market demand, massive product development costs and the existence of critical learning curve effects create market conditions which can only support the existence of a few global players. The result, therefore, is a highly concentrated, oligopolistic market structure with huge potential for monopoly profits. As a result, strategic trade theory implies that one or more national governments can secure national welfare improvements, if trade policies are adopted which improve the competitiveness of key domestic firms in such oligopolistic industries.

Brander cites the principal conditions for such a strategy as a situation in which firms must have mutually recognised strategic interdependence and where the profits of one firm must be affected directly by strategic decisions of other players, a situation which is fully understood by all. In essence, this is an application of non-cooperative game theory using a Nash equilibrium in which all players choose strategies such that each player's own strategy maximises that player's pay-off, given the strategies chosen by others.

In the case of Boeing and Airbus Industrie, market structure takes the classic form of a duopoly with both companies competing in the global market. The theory of duopoly tells us that one firm can drive up its profits if it can increase output while convincing its competitor that the increase in output is *permanent*. If this strategic move is effective, the competitor will be induced to reduce its output. To be fully effective, the strategic move must be *credible*, that is, the competitor must *believe* that the increase in output will be maintained, regardless of its response. This is where the role of government can be critical in determining market outcomes. Where a government wishes to ensure that the strategic move made by its domestic company is credible, it can intervene to provide support by introducing an export or production subsidy which will shift that company's reaction curve in the market outwards, thereby achieving the 'rent-snatching' or 'profit-shifting' outcome desired.

Building on this feature of duopoly theory, Brander and Spencer developed important conclusions from the so-called 'third market' model. Here, two large firms (for example, Boeing and Airbus Industrie) compete in a third market. While both firms recognise that the free trade outcome may well be optimal, evidence that one firm receives some kind of government support (in this case export subsidies) to help it compete in the third market will create a prisoner's dilemma scenario. If one firm receives support, whether overt or covert, it will inevitably reduce the output of the competitor, shift profits to the firm receiving support and will fundamentally alter the terms on which trade in conducted.

In terms of national welfare, both players (and their host countries) would be better off under a free trade regime **but** both have an unavoidable incentive to intervene, even though both are likely to be worse off under the strategic intervention model. The basic point here that is relevant for the trade dispute between the US and Europe over aerospace subsidies is that, given the long-term perception of the European nations of massive US subsidies to its domestic aerospace industry through defence and space funding programmes, the member governments of the Airbus partnership *had no choice* but to intervene to support their much smaller aerospace industry—and their policy action *had to be credible*. Further work by Bagwell and Staiger emphasises the greater robustness of research and development subsidies compared with direct production/export subsidies as a tool of strategic policy. This highlights the critical point that it is a government's decision to implement a research and development subsidy (the principal industrial support device employed in the US) in the first place that constitutes the strategic trade policy rather than the subsidy itself.

Even modest intervention by governments, as the performance of Airbus in the civil aerospace market demonstrates, can prove to be a highly successful strategy enabling their companies to captured both significant market share in a strategically critical, high technology industrial sector and, in consequence, have secured substantial domestic welfare gains which can be considered part of the peace dividend. The scale of the reduction in world welfare is debatable, depending partly on the relative weights attached to profits and consumer surplus.

Adherents of the free market challenge welfare gains on the basis that such strategies cost global welfare dear. As far as individual countries are concerned, however, there is clearly room for significant 'dividends' at the national and corporate level. Nor can free market models necessarily overcome the logic of strategic trade. Indeed, as Brander comments:

> 'When strategic trade policy models were first presented, it was often suggested that some important "correction" of the models would eliminate the apparent role for such policies. Perhaps some characterization of government-level or firm-level rationality, or some plausible informational asymmetry, or entry, or international arbitrage, or general equilibrium effects, or some other powerful force would sweep away the foundations of strategic trade policy ... no philosopher's stone that would transmute the normative analysis of strategic trade policy into free trade was found.'

CONCLUSION

Without question, the competitive environment of transatlantic economic relations has changed considerably in recent years. The US has both consolidated and extended its technological lead during a period of increasingly rapid technological change. Far from practising the free trade approach that it commends for others, it appears to be systematically implementing a 'New Mercantilist' strategy in which international trade, export promotion and security/defence policy are inextricably linked.

The clear US strategy now seems to be to secure superior global competitiveness through mobilising, supporting and integrating all of the available advanced technologies within the US civil and defence industries (see, for example, Stowsky, 1997). This mercantilist strategy involves targeting political, security and economic leverage on key strategic markets. Critically, the Clinton administration appears to have overcome co-ordination problems between departments and agencies in the administration, enabling joint strategic initiatives to be pursued between the Departments of Commerce, State and Defence through the Trade Promotion Co-ordinating Committee. Indeed, such is the momentum behind the new drive for enhanced US economic competitiveness in the global market that some analysts have recently expressed concern about the merits of the evolving strategy which transcends normal definitions of strategic trade policy. As Nau comments:

> 'new policy is anything but strategic—it is almost entirely oriented towards business and export salesmanship ... working against the country's broader security and macro-economic objectives, the trade policy of the US stalls abroad and thrashes around at home amidst a swirl of special interests and misplaced concerns about American competitiveness and jobs.'

Unless European governments and high-technology industries such as defence and aerospace can organise themselves effectively to place countervailing strategic pressure on their global competitors, the implications for European trade performance and industrial competitiveness in the defence and aerospace sector and beyond are serious. In this sense, post-Cold War economic prosperity and the attainment of a genuine, lasting peace dividend seems to be accessible only to those nations which are prepared to fight hardest to obtain it. Despite the reservations of market economists, it may be that the solution to achieving both of these goals lies in the realm of industrial policy and it is to this issue that we now turn.

REFERENCES

ACOST (Advisory Council on Science and Technology), (1989), *Defence R&D; A National Resource*, HMSO, London.

Albrecht U, Lock P, and Cohen J., (1994), The Reluctant Eurofighter Partner, in Forsberg R. (ed) *The Arms Production Dilemma*, MIT Press, Cambridge, Mass., p. 188.

Alic J., Branscomb L., Brooks H., Carter A., and Epstein G., (1992), (1992) *Beyond Spin-Off: Military and Commercial Technologies in a Changing World*, Harvard Business School Press, Boston.

Brander J. A. and Spencer B. J., Export Subsidies and International Market Share Rivalry, *Journal of International Economics*, 18.

Buck D., Hartley K, and Hooper N., (1993), Defence Research and Development, Crowding Out and the Peace Dividend, *Defence Economics*, Vol. 4., pp. 161–178.

Buck D. and Hartley K., (1993), The Political Economy of Defence R&D: Burden or Benefit? in (eds.) Coopey, Uttley and Spinardi, (1993), *Defence Science and Technology: Adjusting to Change*, Chapter 2, Harwood Academic Publishers.

Coopey R., Spinardi G., and Uttley M. R. H., (1993), Defence Science and Technology: Setting The Scene, in (eds.) Coopey, Uttley and Spinardi, (1993), *Defence Science and Technology: Adjusting to Change*, Chapter 1, Harwood Academic Publishers.

Department of Trade and Industry/Ministry of Defence, (1989), *The Potential for Civil Benefit from Defence Research and Development*, DTI Library, London, mimeograph.

Gansler J., (1998) *Military and Industrial Cooperation in a Transformed, NATO-Wide Competitive Market*, XVth International NATO Workshop on Political-Military Decisuion Making, Vienna, Austria, June 22nd.

Gonchar K., (1997), *Research and Development (R&D) Conversion in Russia*, Bonn International Center for Conversion, BICC, Report 10, May.

Griffin R. W. and Pustay M. W., (1995), *International Business: A Managerial Perspective*, Addison-Wesley Publishing Company.

Gummett P. and Walker W., (1993), Changes in Defence Procurement and the European Technology Base, in (eds.) Coopey R., Uttley M. R. H., and Spinardi G., (1993), *Defence Science and Technology: Adjusting to Change*, Chapter 7, Harwood Academic Publishers.

Hartley K. and Singleton J., (1990), Defence Research and Development and Crowding-Out, *Science and Public Policy*, Vol. 17, No. 3, June, pp. 152–156.

Hartley K., (1995), *The Economic Case for Subsidising the Aerospace Industry*, Centre for Defence Economics, University of York, March.

Heckscher E., (1949), The Effect of Foreign Trade on the Distribution of Income, in Ellis H. S. and Metzler L. A., (eds) Readings in the Theory of International Trade, Homewood: Irwin.

Hughes T. P. (1994), Beyond the Economics of Technology, in Grandstrand O., *Economics of Technology*, Elsevier Science, ch.18, p. 426.

Kuttner R., (1991), The End of Laissez-Faire: National Purpose and the Global Economy after the Cold War, University of Pennsylvania Press.

Krugman P., (1981), Intra-industry Specialization and the Gains from Trade, *Journal of Political Economy*, Vol 89, October.

Lancaster K., (1980), Intra-industry Trade under Perfect Monopolistic Competition, Journal of International Economics, Vol. 10, May.

Lawrence P. K. and Braddon D. L., (1999), (eds.), *Strategic Issues in European Aerospace*, Ashgate.

Lawrence P. K. and Dowdall P. G., (1998), *Strategic Trade in Commercial-Class Aircraft: Europe. v. America*, The Royal Institute of International Affairs, Discussion Paper 78.

Leontief W., (1968), Domestic Production and Foreign Trade: The American Capital Position Re-examined, in eds. R. Caves and H. Johnson, Homewood: Irwin.

Lichtenberg (1990), *US Government Subsidies to Private Military R&D Investment: the Defense Department's Independent R&D Policy*, National Bureau of Economic Research, Reprint No. 1415.

Millburn G. P. (1989), International Technology Transfer: Who is Minding the Store?, *Hearing before the Subcommittee on International Scientific Cooperation*, House Committee on Science, Space and Technology, 101st Congress., 1st Session.,July 19.

Smith M. R. (1985), Military Enterprise and Technological Change: Perspectives on the American Experience, MIT Press, Cambridge. Mass.

Nau H., (1994), Making US Trade Policy Truly Strategic, *International Journal*, Summer.

Ohlin B., (1933), *Interregional and International Trade*, Harvard University Press, Cambridge, Mass.

Pena F., (1994), from a speech, Washington D.C., 6th January.

Porter M., (1990), The Competitive Advantage of Nations, Macmillan.

POST (Parliamentary Office of Science and Technology), 1991, *Relationships Between Defence and Civil Science and Technology*, POST, London, May, p. 9.

Scherpenberg J. V., (1997) Transatlantic Competition and European Defence Industries: A New Look at the Trade-Defence Linkage, *International Affairs,* Vol. 73, 1, pp. 99–122.

Stowsky J., (1997), America's Technical Fix: The Pentagon's Dual Use Strategy, TRP and the Political Economy of US Technology Policy, in (eds.) Markusen A. and Costigan S., *Arming the Future: A Defence Industry for the 21st Century.*

Thee M., Science and Technology: Between Civilian and Military Research and Development, UNIDIR, Research Paper 7, United Nations, New York.

Thornton D. W., (1995), Airbus Industrie: The Politics of an International Industrial Collaboration, Macmillan.

Tyson L. D., (1992), *Who's Bashing Whom?,* Washington D.C.

US Department of Transportation, (1994), *Aviation Initiative: The Clinton Administration's Initiative to Promote a Strong Competitive Aviation Industry,* January.

Ziemke M. C. and Souder W. E. (1992), Co-operative International Weapons Development Through Technology Transfer—From the Civil to the Gulf War' in McGovern J. F., Shapira P., and Ziemke M. C. (eds) *Proceedings of the Technology Transfer Society,* 17th Annual Meeting, Atlanta, pp. 165–172.

Chapter 7

PARTNERSHIPS FOR PROSPERITY: POLICY OPTIONS AND THE PEACE DIVIDEND

INTRODUCTION

Considering the somewhat *laissez-faire* attitude of governments to the attainment of a peace dividend since 1990, one would have to conclude that they viewed such a dividend as a natural and inevitable consequence of the historic changes following the end of the Cold War. The approach of most governments, which for the most part appeared to amount to benign neglect, suggested a pervasive belief at the political level that no longer having to commit vast expenditure to maintain the super-power arms race would automatically mean that such expenditure could be simply re-channelled into more worthwhile, civil and commercial projects. In line with the conventional economic wisdom of the age, such re-channelling was argued to be best left to the market so that resources could be reallocated to alternative activities in the quickest and most efficient manner possible.

Consequently, to date in most military-producing nations, there has been only the most modest attempt by government to identify and refocus the skills and employment patterns of redundant defence workers and the organisations that previously employed them. Similarly, there has been relatively little government–initiated strategy to expand the civil sector directly in response to the demand gap left by declining defence spending. In the main, therefore, resource reallocation and structural adjustment to the post-Cold War economic environment has been left to the market. With a few exceptions, individual governments have chosen not to intervene extensively to help the defence and civil markets adjust to a new equilibrium, believing that, ultimately, a market-driven solution would generate an optimum outcome.

In practice, we may observe that the market mechanism, in the context of such a complex and difficult phase of economic history, has been found seriously wanting, leaving fundamental dis-equilibrium in its wake. Certainly the market for defence products has remained surprisingly strong and, as noted earlier, some of the defence companies that have survived the traumas of the 1990s have emerged as profitable entities. There are however fewer of them and they conduct a level of business dramatically lower than that of the mid-1980s. Again, while there are certainly a number of examples of military producers choosing to, and succeeding in, switching part of their operations into civil production during the 1990s, they have been the exception rather than the rule. By far the most visible corporate response to declining defence expenditure during the decade, discussed earlier in this book, has been contraction combined with rationalisation, generating a number of massive waves of redundancies of defence workers in the major prime contractors, adversely affected by defence cuts. Estimates suggest that in the US, some 2.6 million defence-dependent jobs have disappeared in the last five years with little sign that the market, for all its sophisticated dynamics, is capable of restoring employment to those displaced by the defence cuts with a permanence and at a level commensurate with their skills and expertise.

This has been followed, in turn and much less visibly, by a similar adjustment process in the second and subsequent tiers of the defence industry supply chain as suppliers and subcontractors have found their business also declining and have had little choice but to respond by introducing additional employee redundancies. In this sense, the market has certainly adjusted rapidly (and somewhat ruthlessly) to the reduction in demand for military products but not in such a way as to deliver a peace dividend or even a satisfactory equilibrium outcome. Instead, in many instances, the market has generated a sub-optimal outcome in the form of a peace 'tax' rather than 'dividend' for society in the form of corporate failure, market exit or contraction, higher unemployment, idle resources, and the abject failure to transfer these scarce resources into efficient alternative uses.

Furthermore, even the limited funding apparently devoted to economic conversion in the US during the 1990s may now be considered to have been targeted at serving military rather than civil objectives, further diminishing the potential for a genuine peace dividend. Furthermore, some analysts assert that this nominal support for con version is itself already being phased out, with conversion funding by government, falling 16% in 1998 compared with a year earlier. In general, the conclusion must be drawn as we approach the end of the decade that, a full and lasting peace dividend has yet to be attained and governments have yet to accept their role in and responsibility for its delivery.

It is certainly the case that there is an intuitive belief among many analysts that reducing military expenditure should provide the potential for rapid improvement in national economic performance. Most studies have, however, produced results that fail to confirm this supposition. A recent paper by Knight et al. (1998) suggests that evidence exists to support the view that a substantial peace dividend is possible, if it is measured in terms of sustained and significant increases in capacity output but only over the long-term. The Bonn International Center for Conversion has carried out a number of national pilot studies of the peace dividend process (for Australia, Argentina, Central America, Chile, Japan and Spain) and have concluded thus far that an instantaneous increase in social expenditure following a reduction in military budgets should not be anticipated and that the process of disarmament brings with it high costs in terms of personnel retraining, weapon elimination, and base closures.

GOVERNMENT INTERVENTION

Two basic questions lie at the heart of the debate regarding the appropriate degree of government involvement in addressing the economic impact of declining defence expenditure and the objective of securing a peace dividend. First, is the scale of the impact sufficient to warrant specific policy design and implementation or can the interplay of market forces deal effectively with the process of economic regeneration? Second, if government intervention can be justified, what policy measures are actually available and what is their potential efficacy in resolving the adverse economic impacts of the defence contraction problem?

As noted earlier in this book, in general, analysts anticipate that the scale of the problem for most nations with large defence industries and military infrastructures at the *macroeconomic* level, while significant, will be relatively modest despite the scale and speed of the contraction in defence expenditure. In the case of the European Community, for example, the effect of even a 50% reduction in defence expenditure, spread over several years, has been projected to affect the macro-economy by less than 1% annually (Hartley and Hooper, 1991). For the United States, it has been estimated that, incorporating the 1993 Clinton defence expenditure plans, the significant defence cuts from 1986 to 1998 would affect US gross domestic product by no more than 3.3% over a period of 12 years. In a few cases, however, most notably Russia and some of the countries of the Former Soviet Union, economic dislocation due to post-Cold War defence expenditure reduction has already proved to be immense at the macroeconomic level and these special cases will be considered later in this chapter.

Clearly however, as noted in Chapter 2, all countries with large defence sectors are likely to experience significant economic problems at the regional, sectoral and industrial level, given the degree to which the distribution of defence expenditure is concentrated in modern industrial economies. For the defence industry, its supply network, the military infrastructure and the regions, local economies and labour markets that depend on them, the impact of post-Cold War defence cuts have been and are likely to remain profound indeed and sufficiently damaging to warrant policy intervention if a peace dividend is to be attained.

The experience of rapid decline in other important industrial sectors in recent years confirms the need for appropriate policy action to facilitate economic adjustment to declining defence expenditure, particularly at the regional level. Several traditional heavy industries (for example, steel, coal and shipbuilding), especially those located within the European Union, have experienced dramatic contraction over a relatively short period of time, each in turn generating significant adverse regional economic consequences which the market, unaided by government, proved incapable of correcting.

Across the European Union, the industrial, social and economic impacts of industrial decline have been felt most significantly in the regions of North and East France, the Ruhr and Saar regions of Germany, South and East Belgium and in the UK in the regions of West and Central Scotland, the South-West, North and North-West England and in Northern Ireland (Hitiris, 1988).

Despite relatively expansionary overall economic conditions and the emergence of new growth sectors at the national level, market adjustment failed to correct the adverse economic conditions experienced in these regions, since new industrial activity tended to occur in growth centres well away from the deprived areas. Unaided by national or local government policies, markets proved ineffective at coping adequately with the speed and scale of industrial change, particularly in the areas where it really mattered, and the constraints of wage inflexibility in an increasingly competitive market environment.

Measures employed to ease regional problems have included the selective allocation of regional development grants (such as the European Regional Development Grant), allocated on the basis of perceived national economic strength or weakness as well as the scale of the expected industrial change; financial and technical support from government for training, retraining and employment initiatives; measures designed to encourage land reuse and development; and more specific policies at the regional level focusing upon technology, the environment, industrial expansion and social issues.

Some of these policy approaches may be relevant to meeting the requirements of regions adversely affected by defence contraction but will require flexibility in application. For example, large numbers of military personnel with specific attributes (mainly male, young and well-disciplined with focused skills) are likely to become redundant, often in relatively remote regions. At the same time, Defence Ministries in most countries are likely to release large amounts of land for alternative use as their military exercise and associated training requirements diminish over time. Conventional regional policies will need refinement if such problems are to be effectively resolved. The key to dynamic economic regeneration appears to lie in enhancing the adaptive capacity of regions, and a combination of supply-side reforms, together with suitably targeted regional measures, seems to offer the best strategic response.

NATIONAL AND TRANS-NATIONAL POLICIES

a) France

In almost all cases, industrial policy in France is orientated towards national security and national independence objectives as, for example, in the case of the Rafale fighter aircraft project. In France, industrial policies emerge from consultation between the Planning Commission, industry, trade unions and government agencies. While plans are not binding, their objectives are pursued through the use of administrative guidelines, credit allocation, subsidies and tax policies. In addition, much broader sectors of French industry have been nationalised than in most other leading industrial nations, a process which commenced before World War H. Further waves of nationalisation occurred in 1944–1947 (Renault), in the 1960s (Aerospatiale) and in the 1980s (Thomson and Dassault).

The nationalised industries control about 25% of French manufacturing with the French Treasury providing capital endowments and loans to support industry, both public and private. The Ministry of Defence also has a significant influence on the development of industrial strategy. Considerable support is provided through various government agencies and is critical to both the defence sector and to strategies designed to take defence companies into the civil market.

However, French military industry relies heavily on the export market where export financing is provided by the Banque Francaise du Commerce Exterieure, which underwrites loans to finance manufacturing for export. Until 1995, however, there was little concern at government level at the severity of 'shrinkages' in employment and contractor numbers in the French defence sector, due in part to the maintenance of French defence budgets when other nations were implementing cuts in the early years of this decade. The 'official report on Defence, the Planning Law 1995–2000, and the Finance Law 1995 revealed the importance of these shrinkages and their related financial problems (see, for example, Herbert and de Penanros, 1996).

The official approach to conversion in France is also quite distinctive. In France, conversion may mean a deliberate reallocation of resources from the military to the civil sector, if an agreed level of security relative to perceived threat can be attained at lower cost. This is termed 'deliberate conversion'. However, there may also be examples of 'endogenous conversion', where the reallocation of military resources to the civil sector happens not by autonomous choice but an unavoidable and essential requirement to compensate for a significant change in the global geopolitical or military environment. Two possible conversion scenarios emanate from 'endogenous conversion'. First, there may be 'accepted conversion' where both government and defence sector decision-makers recognise the fundamental change in the global business environment, accept that conversion is inevitable, formalise it as part of the military system and forecast, plan and implement carefully the required conversion strategy.

On the other hand, 'contained conversion' may occur. This happens when governments recognise that conversion is now an unavoidable international necessity but fear the consequences for national security. Conversion is then pursued slowly, with the emphasis being placed on safeguarding a secure military base and then delaying conversion adjustments for as long as possible.

It is argued that this 'contained conversion' most closely resembles the approach adopted in France. As a result, a kind of 'creeping conversion' occurs which takes the form of 'a well ordered retreat which limits activity and job shrinkage as far as possible" (for further discussion, see Herbert and de Penanros, 1996).

Over the last few years, under a privatisation strategy, the French government has largely disengaged from direct involvement in the ownership and management of its arms supply companies with the exception of military shipbuilding. More recently, the government has made clear its wish to reduce and remove the bureaucratic controls on the activities of the defence industrial base. Over the last five years, a number of important initiatives have been implemented by the government to tackle the issue of defence sector restructuring such as: the creation in 1991 by the French Ministry of Defence of a restructuring delegation (DAR) and associated restructuring fund (FRED); the introduction of the 'Formation' programme in 1993 to reduce the number of defence sector civilian staff; and the establishment in 1993 of a defence industry restructuring apparatus (ASTRID).

More recently, research in France has explored the role of territory in the conversion process. Operating within what is termed a 'Local Productive System' (where companies within a region, particularly those which are defence-dependent, share problems and opportunities and work together with local authorities to rebuild regional prosperity) can be beneficial in both reinforcing competitive advantages and facilitating the transition to a diversified production base (Le Nouail and Sauvin, 1996).

b) Germany

In Germany, which in the post-war period did not have a strong defence industrial base despite being one of the most militarised areas in the world, few measures have been developed specifically to assist the defence sector, the communities adversely affected by defence expenditure cuts or the conversion and diversification process. Such matters are assumed to be primarily the responsibility of the private company or community affected, although the government does try to place orders with a variety of companies so that undue dependence on the defence procurement process does not occur. The main institutions involved are the Ministry of Economics and the Ministry of Research and Technology.

The range of industrial support programmes offered includes direct funding of specific industrial projects, using additional indirect measures such as tax incentives and support through the Technologically Orientated Firms programme. Although many defence-dependent companies, such as MBB and MTU Munchen, have been trying to reduce their defence dependency, very little real government support has been forthcoming. The only important exception was the provision of support, nationally and regionally, for the shipbuilding industry.

Although there is no overall conversion strategy in Germany to harness the potential economic benefits of the end of super-power conflict, there seems to be an accepted view of what conversion means. In essence, it means taking the broadest approach to include military personnel reduction due to post-Cold War budget limitations and their re-integration into the economy;; research and development refocusing; the redeployment of military land and facilities where appropriate; and the withdrawal and destruction of military equipment. It is perhaps helpful to the cause of conversion and diversification that Germany has developed a powerful military industry focused on aerospace and ship-building which is well-embedded in an industrial structure that produces civil goods as well.

c) Sweden

In Sweden, the primary aim of industrial policy has been to modernise Swedish industry and assist its expansion. The government-owned Procordia AB controls most of the nationalised companies which operate in the industrial sectors with a significant defence element. Government aid has been directed at the shipbuilding industry (Svenska Varr AB) and the iron and steel industry (Svenska Stal AB). Financial support in the form of loans, production cost support and credit guarantees is administered by the National Industrial Board, for example, for shipyards. The Board also provides support for small and medium-sized enterprises which includes regional development grants and assistance with new product initiatives. The National Board for Technical Development assists up to the prototype stage with conditional loans and the sponsorship of pure research. The Swedish Industrial Development Fund was set up in 1979 to encourage high risk industrial projects, including those in the defence sector. Companies such as Saab-Scania and Volvo Flygmotor have been major recipients. Support can amount to as much as 50% of a project's costs and has to be repaid unless the project fails.

Sweden has shown more interest in disarmament and conversion issues than any other European country and has carried out a number of important studies in key areas: for example, defence industrial problems (in 1975), the future of the military aircraft engine sector in Sweden (in 1979), the structure, competence and development conditions of the Swedish defence industry (in 1982), civil production in the Swedish defence industry (in 1982 and 1983), and the pursuit of disarmament (in 1984).

Swedish defence companies have attempted to diversify, although important defence supply companies such as Saab and Bofors have not been able to move far from their core businesses of aircraft construction and ordnance, respectively. At the same time, government policy has tried to ensure that, where offset deals are negotiated in the defence sector, such offset work includes civil development and production work as, for example, with the Swedish JAS 39 Gripen aircraft programme.

d) The United Kingdom

The British defence industry remains the largest in Europe and comprises some of the most important defence contractors in the world outside the US and the former Soviet Union. As in the United States, the industry experienced buoyant market conditions during the major rearmament programme of the 1980s. The sharp and sustained decline in UK defence spending after the mid-1980s, however, precipitated a dramatic restructuring of the British defence industry (Lovering, 1993, pp. 123–140).

In general, the UK government has favoured a strategy which allows the market to operate as freely as possible in resolving the resource allocation issues associated with the decline of the defence industry. The scale and impact of the defence cuts in the early years of this decade were of such magnitude, however, that an element of interventionist policy was introduced. In 1991, the government announced measures to help the county of Cumbria tackle the problems of defence-related unemployment, much of it attributable to a significantly reduced workload for the nuclear submarine yard at Barrow. Again, in the same year, the Scottish Office examined the military sector and the implications of defence cuts for the country with the help of the government-supported Scottish Enterprise Development Agency. As a result of their investigations, a Scottish Defence Initiative was established to operate for a four-year period until 1995 which would involve extensive retraining programmes. This initiative was designed to reduce the worst effects of defence expenditure reductions and to help companies adjust to new market conditions in order to secure new commercial opportunities.

During 1992, the Department of Trade and Industry organised a series of briefing seminars on the changing defence market, targeted at small and medium-sized enterprises across the UK. Again, since defence production tends to be concentrated regionally, in the early 1990s the government issued a consultation paper (DTI, 1992) to seek the views of interested parties on the future of regional policy in Britain and thereby provided an opportunity for local authorities, dependent upon defence expenditure, to raise their concerns. As part of this process, many local authorities across the country presented their defence-related concerns to government and pressed for a recognition of the problem by the awarding of Assisted Area status to regions adversely affected by defence cuts.

Such status confers a range of benefits including the enhanced capacity to attract inward investment as well as the opportunity to modernise regional industry and to utilise new technology. Furthermore, such status increases the chances of attracting assistance from the European Union's regional support fund. The outcome of the Assisted Area review was the establishment by the central government of 31 new Assisted Areas, although it was quite conspicuous that most of the 'defence sensitive' local areas were not among the most successful localities for Assisted Area designation.

The attitude and approach of the British government towards the need to diversify and convert defence industry in the post-Cold War business environment appeared to be changing in a more pro-active direction with the election of the Labour government in May, 1997. The Labour government announced proposals for a Defence Diversification Agency which were presented to Parliament in a Green Paper (Cm3861) in March, 1998. Within these proposals, the government estimated that some 400,000 jobs in prime and sub-contractors in the UK still depended on defence expenditure, despite the post-Cold War defence cuts, with many of these jobs at the leading edge of technology. Additionally, a great many jobs elsewhere in the economy depended on the multiplier effects of this defence-dependent employment. The government made clear their belief that:

'Both for defence reasons, and for wider economic reasons, it is therefore important that there should be a ready transfer of technology and scientific know-how from the military to the civil sphere and vice versa... What is of real benefit to the economy is to make available the fruits of defence scientific and technological advance to the business supply chain of the civil market.'

It is interesting to note here the phrase 'the business supply chain' for, indeed, it is precisely here that the technology-driven competitive edge of the modern defence company will be determined. To assist in making available the information required by industry to enhance their performance, the government (through the Department of Trade and Industry) has announced in 1999 the establishment of a number of national Centres of Expertise, designed to facilitate information acquisition and transfer by companies in key industrial sectors. The defence and aerospace sector has been singled out as a sector requiring this valuable facilitating mechanism and a Centre of Expertise for Aerospace and Defence has duly been established as part of Business Link West in South Gloucestershire, located in the heartland of a region where industrial defence-dependency is argued to be amongst the highest in Europe.

While these are encouraging steps, however, it remains the case, that the British government appears to favour principally a market-driven resolution of the problem of the economic and corporate impact of defence cuts and actively encourages a complete restructuring of the defence industry to create more of a European defence industrial base with, on occasions, the emphasis switching to trans-Atlantic restructuring.

e) The United States

Increasingly through the 1990s, national concern about the damaging impact of defence expenditure cuts on companies and communities in the US was deepening (Cohen and Garcia, 1994). Within the overall decision-making process of the US Department of Defense, the economic impact of defence policy adjustments is a factor taken into consideration with a view, wherever possible, to minimising any adverse economic consequences. An Economic Adjustment Program was established in May, 1961 for this purpose with assistance to facilitate economic adjustment being provided from 1970 through the President's Economic Adjustment Committee (EAC) which comprises 23 federal departments and agencies, chaired by the Secretary of Defense. The permanent staff for this Committee operate through the Office of Economic Adjustment. The role of the EAC is to help communities help themselves, an approach which essentially makes the communities responsible for the productive reuse of former defence facilities.

The EAC works in partnership with local, state and federal agencies (and with the Base Realignment Commission) to establish appropriate strategies and co-ordinate action plans which offer potential new employment opportunities in communities adversely affected by military base closure or run-down. Wherever practical, redundant military bases are converted for productive civilian use, often as airports, industrial parks, housing developments, schools and colleges, hospitals, recreation areas and so on. Resources from federal, state and local government are utilised to encourage private investment in such redevelopment work. To assess the success with which the EAC has addressed its role and remit, base closure experience between 1961 and 1993 was evaluated by the Department of Defense in 1993, focusing the analysis upon base closures affecting 97 communities. This survey concentrated on replacement job generation and base reuse achievements as reported by the communities themselves. The principal findings for the 97 base closure communities surveyed are shown below in Table 12.

In the United States, increasing concern in the early 1990s over the potential economic damage that defence cuts might inflict at the regional level stimulated a modest degree of additional government intervention. In the 1991 Defense Authorization and Appropriations Act additional government support was committed for regional communities adversely affected by defence cuts.

The Act offered US$150 million of aid for defence conversion initiatives and other support for redundant defence employees, specifically targeted at the community level. Under the provisions of the Act, the Department of Defense provided some US$50m directly to the Department of Labour to help fund the Job Training Partnership programmes, while a further US$50m was allocated to the Department of Commerce for allocation through the Economic Development

TABLE 12: PRINCIPAL FINDINGS OF US MILITARY BASE RE-USE STUDIES

Civilian jobs lost due to military base closure (93,424) during the period 1961 to 1990 have been more than replaced by 15 8,104 new civilian jobs, following base redeployment.
Successful office and industrial parks have been developed at more than 75 former bases.
42 former bases and facilities of the Department of Defense have been redeveloped into municipal or general aviation airports.
57 former military bases have been redeveloped to provide educational facilities; for example, 4-year colleges, community colleges and vocational-technical institutes. These facilities have enrolled over 73,000 college and post-secondary students; over 25,000 secondary vocational/technical students; and over 62,000 trainees.

Source: US Department of Defence, 1993.

Administration (EDA) in the form of planning grants to facilitate economic recovery strategies. In addition, further financial support at the regional level is provided through the Office for Economic Adjustment in the form of grants to states or communities adversely affected by defence contract cancellation or military base run-down or closure.

By 1994, estimates suggest that a total of US$6.4 billion has been committed to furthering the disarmament process in the US, of which US$2.7 billion was deployed to assist base closure strategies, US$2.1 billion to conversion and economic adjustment projects, and the remainder to activities associated with the INF, START and CFE Treaties and their implementation (Fontanel, Samson and Spalanzani, 1995). While important, this sum represents only about 2.5% of the defence budget. As part of the strategy to encourage effective restructuring, conversion and diversification, President Clinton suggested a US$20 billion Defense Reinvestment and Conversion Program. However, estimates suggest that about two-thirds of these funds are employed in high-technology projects which enable arms companies to remain in the military sector while taking on some civilian orientated production, especially where dual-use possibilities apply.

The US Defense Conversion Commission has drawn five main conclusions from its recent work. These are shown in Table 13 below.

While the United States government has taken these tentative steps to facilitate military base reuse and community economic regeneration, the scale of the initiative is relatively small compared to the swingeing cuts in US defence expenditure and the dramatic change in business conditions that such cuts have created for defence contractors. However, even minimal support from the Office of Economic Adjustment can be effective in stimulating action in local communities,

TABLE 13: US DEFENCE CONVERSION COMMISSION FINDINGS

The effects of the current disarmament process in the US remain less significant than that following the end of the Vietnam War, although major impacts have been experienced in heavily defence-dependent regions.
Defence conversion is not a panacea for the problems of US industry but does have clear growth potential. Successful defence conversion depends critically upon the capacity of the US economy to grow steadily..
A critical element in successful conversion strategies is the role of public authorities—market forces alone are not sufficient to deliver smooth and rapid economic restructuring
Although a range of government programs to assist restructuring have been implemented in the US, they are rarely effectively co-ordinated and often fail to monitor outcomes efficiently.

Source: US Defense Conversion Commission.

enabling them both to study the regional economic impact of defence cuts from their perspective and to try to create strategies for economic regeneration locally. One example of this in the St. Louis Economic Adjustment and Diversification Program.

At the beginning of the 1990s, the St. Louis region had a high degree of dependence on the defence industry and related business sectors. A large number of important defence contractors were active in the region at the start of the decade, including the McDonnell Douglas Corporation, General Dynamics and Emerson Electric. Within the region, defence business activities employed 73,500 people directly (6.4% of the regional workforce) with a further 85,000 people indirectly employed. The defence-related payroll amounted to over US$2 billion annually, approximately 8.4% of the region's total wage bill.

The industrial impact of defence budget cuts from 1990 onward had an immediate and severe effect on regional employment and income generation. In 1990 and 1991 alone, McDonnell Douglas (the largest regional employer) announced almost 10,000 redundancies, closely followed by announcements of significant additional redundancies at other large employers including both General Dynamics and Esco. This phase marked the beginning of a long-term economic transformation for the region as the effects of sharply declining military expenditure impacted upon defence industry supply companies, local retailers and construction companies, service suppliers and so on.

To address the issue of regional economic transformation and to aid the process of economic conversion and diversification, key institutions such as the Regional Commerce and Growth Association and the St Louis Economic Council formed the St. Louis Economic Adjustment and Diversification Committee with the mandate of assisting diversification through the development of short-term and long-term strategies. Included in their Adjustment and Diversification Task Force were the county economic development councils and agencies, community groups, the University of Missouri, worker re-entry programs, and representatives of the McDonnell Douglas and Chrysler Corporations. Key economic initiatives emanating from their proactive stance include the development of small business incubator schemes, entrepreneurship training courses, skill retraining programmes and the establishment of a Regional Steering Committee to improve regional co-ordination and communication.

Other initiatives across the US, stimulated by initial modest funding under the 1991 Act, are noted in Table 14.

TABLE 14: EXAMPLES OF SUPPORT PROGRAMMES FOR REDUNDANT
US DEFENCE WORKERS.

Arizona

A US$1.5m grant was awarded to Pima Regional County to assist 500 workers laid off at Hughes Aircraft. The funding will be targeted on the expansion of health-related business and upper level service occupations, as well as encouraging the development of environmental occupations.

South Carolina

US$1.2in grant awarded to Charleston County to assist redundant workers at the Charleston Shipyards. The funding will be used for relocation assistance, job placements and retraining

Louisiana

US$1.2m grant awarded to the Rapides Parish Job Training Office to help retrairiing of 500 redundant workers following the closure of the England Air Force Base.

Colorado

US$0.8m grant awarded to Colorado AFL-CIO to assist 700 workers laid off following closure of the Lowry Air Force Base.

Ohio

US$0.56m grant awarded to Job Training Office in Lima to provide effective response to lay-offs at General Dynamics.

Montana

US$0.4m grant awarded to the Fort Peck tribes in Montana to help 124 workers laid off following loss of key defence contracts. The grant will provide for retraining at a local community college while the company seeks civilian contracts (for example, with IBM) in the locality.

Iowa

US$0.26m awarded to Iowa-based non-profit Community Action Agency to provide assistance to 146 workers laid off at the FanSteel/Wefiman Dynamics plant

---

Source: The New Economy, Vol. 3, No. 1, Issue 13, Winter 1993.

A second initiative during the early 1990s, developed and implemented by the defence companies themselves, relates to the establishment of manufacturing networks. This relatively recent development in the manufacturing sector brings companies together to share common problems with the objective of jointly securing a competitive edge in the market. It is anticipated that such manufacturing networks will prove extremely valuable in assisting companies to complete a successful transition from defence to civil markets, particularly for small and medium-sized enterprises.

The significance of the network system for conversion strategies is that such a mechanism can help to reduce or even eliminate two major obstacles to successful conversion: the uncertainty that accompanies a move into a hitherto unknown market and the associated high degree of business risk. As Hoops (1992) commented:

'We have found that many companies would enter new non-defence markets if they knew how and had the confidence to take risks on a new market or product. Many managers see relying on a ... defence market as less dangerous than the risks of unknown market conditions or costly new production factors.'

Since the majority of defence subcontractors are relatively small, they lack the market research capabilities, investment capital, management time or sufficient funding for product research and development. Manufacturing networks can help to overcome such problems through joint strategies that spread both risks and costs. One example of successful network interaction in this area is that in Massachusetts, where a group of precision metal-working companies have joined forces to upgrade both technology and manufacturing capacity. As yet, the network phenomenon is relatively undeveloped in the US, unlike Europe where, in Italy for example, such network arrangements are commonplace and can involve as many as 2,500 small firms in a single network. (For further discussion of the process of conversion in the USA, see Ward, Cohen and Bets, 1995.)

Finally, in 1992, a separate initiative launched by the Transportation Department led to three consortia (for example, Calstart in California) being awarded US$10m to design and develop electric vehicles for personal use and for mass transit. It was made explicit that defence and aerospace companies would be involved in these initiatives to the extent possible (Raffel, 1992).

f) The European Union

Across Europe, to varying degrees as noted above, national governments have implemented relatively few policy initiatives to facilitate regional economic regeneration to counteract the impact of declining defence budgets. Within Europe, it has been left to the European Commission to develop and implement a limited policy response under the KONVER strategy. Under this initiative, the Commission offers limited funding on a competitive, selective basis for regions where defence cuts have created severe problems. In the United Kingdom, KONVER-supported projects include the identification and upgrading of defence sector skills; employer subsidies to recruit redundant defence workers; the creation of technology revival centres; and new employment opportunity programmes for redundant defence workers. Most of these KONVER initiatives commenced operation in 1993 and it is too early to judge their effectiveness. Almost all represent initiatives to help the regional market achieve a relatively smooth adjustment to the new business environment.

TABLE 15: EUROPEAN COMMISSION AGENCIES AND INITIATIVES FOR DEALING WITH THE ECONOMIC EFFECTS OF DEFENCE EXPENDITURE CUTS

DEMILITARISED	A network of European regions where local economies have been adversely affected by cuts in military expenditure.
ERDF (European Regional Development Fund).	A Fund which targets support for depressed regions of the European Union and which contains a range of initiatives which focus on defence-dependent areas, such as PERIFRA and RECITE.
PERRIFRA	A Fund which provides support for regions at the periphery of Europe and those which have been damaged by destabilised market conditions (such as the decline of the defence industry).
RECITE	A group of regions and cities across Europe which include the DEMIILITARISED network and which seek to counter the adverse impact of defence cuts at the regional level.

Source: Coventry Alternative Employment Research, 1992.

Published on 7 April 1993, the European Commission's KONVER programme was established to address the adverse local and regional economic consequences being experienced across the EU following the sharp contraction in defence expenditure. To tackle the problem, KONVER provided support funding to rebuild regional infrastructure with assistance for industrial and military site redevelopment, human capital enhancement and to support other innovative economic and social projects. The KONVER budget constituted a fund of some 130 million ECU derived from EU structural funds, principally the European Regional Development Fund (ERDF) and the European Social Fund (ESF).

The KONVER programme was designed to partially finance (through both ERDF and ESF) a range of policy measures including:

- basic/advanced training for new jobs and qualifications with the aim of facilitating the employment in non-defence-related industries of those made redundant in the rundown of defence expenditure. The focus would be upon the enhancement of existing skills, the acquisition of new skills and the attainment of additional qualifications.
- employment subsidies (excluded in the UK).
- the diversification of regional economic structures through the development of new start-up businesses and existing small- and medium-sized enterprises (SMEs) with a view to enabling defence-dependent SMEs to adapt to new market requirements.

- improvements to the business environment and services.
- the promotion of innovation and technology transfer, specifically to assist SMEs adapt to the needs of new markets.
- the conversion and redevelopment of redundant military sites, together with environmental restoration and land rehabilitation, following the withdrawal of military activities, excluding major infrastructure projects.
- feasibility studies and models for conversion projects, aimed principally at SMEs and/or local areas, as part of a long-term development strategy;
- intra-regional co-operation to enable different regions to exchange information on their experiences to support joint diversification projects and SME development.

Previously in this book, reference has been made to the high degree of defence-dependency experienced in the southwest region of the UK and, not surprisingly, a number of KONVER-funded projects have been undertaken (table 16 below) illustrating the range of support mechanisms KONVER offers.

More generally, the European Union operates a number of agencies and initiatives designed to assist economic regeneration in areas of Europe adversely affected by cuts in defence spending.

Finally, one important dimension of the European strategy towards defence run-down and diversification and conversion initiatives relates to the 'special case' perception of the defence industry within the European Union. Under the Treaty of Rome, the foundation statement

TABLE 16: KONVER PROJECTS IN THE SOUTHWEST REGION OF THE UK

a) Under the European Regional Development Fund:		
County:	Project:	Value:
Avon, Glos, Wilts	Diversifying the economy	> £858,000
South Dorset	Local economy diversification	£240,000
Somerset	Technology development promotion	£ 75,000
Devon	Business support	£500,000
b) Under the European Social Fund:		
Dorset	Redundancy training programme	> £125,000
Somerset	Unemployed support measures	> £ 35,000
Avon, Glos, Wilts	Defence diversification training	> £700,000
Devon	Flexible delivery of IT core skills	> £ 38,000
Devon	Routeways into work	> £ 77,000
Devon	Closure of RAF Chivenor	> £ 6,000
Devon & Cornwall	Customised training programme	> £110,000
Cranfield University	Training audit	> £ 56,000

of the original European Community, a member country is permitted to act in any way which wffi: 'protect the interests of its security which are connected with the production or trade in arms, munitions and war material This key element of the Treaty, stipulated under Article 223, has been used by governments across Europe to allow preferential investment subsidies and procurement for its defence industry.

Recently policy changes have also been implemented to support the conversion process. Scientists in government laboratories with a former role in leading edge military research have been actively encouraged to find new business opportunities and establish links with potential customers. In the US, this has been encouraged through new agencies created by government legislation of which perhaps the best example are the Co-operative Research and Development Agreements (CRADAS), discussed earlier in this book, which are used to promote co-operation between laboratories and the business community. Some defence contractors have learned that An apparently successful strategy to assist the development of new business initiatives that some defence contractors have pursued is to spin off that new business as a separate division or subsidiary of the parent company.

However, it is often the case that for conversion strategies to be truly successful, the existing culture of defence-related design, development and production has to be fundamentally altered to reflect the different demands of an intensely competitive, commercial market. This is not an obstacle that the market, unaided, can easily remove. Appropriate government policy will be required to encourage cultural change by, for example, providing financial support for R&D for civilian-related public goods; removing government-imposed regulatory barriers to conversion of government-operated facilities; and taking further the developing relationships between government defence laboratories and their personnel and the business world, perhaps in the form of business partnerships.

Another more controversial policy alternative would be for governments to provide R&D subsidies or perhaps tax credits to make it more attractive for companies to increase their demand for appropriately skilled scientists and engineers, thereby increasing the number of employment opportunities available for those leaving military-related work. At the same time, government could allocate new investment support to those companies wishing to enter new markets and utilise more fully these additional R&D personnel. As discussed elsewhere in this book, this is a particular and deep-rooted problem in Russia where such policies, currently, would not be financially feasible. To ensure that the post-Cold War world remains relatively peaceful and that the peace dividend, whatever form it takes, can be realised eventually, Western governments need to be more pro-active in supporting the Russian conversion process than they have been in the past.

From a slightly different perspective, governments have another key policy role to play. Their support is not just required in order to facilitate the actual process of conversion but, in addition, to stimulate further the demand for such a change. Intervention designed to encourage society's demand for conversion could include, for example, identifying at the local, regional, national or global level, what specific civil sector requirements could be provided for by the refocusing of military R&D capabilities.

g) Russia

The situation in Russia is, of course, very different. Inheriting almost four-fifths of the Former Soviet Union's defence industry and military infrastructure, the Russian economy was devastated at the macroeconomic as well as the regional, industrial and sectoral levels by the post-Cold War collapse of defence expenditure. With the military-industrial complex at the very heart of the Russian economy and the driving force behind economic growth and prosperity, the macroeconomic impact of the 'outbreak of peace' was inevitably catastrophic.

As a result, the decade of the 1990's has witnessed the relatively stable, if declining, super-power command economy of Russia transformed into a unstable, fragmented and economically weak economy, devastated by the simultaneous collapse of its economic, political and military systems. Over this period, Russia suffered rampant inflation, unsustainable budget deficits, unprecedented levels of unemployment (rising from 2 per cent to 10 per cent between 1992 and 1995); industrial bankruptcies, sharply falling living standards and dramatic losses of both domestic output and trade which, taken together, suggested an economy teetering on the brink of imminent economic collapse. In the midst of such extraordinary economic and political turmoil, the nation was also attempting to introduce the market economy and, at the same time, greatly reduce the role played by its economic powerhouse, the military sector.

Russia adopted a wide-ranging approach to economic reform after 1990, as did most of the transition economies. Economic policy combined planned limits on monetary expansion with specific targets for a reduced fiscal deficit and included price and wage deregulation; extensive privatisation; property rights reforms; the fragmentation of state monopolies; enhanced social provision and progressive steps towards wider currency convertibility. The crucial target of this early policy reform was to create at the earliest opportunity a degree of macroeconomic stability, coincident with a major transformation of the economic base along more competitive, market-driven lines with increased emphasis on civil rather than military production.

With the economic situation further aggravated by the collapse of foreign trade with its former command economy partners and instability heightened still further by the attempted coup of August 1991, the economic contraction deepened and national output suffered a further loss of some 10 per cent of national output in 1994. However, while the advent of market reforms can be blamed for sharp initial falls in national output elsewhere within the transition economies, the output collapse in Russia actually preceded the full implementation of market reforms and is now viewed primarily as 'supply-induced', originating from the fragmentation of domestic inter-enterprise and external trading relationships, exacerbated by sharply declining demand for defence production. Nevertheless, throughout this immensely difficult period, the reform process continued under Prime Minister Gaidar and, somewhat against expectations, under his successor Chernomyrdin, with particular emphasis being placed on the privatisation process which would ultimately generate a market-based, competitive economic and business environment. In many respects, the Russian privatisation process that lay at the heart of the economic adjustment programme was indeed of 'unique proportions', being remarkable both in terms of scale and speed of implementation. By the end of 1993, it was estimated that in Russia some 60,000 factories with less than 200 employees had been privatised, together with about 5,000 large factories placing some 50 per cent of the national product in the market sector.

By far the most important systemic change required in the transformation of the Russian economy is the rapid and smooth reallocation of resources from the military to the civil sector. In this process, for a genuine economic recovery to take place in Russia and in similar transition economies, resources must be channelled by rapid and smooth market adjustment from the defence sector into the production of goods and services required by both the domestic consumer and, especially, the highly competitive global market.

The successful transformation of Russia's economic system to the requirements of a post-Cold War international business environment requires enhancement of critical factors of production. First, improvements in the quantity and quality of important materials (rolled ferrous metal, copper etc.) are required, together with extensive retraining programmes for redundant labour to facilitate the acquisition of new skills in, for example, marketing and contract negotiation. Second, more substantial and carefully focused capital resources are required to ensure a rapid and successful transition of defence-related industry to civil production. The absence of a realistic 'peace dividend' precludes a simple switch of resources from military production and, at the national level, the dire problems with the Russian budget deficit—and the associated risk of explosive inflation—will constrain any significant funding from government.

The only real sources of capital enhancement to facilitate economic transition are from foreign governments, international agencies and, of particular importance in the current situation, from foreign companies. Despite promises of support from Western governments and international agencies estimated at around $24 billions by 1992, the actual amount of external financial support received by Russia is believed to range from $1.5 billion to $8.5 billion, offered principally as short-term loans at market rates. By 1995, initial interest payments of at least $2.5 billions have accumulated. Western economic advisors to the Russian government as well as the leaders of the International Monetary Fund and the World Bank have requested that Western governments reduce military expenditure further in order to free resources to supplement aid for the reconstruction of the Russian economy. The announcement of increased financial commitments from the International Monetary Fund for Russia (and of the possibility of new conditional support from the European Union) in March 1995 represents a welcome recognition of the need for external assistance in transforming the economy.

However, if the Russian experiment with market liberalisation is to be wholly successful, it will be necessary for external involvement in the reform process to be forthcoming from *within* the market system itself. That is, while foreign governments and international agencies clearly have a role to play, the most important and potentially productive gains are likely to be acquired at the corporate level. Foreign companies have, for some time, been involved in joint ventures with Russian enterprises and have enjoyed considerable success. Joint ventures such as East-West Technology Partners, established in 1993, bring together Russian scientific expertise and Western business acumen with the objective of marketing Russian technology in the West, while facilitating the flow of Western technology into Russia. Frequently, however, joint ventures have been in primary sectors of the economy where foreign investment and expertise have been utilised in, for example, the extractive industries. For successful regeneration of the Russian economy and, with it, for the preservation of international peace, it is now essential to build upon such modest beginnings and to create an environment in which Western capital investment and marketing expertise works in a genuine partnership with Russian enterprise.

To achieve this desirable end requires recognition of a 'mutuality of need' on both sides. Virtually all defence supply companies, wherever they are located, are struggling to accommodate defence cuts and to remain viable. Almost all are finding the process of defence conversion difficult. Almost all require access to new markets such as that of Russia where demand is virtually unlimited and where, with appropriate macroeconomic policies and sufficient external financial support, constrained potential can be fully realised. Recognising this mutuality of need, a pooling of common interests would enable sufficient resources to be deployed over the long-term designed to build effective industrial partnerships between foreign and domestic companies in the key sectors of Russian industry. All the ingredients for success are present: high and rising demand levels, enormous supply capacity, leading-edge technology and significant reserves of skilled labour. Furthermore, if it can overcome the current economic malaise, Russian consumers will, in the future, offer a lucrative and almost limitless market for well-positioned Western companies. These companies need to recognise the barriers they will need to overcome in the future and take appropriate action now. To encourage market players to participate in this fusion of common interests in the complex international business environment of the 1990's, however, powerful incentives will be required to help overcome natural risk-aversion. A combination of policy measures at governmental level, designed to encourage international industrial partnership formation will be essential. Such measures could include allocating collaborative ventures preferential future access to the expanding Russian market; devising profit-sharing reward mechanisms for international technology 'pooling'; making the award of additional funding from international agencies conditional upon proof of successful international partnership formation; and underwriting joint initiatives aimed at resolving issues of common concern to governments world-wide, such as environmental action programmes.

While evidence suggests that few governments are good at devising such facilitating mechanisms, it is encouraging that often market players lead governments in the transformation process. For example, while member nations in the European Union continue to debate the merits of full integration, many industrial companies have already taken the necessary steps towards full corporate restructuring and integration on a European basis. Governments can assist this natural tendency towards trans-national integration with respect to the requirements of Russian economic transformation by agreeing a regime for, say, the international protection of intellectual property rights in collaborative ventures and by accepting a share of the burden of additional costs frequently associated with partnership arrangements in industry.

Five years after the end of the Cold War, there remains a real price to be paid for the preservation of peace. The current price being paid in terms of Russian economic and political instability cannot be sustained. The attainment in 1994 of the Partnership for Peace agreement between Nato members and some countries in Eastern Europe clearly defines an important moment in recent political history. At the present time, however, the development of a genuine Partnership for Prosperity encompassing Western nations and the Russian Federation may prove even more critical.

Without a genuine and significant increase in external support, internal political and economic vested interests, fundamentally opposed to the market experiment, may well use deteriorating economic conditions to bring economic and political liberalisation to an end. As far as Russia is concerned, many analysts now view the forthcoming Presidential election with grave concern, given the instability it is likely to engender in an already shattered and chaotic economy.

CONCLUSIONS

Despite the dramatic and historic changes that have swept through geo-political and business landscapes during the past decade, attainment of a compensatory peace dividend to make such dislocation economically worthwhile remains elusive. For the most part, with the exception of a few somewhat limited policy measures, governments have generally fought shy of trying to over-ride market outcomes with intervention measures. The market as been encouraged to work and reallocate resources from military to civil activities in the expectation that rich rewards would flow to society, rapidly and smoothly, as a result.

The market has indeed worked. In the United States and in Europe, the corporate sector has taken the lead in adjusting to lower demand for military goods but it has not succeeded in shifting resources sufficiently quickly or efficiently to avoid economic dislocation. The only way in which the market at the prime contractor level, unaided for the most part by government, has been able to respond as been through extensive restructuring and rationalisation, together with associated unemployment, with the US taking the lead. Yet, this is not a strictly accurate reflection of what has actually happened. There has, of course, been government intervention in this critically important industry: first, through continued, albeit lower, demand for military products and secondly, through a range of government financial stimuli, designed to encourage mergers in the defence sector and duly succeeding at enormous cost to the taxpayer.

The market has also worked after a fashion at the level of the supply chain or matrix. Here, the vulnerability of highly defence-dependent small companies has been seen only too clearly with a great many corporate closures and contractions at the SME level, significant diminution of business and large numbers of redundancies. The market has indeed adjusted to the exogenous shock of major and sustained defence cuts but only by reducing the scale of the industry, creating significant unemployment and eliminating wealth-generating potential—hardly the requirement for the attainment of a peace dividend and enhanced prosperity.

Conversion and diversification strategies, similarly, have emerged as part of the market's response but, in only a few cases, have such developments succeeded in generating as much or more wealth-creating activities as has been lost due to the defence industry's contraction. Dual use technology offers something of an opportunity here to speed up the resource transfer from defence production to civil, harnessing military technology and R&D to the requirements of commercial production. In this area, governments have been more active and with some success. Unfortunately, whether the political will is sufficiently strong to drive this forward to the level required for genuine technology transfer to occur on a major scale remains unclear. Certainly, the retreat observed recently in the US in the area of dual use technology development is regrettable in the peace dividend context.

Not surprisingly, as noted in earlier chapters, when an exogenous shock triggers off an economic downturn and the market is left alone to respond, the results are predictable—corporate contraction, higher unemployment, wastage of scarce resources and reduced prosperity. Often, in the past, such experiences also set in motion forces that lead to serious conflict in trade between competitor nations and the evidence of the last few years, discussed earlier in this book, spells out a dire warning of where such bitter economic rivalry can lead. Market adjustment can only offer a partial solution to systemic changes of high magnitude such as the end of the Cold War and, indeed, may have proved disastrous without the very limited but nonetheless supportive action of governments since 1990.

The peace dividend is there to be grasped. It requires decisive action by governments to stimulate economic expansion and to provide economic incentives that will enable trade to expand rather than contract; employment to be generated not crushed by the need to survive in a declining market; technology to be genuinely dual use in nature not segregated yet again into military and civil components; and the undoubted power of the market to be harnessed to the needs of the community not captured in their own interest by powerful groups within it. As we have seen, there are a great many obstacles that lie in the path of society fulfilling two of its most profoundly important goals: enhanced wealth and a safer world. There is no reason to suppose that the two are mutually exclusive but there is every reason to expect governments to take responsibility at such a critical time for ensuring that the market can indeed fulfil its potential and work in the interests of, and not by default against, greater prosperity from peace. The final chapter reviews the main themes covered in this book, identifying at each stage the central problems hindering the market in its attempt to reallocate resources in a way which would secure a substantial and enduring peace dividend and proposes, in each case, how such problems may be addressed most effectively through government intervention or through the actions of some other agent. In doing so, the discussion will highlight a research agenda, the results of which would better inform governments, defence companies and other interested parties in their efforts to convert a potential peace dividend into a real and lasting phase of enhanced prosperity.

REFERENCES

Cohen S. S. and Garcia C. E., (1994), California's Missile Gap, *California Management Review,* Vol. 37, No. 1, Fall.

DTI, (1992), *Regional Policy: Review of the Assisted Areas of Great Britain,* June, Department of Trade and Industry.

Fontanel J., Samson I..and Spalanzani A., (1995), Conversion for the 1990s: 'Peace Cost' against 'Peace Dividend', *Defence and Peace Economics.*

Hartley K. and Hooper N., (1991), *The Economic Consequences of the UK Government's Decision on a Chieftain Replacement,* Research Monograph 1, Centre for Defence Economics, University of York.

Herbert J. and De Penanros R., (1996), The Role of the State in French Defence Industry Conversion, *Defence and Peace Economics,* Vol. 7, February.

Hitiris T., (1988), *European Community Economics,* Harvester Wheatsheaf, London..

Hoops J., (1992), Manufacturing Networks: Co-operation for Conversion, *The New Economy,* Vol. 3, No. 1, Issue 13.

Knight M, Loayza N. and Villanueva D., (1998), *The Peace Dividend: Military Spending Cuts and Economic Growth,* World Bank Group.

Le Nouail M. N. and Sauvin T., (1996), Is Territory a Factor in the Conversion of Military Activities?, *Defence and Peace Economics,* Vol. 7, February.

Lovering J., (1993), Restructuring the British Defence Industrial Base After the Cold War: Institutional and Geographical Perspectives, *Defence Economics,* Vol. 4., pp. 123–139.

Raffel J., (1992), Calstart: California's *Innovative* Conversion Consortium, *The New Economy,* Vol. 3, No.3, Issue 15, National Commission for Economic Conversion and Disarmament, Summer.

Ward, M. D., Cohen J. S., and Betsil M., (1995), The Three Faces of Conversion in the US, *Defence and Peace Economics,* Vol. 6.

Chapter 8

SALVAGING THE PEACE DIVIDEND: ACTION FOR PROSPERITY

INTRODUCTION

In the previous chapters, attention has focused on the question of whether, following the post-Cold War global decline in defence expenditure, market forces have been able to generate the anticipated peace dividend in a reasonably smooth and rapid manner in the absence of significant government intervention. In essence, the approach of this book has been to challenge the fundamental belief that a substantial and lasting peace dividend can be secured through a market solution alone in such a complex area and at such a difficult time for the industry and economy. The assertion is that market adjustment alone cannot adequately deliver such a dividend; the prosperity-generating power of the market is, in this instance at least, a myth.

Throughout the book, as well as analysing the macro- and micro-economic dimensions of the peace dividend issue, specific aspects of the economic and business impact of post-Cold War defence expenditure reduction were explored including industrial restructuring, labour market consequences, regional effects, supply chain implications, the conversion and diversification process, technological and strategic trade issues and limited policy response from governments. A number of important conclusions were drawn from the analysis and these are summarised below. Key problems obstructing optimal market response are identified, possible remedial action by government and others considered, and important areas for further research highlighted.

THE PEACE DIVIDEND: ORIGINS AND PROBLEMS

Chapter 1 focused upon the end of the Cold War, the geo-political dimensions of that historic development and its consequences and the impact upon national and global defence expenditure, noting that such dramatically reduced military spending gave the world the opportunity to secure a genuine peace dividend as a direct result of sharply declining defence budgets. From a Cold War peak of some $1,000 billion per annum, world military expenditure has declined by about 40% over the last decade, reaching its lowest level for thirty years, with significant reductions in most nations and particularly severe cuts in the former Soviet Union/Warsaw Pact countries.

Such a peace dividend was expected to accrue from two directions: first, through the potential macro-economic impacts of lower public expenditure, or lower taxation, or lower interest rates, or a combination of all three, as a consequence of reduced military expenditure; and second, through the potential micro-economic impacts of defence companies pursuing industrial restructuring and corporate conversion and diversification 'escape routes' which would then be inevitable. It was noted that most governments in the early post-Cold War years seemed to believe that the market would deliver such a desirable economic outcome, given some time for adjustment and sufficient flexibility in factor markets. A relatively smooth and rapid transition from military-focused to civil market-focused production and from public expenditure targeted on defence to expenditure refocused on health, education and welfare provision was anticipated, given the tendency for markets to reallocate resources towards their most efficient use, allied with the urgent need of the defence-dependent sectors of the economy to find new income, profit and employment generating activities.

In Chapter 1, the initial barriers to smooth and rapid market adjustment in response to a major exogenous shock (such as the massive and apparently permanent defence expenditure contraction) were identified, including the abrupt and unexpected end to the Cold War; the dire expectations for future business conditions in the defence market thus generated; the economic and political uncertainty that followed as an inevitable consequence of such dramatic systemic change (especially in the former USSR and eastern Europe); the questions hanging over the future nature of international conflict and its resolution in the aftermath of the termination of Cold War 'certainties'; and the associated vacuum in global security arrangements that could only be filled, ultimately, by the emergence of some kind of new world order. History suggests that markets abhor such volatile and unpredictable circumstances, making unpalatable disequilibrium outcomes more likely than the unhindered and rapid enhancement of prosperity as the appetite of the military sector for government finance is curtailed.

NEW CONFLICTS, NEW ROLES

Far from ushering in the age of global peace, the first decade since the end of the Cold War has witnessed three major international conflicts—the Gulf, Bosnia and Kosovo, in addition to at least thirty other more limited conflicts elsewhere. At once, two problems appear which jeopardise an effective market solution to the problem of declining defence expenditure: the absence of a new world order with clear ground rules for conflict resolution and the fact that, as a result, emerging military commitments and weapon requirements may be considerably greater than the initially optimistic post-Cold War scenarios might have depicted. Each of the three major post-Cold War crises was dealt with by United Nations or Nato allies, after much delay and procrastination, and frequently at odds with each other, eventually managing to agree a strategy (based mainly upon the use of overwhelming air power) with which to finally restore some semblance of order to desperately unstable war zones, while succeeding in the most difficult circumstances in simultaneously providing humanitarian and peace-keeping support.

The fact that, in each of the three cases, the allies still have to maintain a peace-keeping presence in or near the conflict theatre, suggests that, in the absence of a new world order, genuine conflict resolution will be more difficult, more expensive and will be of longer duration than before. The requirements for appropriate high technology weapon systems (and in some cases, their surprising vulnerability as demonstrated particularly during the Kosovo crisis) implies that military expenditure may not continue to decline as far as might have been expected, already eroding some part of the peace dividend as the military and their masters adjust to evolving global security requirements. To deal effectively with these problems requires the most urgent effort by those nations involved in global crisis management (Nato, its allies and Russia) to work closely with the United Nations to establish a new *modus operandi* for the resolution of post-Cold War crises around the world. It may be that the outcome eventually achieved in Kosovo, where Russia became involved in a peace-keeping role in partnership with Nato allies, could become the foundation stone of the new world order. It is crucial that some sense of stability and certainty is restored to the international relations side of global conflict resolution, so that the actions required of participants and, therefore, the military force reconstruction potential they require are clarified.

THE REGIONAL DIMENSION

For those attempting to analyse the economic implications of the transition to the post-Cold War world, one of the main issues of interest is the degree to which specific defence-dependent regions within the major arms producing nations and their constituent defence companies and military infrastructures will be adversely affected by the prolonged downturn in defence expenditure and the extent to which regional economic regeneration can be achieved without government intervention to provide alternative income- and employment-generating programmes of public expenditure. For it is at the regional level of defence-dependency in particular where the defence cuts will inevitably hit hardest—that the market will have to work efficiently if the attainment of a peace dividend is not to be impeded. It was not until the KONVER initiative across Europe that regions, at least in some cases, were able to attract sufficient funding to offer limited programmes of retraining and industrial regeneration. Even then, the funding provided was relatively modest and often had to be utilised in a situation where little was actually known about the true extent of regional vulnerability to defence contraction. For much of the 1990s, there were few significant attempts across Europe at the regional level to calculate the number of defence industry employees or armed force personnel made redundant by the defence cuts; indeed, as research at UWE, Bristol and elsewhere discussed earlier in this book has shown, in most cases there was little real understanding of what actually constituted the 'defence industry' or 'defence sector' in the first place.

Without such understanding, it is scarcely surprising that accurate data on the economic impact of defence cuts was hard to find and appropriate remedial action, therefore, much delayed. A number of important studies conducted during the 1990s (and referenced earlier) provided valuable statistical snapshots of the economic impact of the defence cuts in different locations and at different moments in time. No longitudinal study was carried out, however, with a European or US focus that would have revealed, once and for all, the real economic impacts of such a major exogenous shock. Clearly, as the decade of defence contraction draws to an end, it is too late to pursue such a study. Nevertheless, it would still be extremely valuable to monitor as much information about the transition of the defence sector over the next few years as possible, primarily at the regional level. If market forces are to be left to deal with such significant changes in economic conditions, then the better informed the market is, the more likely it is that the process of economic regeneration will be facilitated. This is a further area where new research is essential to better inform decision-makers of both the precise impacts to be expected and the real economic effects of evolving defence policy in the early years of the new decade.

In the UK, the creation of the new Regional Development Authorities (RDAs) provide a golden opportunity to prioritise this information-gathering process, especially for these critical industries. The government's newly-created Centre of Expertise for Defence and Aerospace, a single point of contact for the industry operated through the Business Link part of the Department of Trade and Industry, would be a highly appropriate body to lead such a national research programme, in partnership with RDAs with strong defence and aerospace interests. Clearly, there is also scope for this partnership to work closely with the Defence Diversification Agency, once in operation, with the opportunity to generate precisely the kind of information that would assist the conversion process and help deliver the peace dividend.

RESOURCE REALLOCATION

Another part of the problem of securing a genuine and lasting peace dividend is that there is no unanimous agreement among analysts and political decision-makers on how best to reallocate the resources released by reduced military expenditures or, indeed, of the costs to be borne as defence expenditure declines. In practice, an estimate from the US suggests that in the peak post-Cold War years, a peace dividend of some $80 billion between 1993 and 1998 was divided between support for conversion projects and a reduction of the federal deficit, with the latter taking about three-quarters of the dividend. This estimate, however, focuses simply on the reduction in military expenditure and where the funds originally ear-marked for this purpose actually went. It ignores the costs, some significant in scale, associated with the decline in defence spending over the period, primarily because such costs are borne by other parts of government (i.e. unemployment pay) or are completely ignored in the analysis.

Understanding the complex nature and temporal dimensions of the policy-making process is also crucial to understanding how and when a peace dividend may appear. Releasing expenditure 'saved' from defence budgets in the form of additional social spending will have an immediate and mainly consumption-led impact on the economy to an extent determined by the current stage of the fiscal cycle. Using these 'savings' to reduce public deficits will tend to have a delayed impact and may eventually result in a peace dividend of a different kind if interest rates fall and consumption and investment respond positively to the stimulus. Again, utilising reduced military expenditure to achieve lower taxation levels and rates will have both demand and supply-side impacts, depending upon which taxes are reduced, the income groups receiving the tax reduction and what they, in turn, choose to do with the windfall.

All of the analyses above assume that the decision to cut defence expenditure and divert the resources 'saved' into alternative forms of economic activity can be achieved in a relatively smooth, rapid and relatively cost-less manner. Such a desirable outcome, however, could only be attained if both market forces and government decision-making respond quickly to the changing environment surrounding the defence sector and ensure that resources do indeed move as they need to in order to minimise transition costs.

The evidence shows, however, that substantial and sustained reductions in military expenditure brings with it many additional costs which must be borne by the local, regional or national economy. Such costs include higher unemployment; the consequent loss of income and expenditure and their multiplier impacts in defence-dependent regional economies; high and unavoidable financial costs associated with the decommissioning of nuclear, chemical, biological and other weapons; and many other important costs associated with personnel retraining and environmental restitution.

Overall, then, in the face of this initial set of issues and problems, it is not surprising that the market has failed to deliver an adequate peace dividend, generating fundamental disequilibrium instead. By far the most widely observed corporate response to declining defence expenditure during the decade has been initial corporate contraction combined with rationalisation, generating waves of massive redundancies of defence workers in the major prime contractors. In response, suppliers and subcontractors further down the supply chain have little choice but to follow suit and create redundancies.

MARKET MYTHS

As well as exploring the inter-relationships between defence spending and economic performance at the level of the national and regional economy, Chapter 2 considered the long-standing free market versus government intervention debate which has, for so long, been a prominent feature of economic analysis. Many of the ideas pertinent to this historic debate are also relevant to the analysis of the peace dividend, in particular the degree to which a market, in the absence of compensatory government spending, can deal effectively with a severe deflationary shock without generating by the actions and reactions of market players even deeper recession, higher and sustained unemployment and declining real income.

Market analysis has evolved over the decades to form a sophisticated 'competition of paradigms' with different models of the market process being relevant for markets in different kinds of goods and services, under a variety of economic conditions and at different times in economic history. Despite the variety of paradigms on offer, political decision-makers still appear to subscribe to the simple notion of a market as an all-powerful, equilibrating mechanism which can easily and rapidly correct for a temporary economic disturbance. Despite the relative technical and mathematical sophistication of modern schools of thought, particularly those of monetarism and new classical macro-economics, the simplistic and fervent belief in free market economics of a very primitive kind often draws political decision-makers into a trap, believing that market forces alone have the power to rectify economic disturbances which they patently do not.

In many areas of the economy in recent years, it has become increasingly apparent that the reformulated market analysis of the neo-classical economists (which in various guises has continued to dominate much of the mainstream economic literature in recent years by offering analysis of a neat, mathematically precise world) in reality bears little resemblance to the turbulent global economy that currently confronts business decision-makers in all industries. As a result, such an approach cannot deal adequately with the economic fall-out of the historic changes taking place on all sides. There is strong evidence that the global economy—once again—confronts an economic malaise that conventional market-based economic theory cannot adequately resolve, and the failure to secure a genuine and lasting peace dividend is part of that malaise.

The response of the labour market to a severe exogenous contractionary shock serves as a good example of the inability of markets to reach a satisfactory equilibrium in such difficult conditions. Studies of employment transition in non-defence sectors of the economy (railways, steel, coal) have found that, following a significant wave of redundancies in the industry concerned, a large proportion of the newly unemployed remained out of work for long periods, often permanently. While substantial numbers also found re-employment fairly rapidly, it was usually outside their original employment area, at a level significantly below that commensurate with their skill and experience and at much reduced pay levels. While those working in the professions or at an executive level faced a much lower chance of becoming unemployed, when confronted with redundancy, such displaced employees remained unemployed for much longer with scientists (a very relevant category in the defence sector context) experiencing particular difficulty finding new employment. Studies focusing on the labour market experience of redundant defence workers confirm this pattern and emphasise the difficulty in obtaining new work, with those finding jobs often experiencing de-skilling; having little choice but to accept lower pay; and in many cases unavoidably having to relocate from manufacturing industry to the service sector.

In almost all cases, the picture is one of considerable labour market disequilibrium with, for many ex-employees, a combination of prolonged unemployment or considerable income loss. It is difficult to find a single example in the literature of a situation where market adjustment has proven capable of restoring a true equilibrium at previous employment and income levels, following the kind of labour displacement in the defence sector that has followed the end of the Cold War. The evidence suggests all too clearly that the potency of market dynamics to resolve such deep and fundamental disequilibrium is a myth, necessitating government intervention to help restore a stable economic environment and rebuild economic prosperity.

Research on defence industry redundancies has been conducted in the UK (see Chapter 2) and in the US but primarily on a regional or local economic area basis. Extending such studies nationally would be valuable with the remit of tracking the skills shed by the defence sector as a result of the cuts in the 1990s. In some cases, human capital deteriorates quickly and these skills will have been lost permanently to the economy. In others, the skills still retained by redundant defence employees will no longer be appropriate to the needs of the post-Cold War economy, although targeted retraining will be valuable here. In the UK, many local and regional studies have been conducted recently, showing clear skill shortages and retraining needs and it should be possible for a pro-active government to create mechanisms both to match skill needs and availability where appropriate or, instead, to establish appropriate retraining programmes, following the advice of the Defence Diversification Agency (once in operation) to ensure that demand and supply remain in reasonable equilibrium at the regional level.

INDUSTRIAL RESTRUCTURING

Critics of the central theme of this book will argue that the market—far from failing—has worked, quickly and smoothly, to deal with the problem of declining defence expenditure through (in the US at least) a remarkable degree of industrial restructuring. In a situation where, probably permanently, demand for military production and personnel had fallen far below existing supply levels, one would expect one of two outcomes. First, in a free market, prices could fall until demand and supply return to equilibrium. The defence market, however, is far from 'free' with an oligopolistic production structure and, often, a monopsonist/monopolist trading relationship between government as purchaser and prime contractor as supplier. In such a situation, prices will not decline and a solution has to be attained elsewhere. The second outcome would be for the adjustment to occur not in price but in quantity. Supply has to decline and proponents of the market adjustment school would contend that this is precisely what has happened. Some companies have divested their defence business (although it has not disappeared since, in most cases, others have taken it up); others have implemented massive redundancy programmes to cut costs. In the US in particular, companies have merged their operations and elsewhere others have formed strategic alliances and joint ventures. Superficially, the market does indeed seem to have worked as expected.

Such adjustment is, however, a myth. What has actually happened, as discussed in Chapter 3, is that companies, merged or otherwise, have actually done little to scale down their production potential. Certainly a few factories have closed, although even then most of the production work has been transferred elsewhere within the company. It is difficult to find many examples of defence companies dramatically reducing the size of their business. Instead, staff numbers are cut while plants remain open, operating well below full capacity. At the same time, as Chapter 3 revealed, these same companies (supposedly reeling from the shock of large and sustained defence cuts) are able to maintain profit levels and satisfy the demands of Wall Street financiers. It is indeed a strange market outcome where, faced with a huge decrease in demand for a product, suppliers simply regroup, do not cut price, retain most of their productive potential, and still manage to generate high profits. When one questions where the peace dividend has gone—or why one never really appeared—part of the answer lies in the sub-optimal outcome noted above. Furthermore, market adjustment along the lines of the US mergers has been hampered within Europe partly by political desires to retain 'national champions' and, at times, by the market behaviour of the companies themselves, as the recent dispute between key European companies over the BAe-GEC merger highlights. It may well be that the real shake-out in the defence business is about to begin—a shake-out in which there will be real corporate casualties at the prime contractor level. It is unlikely however and, if it did happen, the market would have delivered a solution far too late for a real peace dividend to accrue.

THE SUPPLY CHAIN

Despite the comments above, there have undoubtedly been many industrial casualties attributed to the defence contraction of the 1990s. Where market forces have worked with enormous impact has been in the supply chain sector of the defence industry and here the toll has been heavy. Unfortunately, hundreds (maybe thousands, globally) of small- and medium-sized manufacturers and suppliers have perished or had to downsize dramatically as the self-protective actions of the prime contractors and their governments have their effects. It is here that the real impact of declining demand has been felt and where there has been genuine market adjustment. This sector of the defence industry is more free market in nature and, as it has also become more global in nature and prime contractors seek enhanced value for money through a wider geographic purchasing strategy, many important companies have perished. Their demise is not necessarily attributable to corporate inefficiency, weak management or strategic inflexibility. They have simply been caught in a situation from which there is little scope for escape.

Often uncertain of their defence-dependency, becoming aware of vulnerability at too late a stage, last minute attempts to refocus business away from the defence sector have failed due to several factors, including asset specificity, financial constraints, cultural inertia and simple lack of information about threats and opportunities. Once again, a great need is revealed for the kind of information-gathering programme that would enable more effective decision-making in such circumstances. Markets work best when information flows rapidly and smoothly between participants. Deny participants this crucial ingredient and market failure soon becomes endemic. Unfortunately, the damage inflicted on the small- and medium-sized enterprise sector of the defence supply industry spreads far beyond just this industrial sector. For many of these companies are crucial to other sectors of the economy; are involved in a large number of different supply chains; and help to keep this sub-strata of business flexible, competitive and low-cost. Furthermore, these companies represent the potential for an industrial peace dividend, offering new employment opportunities and opportunities for successful conversion, if encouraged. Their elimination or contraction not only presents a future problem should force reconstruction ever necessitate a rapid build-up of the military machine but also calls into question the potential for a peace dividend, particularly at the regional level where these SMEs have a crucial economic role to play.

THE CONVERSION CHALLENGE

Markets are supposed to be effective at switching resources between different uses, always pursuing the most efficient outcome. In theory, then, the conversion process should present few problems to flexible and well-informed markets. Yet, history is littered with the casualties of failed conversion attempts and even the success stories tend to be tinged with comparative failure in the sense that the income- and employment-generating impacts rarely match those of the original military production.

Nevertheless, if the end of the Cold War is to produce a real and lasting peace dividend, conversion has to take place and has to provide compensatory employment and wealth-creating activities. For companies attempting to undertake a conversion process, one of the significant problems they will confront is the need to establish a new set of business relationships, both with purchasers and suppliers in the industrial sector they are entering. However, in this instance the market itself presents a barrier to conversion since buyer-seller relationships will already be in place there which may, over the years, have created a degree of mutual inter-dependency among participants, especially where complex products for major customers are involved. Market entry will therefore be a formidable challenge for the converting enterprise.

As a result, successful conversion may require the establishment of new organisational forms and strategies in order to penetrate these new markets. These will inevitably take time to implement, during which period the targeted market will have moved on. In some cases, urgent conversion solutions might be delayed by socio-cultural and political factors which had been overlooked. For conversion to succeed, it must maintain or improve firms' competitive advantage in the commercial market and must, as a result, be driven by market demand rather than it being simply being viewed as an expedient way of utilising the existing technological capabilities and configuration of the defence companies concerned.

It follows that the conversion process could be assisted by the establishment, at community and/or national level, of facilitating institutions, such as the forthcoming Defence Diversification Agency, designed to create an appropriate infrastructure to aid the conversion process. Their remit could be to identify new economic opportunities and potential regional, national and global markets, encourage the development of supportive regional infrastructure as required, and help devise and direct appropriate employee retraining in line with the needs of these new market opportunities. In doing so, they will need to address the range of barriers to exit which frequently confound attempts to convert away from defence, including: the specialist and sometimes non-transferable skill base of a large part of the defence industry and labour force; very high, 'government-imposed', overhead costs; the ownership of highly specialised capital equipment often unsuitable for alternative use; the lack of experience of many defence supply companies in commercial marketing; and constrained access to the capital markets due to the decline in their current business.

TECHNOLOGY AND TRADE

It is here that there may be a clear role for government to lend their support to the process of dual-use technology development, offering strong military/civil synergies, as a means of stimulating the conversion process and releasing a substantial peace dividend. Although the military-to-civil technology transfer process may have lost some of its earlier potency in recent years, it remains a powerful force in stimulating technological advance and generating new market opportunities. Attempts to pursue technology transfer are often obstructed by vested interests in the military sector and by security problems surrounding many military technology projects.

Furthermore, rapid and smooth transfer from military into new civil market R&D demands organisational and personnel flexibility that are not usually prominent features of the military R&D sector. Again, military R&D tends to focus on 'blue skies' areas of design and development on projects which are both high cost and high risk. Such cost and risk profiles are unacceptable in the highly competitive civil marketplace and such business culture is inherently difficult to reshape in the short time period available for the delivery of a peace dividend.

Can this important development be left to market forces to deliver? Is this where the market proves itself as the perfect resource reallocator? Unfortunately not; the market also cannot provide an effective solution here. Markets abhor unacceptable risk and high cost exposure and military R&D is vulnerable to both to a high degree. Furthermore, we see some governments, particularly in the US, already intervening in the market to enhance the competitive strength of their key industries and to preserve their critical technologies. Most of these critical technologies have clear dual-use applications and are seen by key agencies in the US as crucial to the preservation of national economic and military.

In the US, not only has the Department of Defense, on occasions, publicly encouraged the development of a dual-use R&D policy in recent years but it has also reduced the number of precise and restrictive military specifications which manufacturers are obliged to meet, a development now being adopted more widely in the UK under the 'smart procurement' initiative, opening up the defence supply market to a wider range of civil sector companies. Furthermore, a new kind of 'mercantilist' strategy seems to be evolving in the US, designed to achieve enhanced global competitiveness through mobilising, supporting and integrating all of the available advanced technologies within the US civil and defence industries. Overcoming co-ordination problems between key US government departments, this 'new mercantilist' strategy involves combining and focusing US political, security and economic leverage on key strategic markets. Indeed, such is the momentum behind the new US economic competitiveness initiative in the global market that some analysts view the evolving strategy as something which transcends normal definitions of strategic trade policy.

In such a market environment, any peace dividend that might ultimately accrue is likely to be captured by those governments willing and able to best protect their economic and industrial interests. Such peace dividend gains will then be measured in terms of higher living standards to be derived from targeted strategic policies such as dual-use technology enhancement and industrial competitiveness measures designed to achieve global market dominance. In the longer term, those governments that decline to match such strategies stand to lose market share and will, ultimately, put their own critical technologies, conversion potential, future prosperity and share of the peace dividend at risk.

CONCLUSION

Without question, the end of the Cold War a decade ago must be seen as a momentous and highly desirable development, giving the world the rare opportunity to enjoy both a safer, more peaceful existence and to refocus economic resources from the military sector to other, more beneficial purposes through the peace dividend. Few doubted that the 'outbreak of peace' had the potential to vastly improve human welfare as urgent global priorities in areas such as health, education and welfare could be tackled with expenditure no longer absorbed by the military-industrial complex.

With a few exceptions, in the age of reborn market economics, most governments decided that the process of adjustment to the post-Cold War environment and the delivery of the peace dividend would both be best facilitated by allowing market forces to operate, thereby diverting displaced resources to their optimum alternative use, rapidly and smoothly. After all, companies formerly engaged in defence production, facing a declining market, would have no choice but to convert to civil production or shrink dramatically, freeing resources in doing so for the civil sector to employ. The release of capital from military deployment into a fast growing, profit-seeking civil economy would—under competitive conditions—be certain to generate enhanced prosperity and absorb resources, particularly in the labour market, displaced by the defence cutbacks.

Unfortunately, the experience of the 1990s suggests that this fundamental belief in the efficacy of market forces to restore satisfactory equilibrium to a regional or national economy after a major exogenous shock is but a myth. This book has highlighted the many deficiencies in the process of market adjustment, consequent upon major reductions in defence expenditure, which have obstructed its operation, preventing such a smooth and rapid transition to a more prosperous economy. As we have seen the obstacles to a smooth and rapid market-based transition to the post-Cold War business environment with a substantial peace dividend include:

- the vacuum initially generated by the unexpected cessation of the Cold War and the accepted international relationships and security 'ground rules' that were suddenly thrown into disarray;
- uncertainty about the future trend of defenc expenditure and its unexpectedly rapid decline;
- initial corporate paralysis in the face of unknown market conditions, followed quickly by individual corporate decisions to divest, contract, convert and diversify as best they could in a somewhat haphazard manner;
- eventual corporate restructuring, often through mergers and acquisitions, which have resulted in massive employee redundancies in the defence industry but few real plant closures;
- corporate restructuring in the US which, driven by Wall Street financiers, has been too rapid and corporate restructuring in Europe, driven by a national champions approach which has rendered the European response too slow;
- evidence of 'over-shooting' in terms of overall defence industry redundancies as a result and the inflexibility of the labour market in dealing with such a large and sudden influx of redundant labour, both from industry and also from the armed services;
- the inability of the defence industry supply chain to recognise the full implications for their business following the impact of defence cuts upon prime contractors and the limitations on their capacity to respond as required;
- the economic, cultural, financial and managerial constraints within the corporate sector that cause attempts to diversify or convert defence business into civil sector output to fail;
- the vested interests that call into question the potential viability of strategies that might yield a peace dividend such as the expansion of dual-use technology;
- the growing threat of new mercantilism in international trade, particularly with respect to critical industries such as aerospace.

Each of these factors plays a significant part in delaying or obstructing the market adjustment process. As a result, markets fail to work properly and the process by which a peace dividend can be obtained is impeded. To better understand how and why the peace dividend has so far failed to meet expectations, each of the factors listed above needs to be researched more thoroughly than has been the case in the past to identify the precise nature of the market adjustment problem and assess the degree to which each may be susceptible to appropriate policy action by government.

Even in the absence of such detailed information, the analysis conducted here suggests that there is still much governments could do, however belated it may be, to facilitate the transition process and capture at least some of the benefits of a peace dividend. There is an urgent need to restore a higher degree of global stability through rapid international agreement on a 'new world order' and dovetail this with a clear and realistic remit for Nato members (incorporating a carefully negotiated role for Russia), together with standardisation of weapon procurement and crisis response procedures as a priority. Such an agreement would allow each nation to properly assess its future defence needs and ensure that its defence industry and supply chain were kept fully informed of the future trend in defence spending. With standardised defence procurement within Nato and clear trends in future defence spending now discernible, the trend towards mergers, acquisitions, joint ventures, technology partnerships and so forth could be encouraged, making defence supply a truly global industry like so many others. Recognising that these steps would inevitably lead to a smaller but more efficient globally-based defence industry, the consequences for the defence sectors of individual nations and their companies, large and small, could be better assessed with policies adopted to help counter adverse effects, particularly at the regional level.

In a declining market, resources will not always flow to where they are most required and it must be the responsibility of government to ensure that the most appropriate incentive mechanisms are put in place to correct for market deficiencies in this respect. Much could be done by government in encouraging the conversion and diversification process, particularly at the level of the lower tiers of the supply matrix to the defence industry, where the potential for relatively easy transition is greater. Financial constraints limiting successful transition could be overcome by government-funded, conversion-targeted incentive mechanisms. Again, labour market inflexibility could be addressed by the implementation of more sophisticated and wide-ranging retraining programmes, operated at the regional level through regional development bodies, working in partnership with relevant industry-based agencies. A clear commitment by governments (supported if necessary by tax or other financial inducements) to the development of dual-use technologies and a determined attempt by all nations to resist the slide into a new mercantilist world would also help to rebuild wealth and restore greater stability in difficult times.

It has taken ten years for the world to recognise the mythology of the market with respect to the attainment of a meaningful peace dividend and to understand fully the serious economic damage that has been the unfortunate consequence of the end of the Cold War. However, neither reductions in global defence spending nor the associated transition process have yet run their full course. The post-Cold War world still struggles to come to terms with the dramatic changes that confront it and there still remains time and scope for governments to achieve what the market cannot and deliver a substantial and lasting peace dividend to an expectant world.

Index